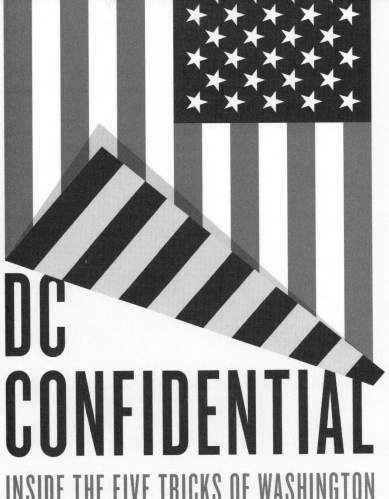

DC CONFIDENTIAL

INSIDE THE FIVE TRICKS OF WASHINGTON

DAVID SCHOENBROD

**WITH FOREWORDS BY GOVERNOR HOWARD DEAN
AND SENATOR MIKE LEE**

Illustrations by Stephen Fineberg

ENCOUNTER BOOKS
New York • London

First American edition published in 2017 by Encounter Books,
an activity of Encounter for Culture and Education, Inc.,
a nonprofit, tax exempt corporation.
Encounter Books website address: www.encounterbooks.com

Manufactured in the United States and printed on
acid-free paper. The paper used in this publication meets
the minimum requirements of ANSI/NISO Z39.48-1992
(R 1997) (*Permanence of Paper*).

FIRST AMERICAN EDITION

LIBRARY OF CONGRESS CATALOGING-IN-PUBLICATION DATA
Names: Schoenbrod, David, author.
Title: DC confidential : inside the five tricks of Washington / by David
Schoenbrod ; foreword by Howard Dean.
Other titles: D.C. confidential
Description: New York : Encounter Books, 2017. | Includes
bibliographical references and index.
Identifiers: LCCN 2016040156 (print) | LCCN 2016059669 (ebook) | ISBN
9781594039119 (hardback) | ISBN 9781594039126 (Ebook)
Subjects: LCSH: Government accountability—United States. | Political
culture—United States. | Political corruption—United States. | BISAC:
POLITICAL SCIENCE / Government / General. | POLITICAL SCIENCE /
Political Ideologies / Democracy.
Classification: LCC JF1525.A26 S35 2017 (print) | LCC JF1525.A26 (ebook) |
DDC 320.973—dc23
LC record available at https://lccn.loc.gov/2016040156

Interior page design and composition: BooksByBruce.com

In fond memory of my mentors:
John Doar, Neal D. Peterson, and Judge Spottswood W. Robinson III

Table of Contents

Foreword by Governor Dean

This is an alarming book, and indeed we should be alarmed. Americans already know that there is total lack of responsibility in Washington. That knowledge helped to produce the turmoil that we experienced during the election of 2016.

Washington and the campaigns of those seeking to get there have become like middle school on steroids: with the raging hormones, complete lack of civility, and, most tragically, abdication of any sense of dedication to a cause greater than ourselves.

As David Schoenbrod points out, this has been some time in the making. The Five Tricks of Washington that he discusses were not invented by the recent crop of candidates but rather are the result of decades of self-absorption by our political class, including the media.

A layperson reading this book may be tempted toward despair. Don't go there!

The Five Tricks are complicated; otherwise they would not have been so successful for so long. But the real recurring theme here is very straightforward: the power to get rid of Washington chicanery is not within Washington, it is in each of us.

Yet, as Americans, we have failed to articulate the most important part of the solution. We debate ad nauseam about our rights as Americans, but it's been a long time since I've heard a serious discussion about our obligations to one another. So, we get pulled into hot-button emotional issues about rights, most of which I support, but we never get around to asking what we ourselves must do to maintain a political system that allows us more rights than almost anywhere else in the world.

Half of us vote, at best, and yet we wonder why the people we vote for can get away with using tricks that wreck the nation to get reelected.

I am, however, optimistic. Not long ago, I heard a conservative North Carolinian interviewed about the election of 2016. I disagreed with him on immigration and much else. After he bemoaned the state of the country from his point of view and talked about his fears for the future—the debt, the loss of jobs, and the prospects for our kids—he concluded by saying, "I am a social conservative, but I think we may need to put social conservativism on the shelf for a while in order to straighten this all out."

I agree, but not because he spoke of putting aside social conservatism. We all, regardless of our favorite cause, need to work "to straighten this all out." Our politics can't be about winner-takes-all anymore. We have to make common cause and talk about real issues, including unpleasant subjects like debt and entitlement reforms. To do that, we must stop the tricks.

As you read this book, think not just about how mad you are at the tricksters. Think, as the social conservative from North Carolina did, about our obligations to one another as we fix the problems. We must refuse to respond to divisive tricksterism, and start to demand accountability from politicians, the media, and, most importantly, ourselves.

Howard Dean, MD
Governor of Vermont, 1991–2003
Chair, Democratic National Committee, 2005–09

Foreword by Senator Lee

Washington is broken and everyone in America knows it.

Every day the chronic dysfunction of the federal government becomes harder to ignore. Nearly $20 trillion of national debt, boosted by massive annual deficits as far as the eye can see. Soaring corporate profits on Wall Street and stagnant wages on Main Street, thanks to unfair tax and regulatory systems engineered by and for the politically well-connected. A bloated bureaucracy—insulated from the consequences of its decisions—that raises the cost and lowers the quality of nearly everything it touches, from health care to higher education to our social-safety-net programs. Meanwhile, our political debates seem to have descended from a contest of ideas to a lot of yelling and finger-pointing.

No wonder recent polls show that a mere 19 percent of Americans say they trust the federal government.

In the pages that follow, David Schoenbrod explains how we got here and how we can start to rehabilitate our government so that it once again is of, by, and for the people. Through a series of riveting—and often infuriating—blow-by-blow accounts exposing the ugly reality of today's deceptive lawmaking process, he shows that the problems in Washington can't be pinned on one party or one president, but have instead accreted over decades. But *DC Confidential* is more than a polemic against a discredited, flailing political establishment. It is equal parts diagnosis and prescription, tied together with a penetrating historical and legal analysis that identifies the proximate cause of the structural dysfunction plaguing our federal government: a weak and timid Congress that seeks above all to avoid responsibility for the consequences of harmful laws by, as Professor Schoenbrod explains, "enacting popular policies" that promise big benefits while "shunting [the] hard choices" of lawmaking to an executive branch agency.

Herein lies the profound insight of Schoenbrod's superb exploration of the tricks of Washington and the key to fixing what's broken in the federal government.

The only way to put the American people back in charge of Washington is to put Congress back in charge of federal lawmaking.

Restoring the legislative branch's proper constitutional role and making Congress once again responsible—in the sense of both discharging its constitutional duties and taking responsibility for the consequences—is *the* reason I came to Washington in 2010. And it's why I recently joined several colleagues in the House and Senate to launch the Article I Project, a network of reform-oriented lawmakers working together on an agenda of congressional empowerment designed to put elected representatives in Congress—rather than unelected, unaccountable bureaucrats—back in the driver's seat of federal policy making.

As Schoenbrod shows, Congress's habitual abdication of its constitutional duties is a problem years in the making, and fixing it will not be easy. But in a democratic republic like ours, the first step toward government reform is always to educate the people, so that they are empowered to hold their elected representatives accountable for their decisions. That's exactly what *DC Confidential* aims to achieve, and it's why this book should be required reading for anyone who believes it's still possible to reform our failing public institutions and put the federal government back to work for the American people.

Mike Lee
United States Senator, Utah, 2011–Present

Rabbits, Hats, and Sleights of Hand

FINEBERG
Washington at Work

Illustration by Stephen Fineberg.

Y ou think you know why our government in Washington is broken,
but you really don't. You think it's broken because politicians curry
favor with special interests and activists on the left or the right. There's
something to that belief and it helps explain why our politicians can't find
common ground, but it misses the root cause. A half century ago, elected
officials in Congress and the White House figured out a new system for
enacting laws and spending programs—one that lets them take the credit
for promises of good news while avoiding the blame for producing bad
results. With five key tricks, politicians of both parties now avoid accounting to us for what the government actually does to us.

While most people understand that politicians seem to pull rabbits
out of hats, hardly anyone sees the sleights of hand by which they get away
with their tricks. Otherwise, their tricks wouldn't work. *DC Confidential*
exposes the sleights of hand behind the Five Tricks of Washington. Once

the sleights of hand are brought to light, we can stop the tricks, fix our broken government, and make Washington work for us once again.

Congresses and presidents of both parties have used these tricks for so long that they now seem like natural features of Washington's landscape, but for more than a century and a half they were contrary to the ground rules of government.

The people who met in Philadelphia in the summer of 1787 to draft a constitution for the United States were not all-knowing, but they did respond sensibly to the challenge of finding a way that a population with clashing interests could get along. They put at the heart of the country's new government an elected Congress whose members would both represent different constituencies and take personal responsibility for the consequences of their decisions. Personal responsibility to voters was essential because the Declaration of Independence held that governments derive "their just Powers from the Consent of the Governed." The legislators' responsibility would spark open debate and so educate both them and their constituents about the consequences of proposed actions. This feedback would sometimes move voters to moderate their demands, but given human nature, there would still be disagreements. Nonetheless, because Congress would resolve the disagreements in the open, legislators would usually be required to balance conflicting interests and voters could generally accept the system as fair. Win some, lose some.

The circle of repeated demand, feedback, moderation, balancing, decision, and acceptance induced by the responsibility of representatives would tend to foster virtue. This virtuous circle could put the goodness in peoples' hearts into the heart of government. And so it was that Congress could legislate on such controversial issues as tariffs in the early 1800s and civil rights in the early 1960s.

Politicians began using the Five Tricks in the later 1960s, an era in which our federal government seemed capable of working wonders. It had gotten the country through the Great Depression, won World War II, invented the atomic bomb, built the interstate highway system, came to preside over the world's richest economy, and enacted meaningful civil rights legislation. In 1969, it even put humans on the moon. The government had achieved all this without needing the Five Tricks.

The successes of the government understandably led voters to demand more from it, and these demands understandably led politicians to want to please voters. So Congress and presidents (rightly in my opinion) addressed additional challenges such as pollution and haphazard health care for the poor and elderly, but (tragically in my opinion) began using tricks in writing the statutes.

The trickery, too, is understandable. Voters did not want to feel the burdens needed to produce the results they demanded from the government. Again wanting to please voters, politicians came to embrace theories, often sincerely, that enabled them to believe that they could deliver the benefits without commensurate burdens, and built such theories into statutes.[1] As I will show, however, the theories usually failed to deliver the benefits without burdens, but promising something for nothing, or very little, had become the course of least resistance. The Five Tricks had begun.

The tricks differ from the spin and deceits with which politicians have always tried to put their actions in the most favorable light. The Five Tricks allow them to act in new ways that shift the blame for unpopular consequences to others:

- *The Money Trick* lets current members of Congress get the credit for gratifying the public's demands for tax cuts, benefit increases, and other spending increases, while shifting the blame for the inevitable tax increases and benefit cuts to their successors in office when the long-term fiscal consequences of these actions require painful adjustments. As a result, Congress has set a course that, unless soon changed, will require draconian tax increases and spending cuts across the entire population.
- *The Debt Guarantee Trick* lets current members of Congress get support from the too-big-to-fail banks and other businesses whose profits it increases by guaranteeing their debts, while shifting the blame for the eventual bailouts to their successors in office when the debt guarantees produce fiscal crises. As a result, Congress grants debt guarantees in a way that encourages these businesses to run risks that will lead to fiscal crises, lost retirement savings, unemployment, and foreclosures.
- *The Federal Mandate Trick* lets members of Congress get the credit for the benefits they require the state and local governments to

deliver, while shifting the blame for the burdens necessary to deliver those benefits to state and local officials. As a result, Congress mandates benefits without considering whether they are worth the burdens they place on us.

- *The Regulation Trick* lets members of Congress get the credit for granting seemingly rock-solid rights to regulatory protection, while shifting the blame to federal agencies for the burdens required to vindicate those rights and the failures to do so. As a result, Congress designs regulatory statutes to maximize credit for its members rather than providing us with effective, efficient regulatory protection.
- *The War Trick* lets members of Congress get the credit for having a statute that requires them to take responsibility for going to war, while colluding with the president to evade responsibility for wars that might later prove controversial. As a result, members of Congress can march in the parade if the war ends up proving popular, but put the entire blame on the president if it does not. Although the presidents must take the blame, they get the power to launch wars.

I am not arguing that deficit spending, debt guarantees, federal mandates, or regulation are always bad. Far from it. And I understand that war is sometimes necessary.

I am arguing that to make government work for us, we need a Congress whose members are responsible for the consequences their decisions impose on us. Such responsibility would give them a powerful personal incentive to produce consequences that we favor. That is why the Constitution sought to put an accountable Congress at the heart of our government. What the Five Tricks do, however, is to short-circuit legislators' personal responsibility for the consequences and, as a result, they give them a strong personal incentive to produce decisions that make themselves look good regardless of the consequences for the rest of us. The bad government hurts us deeply because the federal government controls far more of the peoples' lives than it did before the Five Tricks began.

The presidents, as the most powerful participants in the legislative process, are in on the tricks, too. The tricks also give the president a more

Photograph by Scott Pinney, 2012.

FIGURE 1. Chilkoot Charlie's, Anchorage, Alaska.

powerful federal government and absolute power to start wars. This is a concern now that Donald Trump has gotten elected in 2016, but should have also been a concern had Hillary Clinton won.

With Congress and the presidents promising everyone something for nothing, the Capitol's dome might as well bear the sign that is posted in front of Chilkoot Charlie's bar in Anchorage, Alaska: "We Cheat the Other Guy and Pass the Savings on to You."

Voters, of course, sense that trickery is going on, even though they don't understand the sleights of hand that allow elected officials to seem to pull rabbits out of hats. The well-connected and the well-organized do, however, understand the sleights of hand and so know how to work the system for their own special benefit. The rest of us end up feeling cheated. All of this prevents broad agreement on the fairness of a system that can maintain legitimacy despite clashing interests.

As the tricks brought bad government and bad feeling, the public's trust in the government plummeted. In 1964, shortly before the trickery began, trust in Washington stood at 76 percent, but by 1980, with the trickery underway, trust had fallen to 25 percent. Today, only 19 percent of Americans trust government in Washington to do what is right "just about always" or "most of the time." Pew Research reported that we are now in "the longest period of low trust in government in more than 50 years." According to *Wall Street Journal* columnist Peggy Noonan, "Over 80% of the American people, across the board, believe an elite group of political incumbents, plus big business, big media, big banks, big unions and big special interests—the whole Washington political class—have rigged the system for the wealthy and connected.... People feel they no longer have a voice."[2]

Of course, the tricks are far from the only change since 1964 likely to breed distrust in the government. Other possibilities include big campaign contributions, downturns in the economy, and polarization. Yet, as I will show, the tricks contribute to these problems, especially in Washington. Meanwhile, trust in state and local government remains high.[3]

While voters from across the political spectrum distrust the federal government and openly blame Congress, members of Congress privately blame voters. Tim Penny wrote after serving in the House as a Democratic representative from Minnesota, "Voters routinely punish lawmakers who...challenge them to face unpleasant truths." He is correct. We voters demand something for nothing. The trickery takes place in the legislative process, but We the People are complicit. *New York Times* columnist Thomas Friedman wrote that we need better citizens rather than better leaders.[4]

Yet, as I will show, we can be better citizens only if we get Congress and the presidents to stop the tricks. It is the Five Tricks that allow us to escape responsibility for weighing whether we are really willing to bear the burdens needed to produce the benefits we demand from government. We have thereby come to regard the government as a Santa Claus capable of conferring sugar plums from on high, rather than as a system through which We the People take care of ourselves.

DC Confidential holds up a mirror to the people. If we have the courage to look in that mirror, we will see a citizenry that goes along with being tricked and, as a consequence, suffers. If we see our own part in the dishonesty and stupidity, we can force the politicians to stop the tricks.

★ ★ ★

Recognizing that the selfishness inherent in the human nature of voters and officials could, unless tamed, bring bad government, the drafters of the Constitution quite consciously came up with a solution that worked in their time and long after. In recent decades, however, the Five Tricks have rendered that solution ineffective. We need to implement a solution that works for our times.

With voters frustrated with the government in Washington and members of Congress frustrated with voters and Congress itself, we have come to a crossroads at which we can stop the tricks. This would be a constructive response to the anger that Americans from across the political spectrum feel toward politicians. To point the way, I wrote this book.

CHAPTER 1

☆ ☆ ☆

The Left and the Right Agree on One Thing: Congress Misrepresents

On June 30, 2010, transportation officials closed Seattle's South Park Bridge because it was on the verge of collapse and beyond repair. The bridge had received a grade of four out of a hundred on the Federal Highway Administration's safety scale, far worse than the fifty-out-of-a-hundred grade given to a bridge in Minneapolis whose collapse in 2007 killed thirteen people.[1]

Spanning the Duwarmish River, the Seattle bridge had linked South Park, a working-class neighborhood, with a Boeing plant and other large workplaces on the opposite side of the river. No longer could Boeing employees pop across the bridge to eat in South Park during their half-hour lunch break. The shortest alternative route required traveling an extra five miles in urban traffic. "It's going to kill us," said Chong Lee, the owner of one of the lunch spots.[2]

On the bridge's final day of operation, the residents of South Park mourned their loss. Thousands of them, led by Native American drummers and followed by bagpipers, walked across the bridge one last time. At the foot of the bridge stood a couple with handmade signs reading, "Rest in peace dear old bridge, you'll be greatly missed."

The loss of the bridge also harmed people far beyond South Park. The bridge had been crossed every day by twenty thousand cars and trucks

Photograph by Meg Brown, 2010.

FIGURE 2. South Park mourns its bridge.

plus the buses on three urban routes. The trucks had carried ten million tons of freight per year.[3]

Even with emergency funding from every level of government, it took four years to replace the bridge. These years of disruption were unnecessary. Transportation officials had known for years that the bridge was beyond repair and repeatedly sought money to build a replacement before it had to be closed. Only five months before the bridge closure, federal officials rejected a proposal to fund a replacement, allocating funds to other projects instead.[4]

The old South Park Bridge was in sad shape, and so, too, is our nation's overall transportation system. One in nine of the nation's 607,380 bridges are structurally deficient, according to the (not-altogether-disinterested) American Society of Civil Engineers, and it finds roads and mass transit to be in even-worse shape.[5]

Yet, only a half century ago, the federal government paid for building and maintaining a highway system that was the envy of the world. In 1956, Congress imposed a three-cents-a-gallon tax on gasoline to finance the Highway Trust Fund, which would pay for building and maintaining the Interstate Highway System and some of the lesser highways connecting it to homes, factories, and farms. Three cents might not sound like much, but back then a gallon of gas cost only about twenty-three cents, tax included. As the years went by, Congress increased the gas tax to keep up with inflation and changing needs, and in 1982 it started using the trust fund to pay for mass transit as well. In 1993, when the price of a gallon of gasoline was $1.16, Congress increased the gas tax to 18.4 cents per gallon.[6]

Since then, Republicans in Congress, with significant support from Democrats, have refused to increase the gas tax. At the same time, inflation has reduced the buying power of the tax on a gallon by 39 percent. Moreover, with cars and trucks getting more miles per gallon, drivers pay tax on fewer gallons while causing much the same wear and tear on the roads. As a result, the Highway Trust Fund pays a smaller share of the cost of providing decent roads, bridges, and mass transit. Bad transportation hurts the economy, which is why the usually tax-shy Chamber of Commerce urged Congress to increase the gas tax in 2013.[7] Congress didn't act.

Of course, increasing the federal gas tax isn't the only way to increase funding for transportation. States and localities provide three-quarters of the funds for highways. Congress was not, however, about to say that the states should be the source of any additional transportation funding. With the money gauge on the Highway Trust Fund pointing toward empty by the summer of 2014, federal officials would have to stop authorizing any new projects after September. That threatened to idle the contractors that were paid by the Highway Trust Fund and their employees.[8] If that happened, many corporations and unions would have used their money and manpower to unseat members of Congress in the 2014 elections. That prospect, unlike broken bridges for constituents, stirred Congress to act.

On July 31, 2014, Democrats and Republicans in the House and Senate joined in passing, by wide margins, a statute that kept the contractors and their employees working, but without increasing the gas tax. Signed into law eight days later by President Barack Obama, the Highway and Transportation Funding Act of 2014 put $10.8 billion into the fund to pay for projects from October 2014 through May 2015. Spending at that rate is too slow to fix our broken transportation system. Fixing just the fifteen structurally deficient bridges on *one* interstate highway (I-95) as it runs through *one* city (Philadelphia) would, according to former Pennsylvania governor Ed Rendell, cost $7 billion.[9] However, the $10.8 billion saved the legislators from the wrath of the contractors and unions during the 2014 elections.

From here on in, the plot thickened, but it's not important to recall all of its twists and turns. Just note the various kinds of blame that members of Congress have ducked, and continue to duck, as the plot unfolds. There have been two so far: they ducked the blame that would have come their way had they (1) *increased the gas tax* or (2) *inflicted losses on construction contractors and layoffs on their employees.*

Legislators, of course, had to get the $10.8 billion from somewhere and in this, too, they ducked blame: they ducked the blame that would have come from (3) *having the government borrow it.* To avoid being accused of adding to the deficit and the national debt, they claimed to have generated additional revenue. How they got away with this claim is really bizarre, so take a deep breath and read the next sentence slowly. Legislators temporarily eased a law that requires businesses to put aside enough money to honor their promises to their employees to pay them fixed-benefit pensions after they retire. Because putting money into a pensions fund counts as an expense in calculating a corporation's profits, cutting payments to the fund increases corporate profits and therefore increases the current revenue the federal government earns from the tax on corporate profits. Largely because of this increased revenue, the Congressional Budget Office concluded that the Highway and Transportation Funding Act of 2014 would not add to the budget deficit for the coming ten-year period.[10]

This change in the pension law delighted corporations because it meant they would have more profits to keep even after paying taxes. "It means more cash for us," stated International Paper's chief financial officer Carol Roberts.[11]

Congress had thus seemingly produced more money without increasing the tax rate on corporate profits. So members of Congress thereby also ducked blame for (4) *increasing the tax rate on corporate profits.*

Congress did not, however, produce something for nothing. Businesses will have to make up for their temporarily reduced pension contributions by increasing contributions years from now, which will then reduce the taxes they pay. So Congress did not increase tax revenues long term but rather arranged to collect future taxes early. To make up for this advance, Congress will have to raise taxes or cut spending later on. The legislators, in effect, borrowed the money but finagled to keep the borrowing off the official books. For that reason, reporters and editorial writers working for newspapers as diverse as the *New York Times*, the *Wall Street Journal*, and the *Washington Post* called the statute's funding mechanism a "gimmick."[12]

The gimmick increased the risk that some businesses would not be able to pay the pensions that they had promised employees. Congress had in 1974 required companies promising defined-benefit pensions to their employees to make minimum payments to their pension funds to ensure the employees would get the promised pensions. Even with that 1974 law, however, some companies still stiffed their employees. As a worker who baked Wonder Bread in Hostess's Lenexa, Kansas, plant explained:

> In July of 2011 we received a letter from the company. It said that the $3+ per hour that we . . . contribute to the pension was going to be "borrowed" by the company until they could be profitable again. Then they would pay it all back. . . . This money will never be paid back. The company filed for bankruptcy and the judge ruled that the $3+ per hour was a debt the company couldn't repay.[13]

Hostess Brands, which produced Twinkies, Ding Dongs, and other confections along with Wonder Bread at thirty-three plants across the country, used the pension money for corporate expenses including compensation for executives. When the company went bankrupt, it owed huge sums to the pension funds for its 18,500 employees.

This outrage at Hostess suggests that Congress should have strengthened the 1974 law to protect pensions, but it instead weakened it by resorting to its transportation-funding gimmick. This has put many people at risk. According to Milliman, a leading pension consulting firm, just before Congress passed the gimmick, the hundred largest pension plans operated by individual corporations were underfunded to the tune of $257 billion. This figure does not include the shortfalls with any of the twenty-seven thousand smaller pension plans. The transportation-funding gimmick weakened pension plans that cover thirty-two million workers.[14]

In the course of debating the 2014 transportation statute, a few members of Congress warned that it was leaving members of future Congresses to impose the tax increases and spending cuts needed to fund the $10.8 billion in current transportation spending and that it also put pensions at risk. Yet, no legislator responded to these concerns. The lengthy congressional report on the statute also failed to do so.[15]

Because Congress had in 1974 established the Pension Benefit Guaranty Corporation "to insure the defined-benefit pensions of working Americans,"[16] it might seem that legislators need not have addressed whether they put pensions at risk with the transportation-spending gimmick. The PBGC collects insurance premiums from employers with defined-benefit pension plan, puts the money collected into a fund, and uses the fund to pay pensions to retirees if their former employer's pension plan goes broke. Yet, the PBGC's maximum guarantee for an employee is less than $13,000 per year, meaning that the transportation-funding gimmick does in fact endanger employees.

Worse still, according to Joshua Gotbaum, the PBGC's director appointed by President Obama, speaking two months before Congress passed the transportation-spending gimmick, "Congress has continued to set PBGC premiums and has done so in ways that . . . [underfund] PBGC." As a result, according to a footnote buried deep in its November 2014 annual report, the corporation lacks "the resources to fully satisfy PBGC's long-term obligations."[17] The PBGC as a whole had a net worth of *minus* $62 billion. In underfunding the corporation, members of Congress also ducked blame for (5) *charging employers premiums adequate amounts to insure the pensions they promised.* This is a relatively small instance of the Debt Guarantee Trick.

The PBGC's lack of cash raises the question of what would happen if in a crisis it can't pay even its meager guaranteed pension. Its 2014 annual report states, "The U.S. Government is not liable for any obligation or liability incurred by the PBGC." That is what Congress has said, but if you believe that, "I have a bridge to sell you," as the saying goes. Congress similarly disclaimed liability for the debts of government-sponsored mortgage firms Fannie Mae and Freddie Mac, but paid their debts anyway. We the taxpayers will foot the bill if the PBGC goes broke. However, by taking the position that the taxpayers will not have to pay, members of Congress also ducked the blame for (6) *the potential costs of bailing out the PBGC.*[18]

Meanwhile, Congress uses the PBGC to fudge its budget accounting by including the corporation in the federal government's books on the basis of its current cash inflows and outflows. This means that, according to Professor Howell E. Jackson, the PBGC seemed to have made "a positive contribution to the federal budget (reducing deficits) over the past five years," even though it would likely produce an immense long-term loss to the public.[19]

In sum, members of Congress maneuvered to duck many kinds of blame:

1. blame for increasing the gas tax
2. blame for losses and layoffs in transportation construction
3. blame for borrowing more money, and thus blame for adding to the deficit and the national debt
4. blame for raising the tax rate on corporate profits
5. blame for charging employers premiums an adequate amount to insure the pensions they promised
6. blame for the potential costs of bailing out the PBGC

Essentially, members of Congress twisted and turned to avoid blame without regard to the ultimate impact on the people.

Moreover, having escaped responsibility for the burdens required to raise the money for transportation, legislators also didn't feel pressure to focus the money on the projects that would do the most good for voters—projects such as replacing the South Park Bridge before it had to be closed. This they have pervasively failed to do.[20]

At every step in the South Park Bridge story, members of Congress structured policy to maximize their credit and minimize their blame. For them, it was "every man for himself, and the devil take the hindmost." We the People are the victims.

The Highway and Transportation Funding Act of 2014 is no worse than most statutes that Congress enacts today.[21] Congress-as-usual routinely uses tricks that let its members promise something for nothing or very little. One trick is to leave to members of future Congresses the job of imposing the burdens needed to pay for the things Congress promises now. This is the Money Trick.

Most people know that Congress plays this trick but do not know the scale on which it does so. Congress has used this trick so repeatedly that current policy, if continued into the future, will leave a roughly $100 *trillion* gap between future spending and future revenue. This is about ten thousand times greater than the $10.8 *billion* bill left by the 2014 transportation statute. In chapter 6, I will explain why the gap is so large and what the consequences are for us and our children, but here is the bottom line: Future Congresses will inevitably have to increase taxes and cut spending from the levels reflected in current policy to a painful extent. Detailed studies from the left and the right conclude that an increase in economic growth won't close the gap.[22] Yet, by "kicking the can down the road," as members of Congress have described their conduct, they make the gap bigger and thus will inflict upon us even-more pain in the future.

The trick that Congress uses for taxing and spending is only one of those for ducking blame that members of Congress have been using since the late 1960s (see chapters 3, 4, and 7). The tricks have changed the role of legislators, which under the Constitution is to make themselves accountable at the polls for the consequences of the acts of Congress. When they do so, they align their interests with those of their constituents. By avoiding doing so, however, they create a conflict between their interests and those of their constituents. They accept responsibility for the self-professed "hopes of Congress," but not the unpopular consequences of the "acts of Congress."

As agents of the people, legislators have a plain moral duty to make clear to us, their constituents, the unpopular as well as the popular consequences of their decisions whether we want to hear of them or not.[23] Yet legislators are dishonest, even though they expect to be addressed as "the Honorable." If they are to act honorably, as they should, they will need to stop the tricks that relieve them of personal responsibility for the choices that so profoundly affect our lives.

Their dishonorable conduct wounds us, their constituents. Having evaded blame, modern legislators have little reason to grasp, let alone discuss, what effect their statutes will have on us. In particular, they don't need to analyze whether the government can actually deliver the benefits they promise and the scope of the burdens they impose upon us, or whether the benefits are worth the burdens. They also don't need to design statutes to give us the most benefits for the least burden. They only need to know their talking points on bills, not what's actually in them or how it will actually affect us.

Oscar Wilde defined a cynic as "a man who knows the price of everything and the value of nothing."[24] It is not much of an exaggeration to say that our legislators know the popularity of everything and the effect of nothing.

Legislators' seeming cynicism makes us cynical about them. Approval ratings of Congress have dipped as low as the single digits. According to one recent poll, "Just 14% of voters nationwide think most members of Congress care what their constituents think."[25] Even though overwhelming majorities of Americans believe that most members of Congress don't deserve reelection, most people like their own members of Congress in no small part because they provide services to constituents.

We cannot escape the tricks of Congress by looking to presidents for salvation. As I will show, presidents have often instigated the tricks that Congress uses. With the power to veto bills, the president usually has more power over legislation than anyone and therefore more responsibility. As the legislator-in-chief, the president is the trickster-in-chief.

The tricks poison the entire government rather than just the legislative branch. The executive branch's primary job is to execute the statutes legislated, and the judicial branch's primary job is to apply those statutes in litigation. Statutes once gave the executive more leeway, but to take full advantage of the blame-shifting tricks, the statutes enacted since the 1960s have imposed so many precisely specified duties on the executive branch that it has much-less leeway to rescue us from the bad decisions that statutes make. So, for example, in December 2008 the newly elected president, Barack Obama, asked Congress to pass a bill to stimulate an economy in the depths of recession by putting people to work on "shovel-ready" projects repairing roads and other deteriorated infrastructure. Later, however, he lamented that "there's no such thing as shovel-ready projects." The White House reported in February 2014 that the government could devote only 3.6 percent of the $832 billion program to fixing bridges, roads, and the rest of our transportation system. As Philip

Howard explained: "The President had no authority to build anything, and most of the money got diverted to a temporary bailout of the states. The money was basically wasted." Howard showed that the president's hands were tied again and again by old statutes.[26]

Presidents are often tempted to circumvent Congress by usurping the legislative powers that the Constitution assigns to the legislature. In this, commentators on the left and the right see grave danger. For example, on the left, Bruce Ackerman, a prominent progressive professor of law and political science who had vigorously defended the growth of executive power during the New Deal, expressed alarm at more recent changes in our government. In *The Decline and Fall of the American Republic*, Ackerman noted presidents disregarding the decisions of Congress and daring the courts and Congress to do anything about it. He also predicted that someday extremists would have a chance to get the Democratic or Republican party's nomination for president. This prediction, published in 2010, gained in credibility during the presidential primaries of 2016. To follow his prediction, Ackerman wrote, "We face new constitutional realities—on the one side, a potentially extremist presidency with the institutional capacity to embark on unilateralist action on a broad front; on the other side, a politicized [military] high command, which has assumed a powerful role in defining the terms of national debate."[27]

Ackerman also warned that although presidents try to dress their unilateralism in high purpose,

> in America, it is not enough to be right. Before you can impose your views on the polity, you have to convince your fellow citizens that you're right. That's what democracy is all about. So it makes good sense to require the president to gain the support of Congress even when his vision is morally compelling. He should not be allowed to lead the nation on a great leap forward through executive decree.[28]

Nor do the American people want their president to usurp the powers of Congress. Although opinion polls for decades have reflected disapproval of Congress, the public continues to believe that Congress rather than the president should make the major policy choices. I share that belief, because systematic studies show that nations with strong executives and weak legislatures tend to suppress political liberty, go to war more frequently, and suffer from more corruption.[29]

So we must fix Congress. At first blush, however, the barriers to doing so seem overwhelming. Although many members of Congress went into politics in the hope of exercising power responsibly, these legislators find that they must engage in trickery in order to have power to exercise. The reason is that many voters want something for nothing and will reject politicians who fail to promise it. So legislators are "running scared," as the political scientist and professor Anthony King put it.[30] Moreover, when they were first elected to Congress as junior legislators, these politicians found themselves in an institution that did business through tricks. They had to go along or become irrelevant. They found that using tricks to get credit and avoid blame was a recipe for getting reelected, and showing other legislators how to do the same was a recipe for getting the power to shape legislation within Congress. In sum, powerful evolutionary pressures have turned Congress into the trick-playing institution that it is today.

As a result, we can't simply get rid of the tricks by ousting the members of Congress who join in using them. Their replacements would also feel pressures to deceive voters.

The 2014 transportation statute neatly illustrates these pressures. The statute might seem to have been a good candidate for stopping the trickery as newspaper articles on the left and the right noted the funding "gimmick" involved. Yet, even voters who read such articles would have seen only a small portion of the sleights of hand at work. And even those who understood all the sleights of hand at play in the 2014 statute would have had scant reason to feel injured by it. The costs that it left to the future added only a tiny bit to the total bill that the Money Trick had already kicked down the road. Besides, no one knew who would end up having to pay that tiny portion of the bill, or who might lose their pension because of the statute or when. In contrast, the contractors and unions that stood to gain from the transportation statute knew they would gain a lot and soon. So, most legislators would have gotten far-more votes by supporting the bill than opposing it.

Few if any voters would have taken the time to learn about all the sleights of hand in the bill and then criticize a legislator for supporting it. Even if they had, the legislator would have had a pretty-persuasive defense, which might have gone something like this:

> "If I had opposed the bill, I would have been less effective in securing projects to help our district. And, even if I could have gathered enough legislators to slow down the bill, the bills' supporters would rightly complain that an alternative bill that did not shift blame so much would have had even more trouble passing. We would have ended up wasting time, but probably passed a bill that was just as bad. That's how Congress works."

So we can't stop the Five Tricks by voting against the reelection of incumbents who have voted for bills that use them. We can, however, succeed in stopping the tricks by calling upon candidates for office to pledge to change how Congress works. *DC Confidential* proposes new ground rules for the game of politics to block the Five Tricks. As the saying goes, "Don't hate the players, hate the game." Or, if you are determined to hate the players, recognize that the best chance of changing their behavior is by changing the game.

Switching the focus from whether legislators previously supported a tricky statute to whether legislators should stop the tricks will make it far more apparent to voters how the tricks hurt us. The stakes are ten thousand times greater with the Money Trick as a whole than they were with the individual instance of its application in the 2014 transportation statute. With this trick and the four others in regular use, almost all of us can be sure that on balance, the trickery harms us gravely.

The question then becomes how, despite the powerful pressures that gave rise to the tricks, we can get Congress to adopt new trick-stopping, game-changing ground rules. Archimedes, the most celebrated scientist of antiquity, having shown how a properly designed lever can move any weight, said, "Give me a place to stand on, and I will move the Earth." The place to stand to stop the Five Tricks of Washington is the vantage point that lets us see clearly the sleights of hand with which members of Congress and the presidents get away with the tricks and how they hurt us. This book provides that vantage point. From here, we can stop the Five Tricks.

Voters on the left and the right agree that Congress has become ineffective, self-serving, and more beholden to special interests than to the American people. Yet, voters on the left see conservatives as the problem, and voters on the right see liberals as the problem. What neither side sees is that a Congress that lets its members fool the people (and lets the people fool themselves) is the even-more-fundamental problem. Policy analysts on the left and the right agree on substantive policy to a surprising extent, and the electorate is less polarized than those who are active in politics.[31] Nonetheless, Congress fails to enact such policy because the tricky legislature is stacked against doing what makes sense for us.

So, while the Left and the Right fight over legislative priorities, the real battle remains unfought. That battle is the struggle between honesty and trickery in Washington. *DC Confidential* will start the fight by stripping away the veils through which members of Congress and the presidents misrepresent their legislative actions and show how we can win the battle by making them once again shoulder the responsibility that comes with their job and thereby actually work for us.

Placing responsibility on them for the consequences of their decisions will change how they legislate. I will not attempt to forecast those changes, let alone show that they are good. Voters will decide. That is how things should be with a government that derives its "just Powers from the Consent of the Governed." What I will show is that were voters no longer fooled by the Five Tricks, they would act more wisely.

- Chapter 2 explains how Congress is supposed to and did work for a century and half.
- Chapter 3 describes the beginnings of the trickery in the 1960s and '70s.
- Chapter 4 explains the four tricks that Congress uses in making domestic policy (the Money Trick, the Debt Guarantee Trick, the Federal Mandate Trick, and the Regulation Trick) and how Congress came to get away with using them.
- Chapter 5 shows how these tricks harm us now.

- Chapter 6 shows that these tricks cannot continue indefinitely, because, unless stopped, they will eventually bring ruin.
- Chapter 7 explains the War Trick.
- Chapter 8 proposes a statute that would stop the Five Tricks: the "Honest Deal Act."
- Chapter 9 shows how voters could get Congress to pass the Honest Deal Act.

CHAPTER 2

How Congress Is Supposed to Work—and Long Did

The people who met in Philadelphia in the summer of 1787 to draft a constitution for the United States faced a formidable challenge. They knew that most new democracies ended in tyranny or anarchy.[1] Yet, they designed a system of government that pleased most Americans until 1964. That year, as described in the introduction, an overwhelming majority still trusted our government to do "the right thing." Yet, today most Americans distrust the federal government.

The drafters of the Constitution pinned their hopes for the new government upon representatives in Congress taking personal responsibility for critical policy choices. This would make them accountable at the polls for the consequences. The legislators' accountability would force them to engage in *open debate* about those consequences.

Insight into the value of open debate can be gained by considering—strange as it may seem—how honeybees choose a new home. If a bee colony in the wild is thriving in the late spring or early summer, the queen bee and about ten thousand companions will depart from the hive in a swarm, leaving their original hive to the bees (and a new queen) that stay behind. That is how bee colonies multiply. The swarm will alight on a nearby tree branch and then choose a site for their new hive.

William Shakespeare suggested in *Henry V* that the queen bee rules her colony in the same way as a human monarch rules a country; the bard notwithstanding, monarchy is not how the bees pick a home.[2] The queen bee plays no part. If she were to be injured house hunting, the colony would perish. So, like American revolutionaries who rejected rule by a king, in locating their new hives honeybees must have a workable alternative to monarchy because making a smart choice is critical to survival.[3]

The bee colony leaves picking a new hive to several hundred worker bees. They spread out for miles in every direction to scout for potential sites. Each scout inspects a site, returns to the swarm, and performs a dance that communicates the location of the potential site and the bee's degree of enthusiasm for it. Yet, the colony cannot simply opt for the site that draws the highest praise from an individual scout. The scouts vary in how much enthusiasm they show for the same site. That is understandable. The suitability of a site depends on many considerations, some of which are difficult to assess. For example, the hive's interior must be big enough to store sufficient honey to keep the colony from starving over the winter but not so big that the bees can't fight off the cold by huddling together. The hive's entrance must also be small enough to bar raccoons and other honey thieves from entering. The small entrance means the scouts must estimate the honey-storing capacity of the interior in the dark.

While the colony cannot leave the choice up to a single scout, it cannot have every scout visit every potential site, either. The colony would starve before that could happen.

Here's how the honeybees solve their problem of self-government: After the returning scouts initially report back to the group, they visit sites the other scouts have gone to, especially those that previously drew high praise from the others. When the number of scouts at a site showing enthusiasm for it reaches a threshold of around thirty, that site it is. These scouts communicate the decision to the swarm, which then flies to its new home.

Scientists have found that the bees' method strikes a smart balance between the care needed to pick an excellent site and the speed needed to keep the colony from weakening from hunger while waiting. Evolution thus equipped honeybees with a smart search engine long before computer engineers ever wrote code for searching the Internet.

The genius of the honeybees' search engine lies in using open debate about the comparative quality of competing alternatives to increase the group's collective information, thereby overcoming a daunting set of difficulties including:

- many alternative sites
- multiple considerations applicable to making the choice
- many community members, without a single bee that can gather all the relevant facts in the time available and with many bees evaluating the same facts differently

The people of the United States would face analogous difficulties, as the drafters of the Constitution knew.

Yet people differ from the honeybees in a way that compounds these difficulties. Humans compete with one another for advantage and so have clashing interests. During the drafting of the Constitution, James Madison described the clashing-interest groups as "rich & poor, debtors & creditors, the landed, the manufacturing, the commercial interests, the inhabitants of this district or that district, the followers of this political leader or that political leader, the disciples of this religious Sect or that religious Sect."[4] In contrast, worker bees within a colony don't compete. Evolution has seen to that because only through the colony's queen can individual workers propagate their genes.

It's human nature for voters to want government to further their own interests, for elected legislators seeking their own advancement to attempt to gratify such wants, and for both groups to tend to ignore the burdens that exchanging votes for benefits imposes on other people.

To deal with this whole array of difficulties, the drafters of the Constitution saw open debate as essential. The Constitution contains two features mutually designed to promote such debate. First, it gives responsibility for critical policy choices to a group called Congress, so named because it is a coming together (or congress) of members elected by widely varied interests. It assigns to this Congress the power to levy taxes, appropriate money, impose laws, declare war, and more. Second, the Constitution requires Congress to publish "the Yeas and Nays of the Members of either House" on controversial issues. In contrast, in Britain, members of Parliament were allowed to keep their doings secret, thereby shielding them from responsibility.[5] These two features of the Constitution, together with the original expectation that Congress would legislate in a way that made benefits and burdens apparent, meant that voters could hold legislators accountable for the consequences of their choices.

The personal responsibility of members of Congress would tend to generate open debate. If, for example, citizens of one city pressed their representatives to get Congress to spend money to improve their harbor, those representatives might run up against other representatives whose constituents would resent the cost but garner support from still-other representatives whose constituents wanted to ship goods through the improved harbor.[6] Congress would thus collect information from far afield about the consequences of proposed legislative actions, much as the congress of honeybee scouts collects diverse information about the merits of potential homes for the colony, more than any one scout could collect separately. So, however Congress resolved an issue, the clash between representatives would make it evident to both representatives and constituents who would gain and who would lose from the proposed action and in what ways.

Moreover, the open debate between clashing interests together with the personal responsibility of members of Congress would mean that they would get the credit for conferring a benefit on one group of voters only if they also shouldered the blame for any harm the decision inflicted on other voters. This should give them strong incentives to take into account the interests of both groups. This was the case, for example, during the early 1800s when domestic manufacturers of cloth wanted Congress to set high tariffs on imported cloth to protect them from "the greatest evil—the arts and designs of rivals abroad." Others opposed higher tariffs because they would increase the price of cloth, and they told their representatives so. These representatives, as Daniel Webster observed at the time, were "afraid of their constituents," and Congress ultimately produced legislation that balanced the interests of both manufacturers and purchasers.[7]

Moreover, the drama of open debates would educate citizens about the choices facing the government, even those who didn't take to schooling in classrooms. The people desired this education. Once the states ratified the Constitution, voters insisted on transparency in the political process. For example, when the Senate violated the Constitution by keeping its proceedings secret, public pressure forced it to relent. As the historian and professor Robert Wiebe stated, "The anger at secrecy, the demand for openness, was a functional response to situations that made democracy impossible." In the decades after the Constitution was ratified, Congresses actually voted on the great issues of their era, deciding the law itself on hot-button issues such as tariffs. Legislators took positions on the hard choices and constituents understood.[8] The Constitution had made the government a drama.

Desire to read about the drama contributed to an upsurge in literacy. From 1800 to 1840, literacy rates among white adults increased from 75 percent to around 95 percent in the North and from 50 percent to 80 percent in the South. With a largely literate public, the United States had more newspapers in 1822 than any other country despite its smaller population. According to the historian and professor Daniel Walker Howe, "Foreign visitors marveled at the extent of public awareness even in remote and provincial areas."[9]

One might suppose that the combination of an informed public, open debate, and the selfishness inherent in human nature would tear the country apart. This did not happen because there is another side to human nature—the deeply seated desire to be fair to others in one's own community. Learning how one's demands will affect others, as happens in the process of open debate, sparks the desire to be fair. Modern behavioral scientists have found that people are less apt to try to grab for themselves something that a stranger leaves behind if they actually see the stranger.[10]

The desire to be fair can be seen in everyday events. When many people are waiting to, say, buy tickets for an event, they will usually line up to take their turn and newcomers will generally join the end of the line rather than butt in. First come, first served.

People also behave that way even in extraordinary events. After the Allies liberated Paris in 1944, Coco Chanel offered bottles of her famous Chanel N° 5 perfume to American GIs at a price even they could afford. The soldiers had grown up when travel overseas was a rarity and the Great Depression made money scarce. They could thus barely believe that they were in Paris, let alone that they had survived the Normandy invasion. Now, despite their scant pay, they could bring home to their wives, girlfriends, or mothers a luxury that epitomized Parisian glamour. That luxury was indeed hard to come by. When, the following year,

Photograph by David Schoenbrod, 2016.

FIGURE 3. The bottle of Chanel perfume my father bought for my mother during World War II.

President Harry Truman met with Winston Churchill and Joseph Stalin in Potsdam, Germany, he had to write home to Bess that he couldn't get a bottle of Chanel for her.[11] Yet, as much as the GIs wanted the perfume, they lined up first come, first served—regardless of rank. Fair is fair. Standing in that line to buy a bottle of perfume for my mother, my own father, an enlisted man, saw the supreme commander of the Allied Forces in Europe, General Dwight Eisenhower, arrive at the Chanel store and go to the back of the line.

Scientists see no paradox in seemingly selfish people desiring to act fairly, because in the millennia-long competition among societies, those societies whose members tend to treat one another fairly work better and therefore are more likely to thrive. Being fit to survive includes fairness as well as selfishness.[12]

Yet circumstances can make it tough to be fair. This, again, can be seen in everyday events. When, long ago, I started to take the Amtrak train from New York City to upstate New York, passengers dutifully lined up in the waiting room to board the train, but as the space became increasingly congested over the years, a few passengers, pretending that they saw no line, butted in at the front. Noticing that others were cheating, more and more of the passengers butted in. What had been an orderly line in time turned into a crush of individuals elbowing to get to the head, with most trying not to be too obvious about it. Most nerve, first served.

Thankfully, Amtrak put Charles John Jackson in charge of boarding the trains. He could see that passengers felt horrible about being put in this situation and set about creating circumstances in which people would act fairly despite the congestion. His solution: put up cordons to make the line plainly visible in order to communicate to passengers that "we do care about people waiting in line patiently." He found that about 98 percent of people complied voluntarily and assigned three subordinates to stop those who didn't. Now that passengers have become accustomed to circumstances that make for fairness in boarding the trains to upstate New York, hardly anyone tries to cheat. Behavioral scientists would approve of Mr. Jackson's strategy. Some of them have found, for example, that people are less apt to cheat when they sense that others aren't doing it.[13] I saw an instance of the payoff take place on the day before Thanksgiving in 2014, when 649 people waited to board the midmorning Amtrak train. They formed a line seven hundred feet long. The line required six right turns to fit into the cramped and crowded station. And, as far as I could see, no one tried to butt in line.

The people who wrote the Constitution sought to structure the government to create circumstances that would encourage the fair side of human nature and discourage the selfish side. The Constitution gave members of Congress the job of taking responsibility for the benefits and burdens of legislation, and, as a necessary consequence, the job of educating themselves and their constituents on who would gain and who would lose from the proposed action.[14] In sum, to do its job well, Congress needs to have open debate, just as the honeybees need to have open debate to find good sites for their hives.

There was open debate when Congress attempted to pass civil rights legislation in the early 1960s and the fair side of human nature won out with the passage of the Civil Rights Act of 1964. The act forbids discrimination on the basis of race, color, sex, religion, or national origin. Dr. Martin Luther King Jr. and President Lyndon Johnson as well as Congress deserve great credit for its passage, but there are other heroes who don't get the credit they deserve: the ordinary Americans who supported the legislation because they wanted their country to be fair.

In the summer of 1962, Senator Hubert Humphrey of Minnesota, the most outspoken proponent of civil rights in the Senate, had nowhere near the two-thirds vote from the senators needed to stop the filibuster by Southern senators. His despair was palpable. I had the chance to talk with Senator Humphrey because I worked in his office as a summer intern.[15] These Southern senators had no self-consciousness about their opposition to civil rights legislation. They would never relent. In 1962, Southern opposition to civil rights legislation seemed like an immovable object. That's why its passage in 1964 was a surprise.

In 1963 came the March on Washington amid growing unease in the heartland of America about Jim Crow segregation. When the leaders of the march assembled on the high stage built in front of the Lincoln Memorial, they saw below them a host of marchers stretching out a mile along the Lincoln Monument Reflecting Pool. This host—of which I was a part—seemed to me like a community, a *communion* in the root sense of the word. It was vast and it was determined. The immovable object of bigotry had met an irresistible force.

Dr. King's speech, and, in particular, the "I have a dream" passage, which he added on the inspiration of the moment, convinced the marchers that the irresistible force would prevail. As Clarence Jones, whom Dr. King commissioned to write a draft of the speech, stated a half century later:

> If you read the text of the speech, while you might be impressed and moved by certain parts of it, you would probably think it was a good speech, but not necessarily a profound or powerful speech.... What made the speech an extraordinary speech was a combination of factors. [It was delivered] at a gathering of the largest group of people assembled anywhere in the country at any time in the history of the United States for any purpose, 25 percent of whom were white. [It] was in the capital of the United States. [It was] at the foot of the Lincoln Memorial one hundred years after the Emancipation Proclamation.... Dr. King, to me,

spoke on that day in a way I had never heard him speak before, and had never heard him speak since.[16]

Dr. King's words moved the marchers, and the marchers' reaction moved King. Then, too, everyone there understood that the march would have a vast audience through television. As we listened, we knew that his words would sway the people watching at home. As Jones put it, "Once those words hit the ears of the listener at home, all that was left was to let their meaning take hold and stir the conscience of everyone who was tuned in."[17]

Dr. King's Dream, it seemed, would move the immovable object. And so it would, but not at first. Immediately after the march, King and other leaders met with President John Kennedy and asked him to put some real effort into getting Congress to pass the Civil Rights Act that he had endorsed. What they heard from the president was, in Jones's words, "the March hadn't done much for him.... [Kennedy] was more worried about his party's chances come election day than about the Negroes' chances for justice. Despite the rousing success of The March, he wasn't going to give The Movement any genuine support."[18]

In 1964, only five months after the march and two months after the assassination of President Kennedy, Dr. King and other key civil rights leaders met with President Johnson. The leaders walked into the Oval Office with little hope that the Civil Rights Act would pass soon, but by the time they left, they were confident that it would. According to Johnson biographer Robert Caro, the president needed a strong civil rights bill to secure the support of liberals in the 1964 election, but, more than that, he believed passionately in civil rights. Ironically, one tactic that President Johnson used to sell the legislation to the country is that its passage would honor John Kennedy.[19]

In the end, the Civil Rights Act got passed only because the Senate voted to stop the Southern filibuster, which had blocked the bill for fifty-seven days. In 1964, a motion to stop a filibuster required sixty-seven votes. The motion passed 71–29. Senator Humphrey, who was the floor manager of the bill, a diverse team of other senators, and President Johnson eked out this victory by winning over not only a few reluctant Democratic senators but also the overwhelming majority of the Senate's Republicans.[20]

Photograph by David Schoenbrod, 1963.

FIGURE 4. Some members of the "communion" listening to a speech at the March on Washington.

Because by 1964 the northern heartland of America had come to share the Dream, the Senate finally had the votes to stop the filibuster that year, where it had not in 1962. The bulk of the swing senators who voted to stop the filibuster owed their elections to voters who, as Caro described them, were "traditionally conservative midwestern Republicans"—and who increasingly supported civil rights.[21] These voters wanted their representatives in Congress to vote for civil rights for African Americans. Their clergy told their senators so. The Dream had reached and touched Americans in most of the country because, in the end, most people want to be fair.

There was open debate on the Civil Rights Act. Members of Congress made clear the burdens as well the benefits. They not only promised the right not to be discriminated against in employment, schools, hotels, restaurants, and other public accommodations but also imposed the corresponding duties—duties not to discriminate—on employers, schools, and businesses that provide public accommodations. Businesses and governments that failed to do their duty would have to lay out large sums of money to comply with court orders and pay damages. By taking responsibility for the burdens as well as the benefits, the legislators produced an act of Congress rather than just a hope of Congress. They took real personal responsibility for important legislation.

I emphasize the role of Midwestern Republicans in the passage of the civil rights legislation because, today, some on the left view those on the right as devoid of the capacity to be fair, and some on the right return the favor. My point is that although the parties are different today, most citizens on both the left and the right have the capacity, somewhere down deep, to be fair. The trickery is one of the things that gets in the way. Based upon an exhaustive analysis of thousands of questions asked in polls over fifty years, political science professors Benjamin Page and Robert Shapiro reported that "people of all sorts, in all walks of life, tend to form their policy preferences not only on the basis of narrow self-interest but in terms of group interests and—especially—the public good, or perceived national interest."[22]

Trickery gets in the way of fairness because it masks the responsibility of elected officials and thereby lets them avoid the open debate that, as discussed throughout the chapter, educates citizens on how proposed acts of Congress will affect other people. The sense of fairness thus awakened can get people to moderate their positions. Human nature being what it is, there will always be many fights in Congress, but when Congress resolves the disagreements in the open, taking responsibility for the burdens as well as the benefits, voters can accept the overall system as fair and therefore accept the results. Win some, lose some. The *Economist* approvingly summarized the viewpoint of Nobel Prize–winning political economist and professor of economics James M. Buchanan as follows: "A democratic system can maintain legitimacy despite rancorous politics if broad agreement exists on the fairness of the underlying rules [of decision]."[23]

The circle of repeated demand, feedback, and decisions resulting from open debate promotes virtue. This virtuous circle could, as previously noted, put the goodness in peoples' hearts into the heart of government.

With open debate, Congress's function becomes like that of an orchestra conductor. By beating time and setting the mood, the conductor provides a context in which the ensemble can make music together even as its members express themselves individually. Analogously, Congress is supposed to provide a context in which society can prosper even as its members pursue their individual aims.[24] To do so, Congress must make

clear what benefits and burdens it is enacting and thereby set realistic
expectations of what people can expect from one another and their government. A Congress that does this job well helps people respect rather
than hate one another.

In contrast, when a system seems unfair, as when people butt in line
or Congress uses tricks to evade blame for the unpopular consequences
of its decisions, fairness to our fellows goes out the window and harmony
becomes acrimony. That is why the drafters of the Constitution were
smart in putting stock in members of Congress taking responsibility and
openly debating the consequences of its critical choices.[25]

Open debate has produced decisions on behalf of the American
electorate. As one visitor from overseas, the French aristocrat Alexis de
Tocqueville, wrote in 1835, because "the people participate in the drafting of the laws by the choice of the legislators, in their application, by
the election of the agents of the executive power; one can say that they
govern themselves."[26]

Such government was a source of good will and pride. At Gettysburg,
President Abraham Lincoln celebrated this government with his ringing
conclusion that "we here highly resolve that these dead shall not have
died in vain—that this nation, under God, shall have a new birth of freedom—and that government of the people, by the people, for the people,
shall not perish from the earth."[27]

Perhaps because this passage is so familiar, perhaps because we hear
it in an era of tricky government, some are prone to dismiss "government
of the people, by the people, for the people" as a Fourth of July pie-in-
the-sky aspiration. For Lincoln, however, this people's government was a
present accomplishment rather than a distant aspiration. Otherwise, he
could not have resolved that it "shall not *perish*." It was a people's government because voters could hold their representatives accountable at the
polls and the voters included folk of modest means. In contrast, in Britain
at the time, a property-ownership requirement kept the overwhelming
majority of adult male citizens from voting. On this side of the Atlantic,
almost every state had abolished the property qualification for voting.
Thus, it was quite ordinary folks, We the People, who supervised high officials. In Lincoln's view, what was missing from the people's government

was the inclusion of people of all races. Lincoln in the Gettysburg Address framed the Civil War as a struggle to pair the liberty that comes from accountable government with equality.[28]

Lincoln's celebration of the people's government reached poor people as well as rich ones. Consider, for example, the teachings of Jane Addams, who established Hull House in Chicago to help poor immigrant families. Addams taught the aspirations and personal responsibility needed for people to move from the back streets to Main Street. In particular, she told poor immigrants that they had no less capacity for leadership than their supposed betters. In her view, ordinary people are entitled to the dignity of their own values and high officials should be accountable to them no less than to the elites. For this reason, she particularly revered Abraham Lincoln, whom she described as having taught that "democratic government, associated as it is with all the mistakes and shortcomings of the common people, still remains the most valuable contribution America has made to the moral life of the world."[29] Jane Addams won the Nobel Peace Prize in 1931.

One of Addams's early pupils was my mother's father, Louis Marschak. My grandfather was six years old when Hull House opened in 1889. He, his six brothers, and his one sister frequented it. It was Hull House, I suspect, that taught my grandfather to revere the Gettysburg Address about one score and seven years after President Lincoln delivered it. Its message of equality and democracy must have had special meaning to my young forebear whose poor Jewish family had recently faced oppression in Europe. For him, "All men are created equal" and "Government of the people, by the people, and for the people" were not just pretty figures of political speech. When I was a tot and my own father was at war in Europe, my grandfather taught me to recite the Gettysburg Address by heart. I didn't understand the words but knew they were sacred.

If you think "Government of the people, by the people, for the people" presumes that voters have more rationality than they actually do, consider this finding of professors Page and Shapiro: "Despite the evidence that most individual Americans have only a limited knowledge of politics (especially of proper names and numbers and acronyms), [the data] reveal that collectively responses make sense; that they draw fine distinctions among different policies; and that they form meaningful patterns consistent with a set of underlying beliefs." They qualify this conclusion

Photograph taken from the bio. Web site. http://www.biography.com/people/jane-addams-9176298.

FIGURE 5. Jane Addams in 1892, around the time my grandfather frequented Hull House.

with the caveat that politicians can, by misinforming voters, sabotage their capacity to make sound judgments.[30] Misinforming voters is the function of the Five Tricks.

Legal philosopher Professor Jeremy Waldron neatly captured the essential point of the current chapter when he urged us to

> see the process of legislation—at its best—as something like the following: the representatives of the community come together to settle solemnly and explicitly on common schemes and measures that can stand in the name of them all, and they do so in a way that openly acknowledges and respects (rather than conceals) the inevitable differences of opinion and principle among them.[31]

This passage describes Congress's most fundamental duty under the Constitution: to forthrightly decide issues of legislative policy and, as a consequence, engage in open debate. The open debate widens the information available for making decisions and insures that our elected representatives take personal responsibility for those decisions. This duty is so fundamental because its performance helps citizens who have differences of "opinion and principle" accept those decisions and get along with one another.

Open debate is the process through which Congress generally worked from 1789, when it first convened, through the early- to mid-1960s, a period of more than a century and a half. The differences of opinion and principle were not always pretty—in fact, sometimes, they were downright ugly—but the open debate helped.

CHAPTER 3

When the Five Tricks Began

For too long, Washington has operated on the "something for nothing" principle. Both parties have promised their constituents the world.
—FORMER NEW YORK CITY MAYOR MICHAEL BLOOMBERG (2011)[1]

In 1970, Senator Edmund Muskie of Maine had a problem. He had been the Democratic Party's nominee for vice president in 1968 and was a leading contender for its nomination for president in the 1972 election. His hopes of taking the White House soared with the surprisingly large turnout for the first Earth Day on April 22, 1970. This surge in concern for the environment helped Muskie because he was known as "Mr. Environment" in Congress. This distinction came from his having authored key environmental legislation, especially on air pollution. Therein lay his problem.[2]

Only three weeks after Earth Day, Ralph Nader charged that Muskie's air pollution statute sold out the public's health because of his "preoccupation with the 1972 election." According to Nader's study, Muskie's statute shirked the "hard choices" needed to protect the public's health by leaving them to bureaucrats under the control of the White House and members of Congress working in cahoots with industry. In Nader's words, the government "starting with Senator Edmund Muskie" had failed to clean the air.[3]

Muskie's statute had neither defined the rights that people have to clean air nor the duties businesses have to emit less pollution. In it, Congress had left those critical choices to administrative officials. That is also what it had done in many previous statutes, saying to an agency, in essence, "Here's a problem, solve it." By shunting hard choices to an expert agency, such statutes often give legislators political cover,[4] but Muskie stood exposed to Nader's attack because it came at a time of escalating environmental concern and was directed against a leading candidate for president.

To keep his title of Mr. Environment and his hopes for the presidency alive, Senator Muskie needed a statute that would give him credit for cleaning the air. Yet, a statute that actually imposed the burdens needed to deliver clean air would also bring him blame, and thereby cost him votes and campaign contributions in the 1972 election. Yes, the Civil Rights Act, for which he had voted in 1964, also imposed burdens that were unpopular with some voters. That vote, however, was an easy choice for him because the civil rights statute imposed duties to stop bigoted conduct, which voters in most parts of the country viewed as evil. In contrast, legislating clean air would require imposing burdens not only on reckless polluters but also on reasonably responsible businesses as well as city governments and ordinary citizens in their capacities as motorists, employees, and consumers of electricity and home heating fuel.

To get credit but avoid blame, Muskie cleverly came up with a different sort of regulatory statute. While his earlier statute had said to the agency, "Here's a problem, solve it," the air pollution bill that he introduced in 1970 appeared to say, "Here's our solution, implement it." The new bill promised everyone healthy air in seemingly precise terms, but generally left an agency to define the duties needed to clean the air. In contrast, in the Civil Rights Act of 1964, it was members of Congress who imposed the duties to enforce the right against discrimination.

Because President Richard Nixon didn't want to leave the environmental glory to a potential rival in the 1972 general election, he, too, proposed a bill that promised benefits but shifted responsibility for imposing the commensurate burdens. Competition between Muskie, Nixon, and others who wanted to run for president in 1972 helped to produce a Clean Air Act that Muskie sponsored, both parties in Congress joined in passing with hardly a dissenting vote, and Nixon signed with fanfare on December 31, 1970.[5]

The Clean Air Act would mean, according to Muskie, that "all Americans in all parts of the country shall have clean air to breathe within the 1970s." The statute gave the job of deciding which duties to place on various pollution sources to a newly created administrative agency, the Environmental Protection Agency. Nonetheless, Muskie insisted that the statute "faces the air pollution crisis with urgency and in candor. It makes *hard choices*."[6]

Only on auto manufacturers did Congress directly impose a duty to clean the air. The Clean Air Act decreed that new cars sold from 1975 on must emit 90 percent less of three key pollutants. Because administrators had failed to impose significant duties on auto manufacturers under the pre-1970 legislation—a failure for which Nader gave Muskie particular grief—Congress itself had to impose a major duty on them. The legislators were able to impose this duty without shouldering too-much blame because auto manufacturers at the time were in bad repute for making unsafe as well as dirty cars.[7] Voters would, of course, end up paying more for cars with effective pollution-control devices, but that would be years after the statute passed, and voters would get the bad news from auto manufacturers rather than legislators. They would also, of course, get cleaner cars.

The cleaner new cars manufactured in the 1970s would, however, fall far short of producing the "clean air...within the 1970s" that Congress had promised. To meet the statute's targets for clean air would have required cuts in emissions from power plants, steel mills, municipal incinerators, and dozens of other facilities including homes, as well as requiring motorists in some areas to use their cars less. None of this was made explicit in the statute.

To bolster the legislators' claim that they had made the hard choices needed to produce healthy air by the end of the 1970s, the statute

- required the EPA to issue regulations sufficient to protect the public's health from all pollutants everywhere in the United States;
- established deadlines by which the EPA must do each part of this job; and
- authorized citizens to sue the agency for failing to meet the deadlines.

So Congress granted everyone the welcome right to healthy air, but told an agency to impose the unpopular duties needed to vindicate the right. That shifts most of the blame, political scientists find, to the agency.[8]

With the 1970 Clean Air Act, Congress began to deal with regulation in a new way. During the progressive era that began in the late 1800s, Congress had given agencies broad discretion to shape regulation. The theory was that experts insulated from political pressures would staff these agencies and use a scientific approach to make the correct choices. Viewing the work of these agencies as scientific rather than political, Progressives saw this arrangement as consistent with "government of the people, by the people, for the people."[9]

Another strain of progressivism, however, looked down on the people's government that President Lincoln celebrated at Gettysburg. Herbert Croly, cofounder of the *New Republic* magazine, wrote in 1909 that "the average American individual is morally and intellectually inadequate to a serious and consistent conception of his responsibilities." Captains of industry such as J. P. Morgan and John Rockefeller shared that view. So, too, did many socialists.[10] One of them was my father's father, Nathan Schoenbrod. As a young man in Chicago at the dawn of the twentieth century, he was one of a group of students who worked their way through law school by making cigars. They took turns reading their textbooks aloud while the others rolled the tobacco. Socialists all, they hoped that sooner rather than later people would see that the individual pursuit of private advantage leads to inhumane results. They would then cede power to expert leaders who would run the world as good parents run a family—lovingly but with complete authority. Why complete authority? Because if the leaders had to account to voters, selfishness and shortsightedness would inevitably return, or so they thought. These socialists, too, believed in rule by experts.

In sum, highly educated people with divergent policy preferences wanted Congress, when establishing federal regulations, to state only general objectives and leave the pivotal choices to experts in agencies supposedly insulated from politics. And Congresses professed to do so for many decades. In experts we trusted. That trust continued into the 1960s but came undone with the increasingly widespread realization that members of Congress, the president, and their staffs interfered with the decisions of these experts who were supposedly insulated from politics.[11] Nader drove the point home.

In the 1970 Clean Air Act, Congress pretended to make the hard choices sufficient to protect people's health from air pollution by ordering the EPA to make those choices and directing the courts to require the agency to fulfill that order. Supposedly, the public's health would still be protected and the experts would decide how to go about it. Everyone would have an ironclad right to healthy air, or so the statute promised.

Now, let us consider whether the 1970 Clean Air Act fulfilled that promise.

To bring lawsuits to enforce the rights that the Clean Air Act and other environmental statutes seemed to confer upon citizens, a group of ardent young attorneys set up an environmental advocacy organization, the Natural Resources Defense Council. I joined them in 1972 and, during the 1970s, litigated to get the EPA to protect the public's health from an air pollutant particularly dangerous to children—lead.

Refiners had long put lead additives in gasoline as a means of reducing refining costs. But because the Clean Air Act required that, starting in 1975, cars must have newly manufactured pollution-control devices that would be destroyed by lead, legislators made quite clear that they expected the EPA to order the petroleum industry to allow only lead-free gas in the new cars. Otherwise, Congress would have looked stupid for requiring motorists to pay for the pollution-control devices and then allowing them to be destroyed by gas containing lead. So with this order the legislators were protecting their own reputations, not the public's health from lead. After all, the statute gave no explicit directions about what the EPA must do about the lead in the gasoline used until 1975 and in the hundred million old cars that would still be on the road when the 1975 cars came on the market.

To protect children from all this lead, the EPA would have to order refiners to limit the lead that they added to the gasoline used by those cars. This would, however, raise the price that motorists paid at the pump and cut the profits of some companies. Because the statute left it to the EPA to decide how much pollution would have to be cut to protect health, and how to go about cutting the pollution, *motorists would place most of the blame for any increase in the cost of gasoline on the agency rather than the legislators.*

When the EPA began to develop the regulation to protect public health by cutting lead in gasoline, the petroleum industry sought help from members of Congress. Legislators—liberals as well as conservatives—quietly lobbied the agency to stop the regulation and it did. Because the statute had assigned the protection of health to the EPA, *voters would place most of the blame for failing to protect children from lead in gasoline on the agency rather than the legislators.*

The Clean Air Act instructed the EPA to cut lead to healthy levels by 1976, but the agency failed to meet this deadline. On behalf of environmental and antipoverty organizations, I personally filed lawsuits and won judgments on the basis of the agency having violated the law, but the action the agency produced in response fell far short of the statutory promise. Early in the litigation, the EPA's deputy administrator, John Quarles, candidly told me that even if the court ruled in favor of the children whom I represented, the agency would drag out implementation so that the victory would have no impact. I ended up winning the suit and the victory did have some impact, but not nearly that which the statute promised. Forcing the EPA to take its time were the White House and members of Congress of both parties, who played both sides down the middle. The upshot was that children's exposure to lead from vehicles *increased* over the first half of the 1970s.

For the EPA's failure on lead, I initially blamed the Republicans who occupied the White House and therefore controlled the agency until 1977. When the Democrat Jimmy Carter became president that year, I hoped that his tough campaign talk on the environment would translate into tough action on lead. To the contrary, under President Carter the EPA reduced the already-weak protection of children that his Republican predecessors had issued.[12]

If the 1970 statute had openly decided how fast to cut the lead in gas rather than leaving the choice to the EPA, Congress itself would have required the lead to be taken out much more quickly than the EPA did. Public demand drove Congress to legislate on air pollution in 1970, just as public demand had driven it to legislate on civil rights in 1964. Of the air-pollution problems, the public cared most about the lead pollution from gasoline. Bumper stickers of the time read "GET THE LEAD OUT." Of course, the pressure to cut lead would have run up against resistance from industry, but that happened with new cars, too, and the result was a 90 percent cut in emissions by 1975. Moreover, the auto industry had much-more power than the chief opponents of cutting lead in gasoline—the lead-additive makers and the small refiners. In my opinion, if Congress had decided how much to cut lead in gasoline, by the mid-1970s the reduction would have been, *at the very least*, 50 percent.

By leaving it up to the EPA to decide how much lead to cut from gas, Congress delayed getting most of the lead out by at least a decade. Based upon EPA calculations of the health benefits of eventually eliminating lead in gas, *this delay cost approximately fifty thousand lives* (about the number of American deaths in the Vietnam War), *and so severely injured the brains of a hundred thousand other people that their IQs fell below seventy.*[13]

This ending may seem too awful to be credible, but consider this: In 2016, President Obama declared a state of emergency because one-twentieth of the children of Flint, Michigan, had blood lead levels above five micrograms. In the 1970s, virtually 100 percent of New York City's children had blood lead levels above that level, and the average blood level in children across the United States was three times that level. The great bulk of these children got their lead primarily from gasoline, which is what led to the EPA's finding that removing lead from gasoline produced big benefits.

The legislators left the hard choice of how much lead to cut in gasoline to the EPA rather than making it themselves because handing it off was better for them. If Congress had made the decision, its members would have faced blame, both from voters who wanted more protection of health and from voters who wanted lower burdens. That would have been a "hard choice." In contrast, by telling the EPA to "protect health," legislators from both parties feigned making a hard choice and got credit for protecting health but in fact shifted the blame for the burdens and failure to protect health to the EPA. That's the trick.

The members of Congress did not agree on what to do about pollution, but they did agree that they should get credit and not blame. That's why they voted for the Clean Air Act almost unanimously. The legislators neither rose above their differences nor dealt with them openly but rather hid them, which of course stifles open debate.

If Congress had to make all the hard choices in 1970, it might not have passed a Clean Air Act. Yet, as chapter 8 explains, my proposal is not to require members of Congress to make these choices when enacting regulatory statutes but instead to require them to vote on the major regulations the regulatory agencies later produce. Having already passed the Clean Air Act and many other regulatory statutes, they lack the nerve to repeal those statutes.

The needless deaths resulting from lead added to gasoline in the twentieth century are now history, but the Clean Air Act still costs lives today, even though it also does much good.

The EPA tells us about the good. The Clean Air Act did get rid of lead in gasoline in the end and will continue to do more good. By 2020, the statute as amended in 1990 will halve the emissions coming from the pollutants that harm our bodies. The most harm comes from fine particulates in the air we breathe. The particulates are so tiny—several thousand of them could fit inside the period at the end of this sentence—that they get deep into our lungs and pass into our blood. According to the EPA, halving them will prevent at least 200,000 heart attacks; 255,000 bronchitis cases; and many other diseases each and every year. If the EPA is correct, the average American thirty-year-old will live one year longer as well as many years healthier as a result of the reduction, and the cost of halving pollution is paltry, only one-thirtieth the value of the benefits.[14]

Moreover, according to the EPA's interpretation of the science, cutting the emissions by another half would likely have proportionate benefits. So, for example, cutting pollution by three-quarters rather than a half would add another half year to the life of the average thirty-year-old. The technologies needed to do so already exist. (All of these assertions are based upon the Obama administration's conclusion that cutting pollution will have proportional benefits down to low levels of pollution, and the Bush II administration also reached a similar conclusion.)[15] Nonetheless, the agency still says the Clean Air Act will cut pollution by a half, rather than three-quarters.

In sum, the EPA can count the extra lives that it could save, but can't under the current Clean Air Act. The reason is that to take advantage of something-for-nothing trickery, Congress has built two false assumptions into the statute and left them there.

False Assumption 1: "All air pollutants have safe levels." Congress in 1970 instructed the EPA to reduce pollution below the level at which it harms health. This instruction is based upon the assumption that for each pollutant, there is a level above zero at which it does no harm to human health. Yet, in 1970, Senator Muskie believed that assumption to be false. As he later stated, "Our public health scientists and doctors have told us that...air pollution [at any level] is harmful," adding that the Clean Air Act is based on the assumption that there is a threshold below which pollution does no harm, "although we knew at the time it was inaccurate."[16]

This assumption was a politically convenient lie. It enabled legislators to instruct the EPA to set mandatory air-quality goals at "safe levels" and achieve those goals regardless of the cost. While this instruction led them to claim they had made the "hard choices" needed to protect health, this was gibberish. The only safe level for many pollutants is zero, or so close to zero that achieving it would cost so much that even eco-ardent legislators would freak out.[17]

This assumption is still in the statute. To avoid imposing politically impossible costs, the EPA under every presidential administration claims to comply with the statute, but each continues to violate it by setting the goals at levels insufficient to protect health completely.[18] Because Congress uses a trick, the EPA gets tricky, too.

Congress could stop the lying now by choosing how much to cut total emissions of the most-widespread pollutants, but that choice would necessarily be a compromise between protecting health and holding down the costs of pollution control. In making that choice, the legislators would have to subject themselves to blame, both from voters who want more complete protection of public health and from voters who want lower pollution-control costs. Because Congress refuses to shoulder responsibility, the EPA must continue to set the supposed "health" goals on the basis of political feasibility. The second false assumption that the legislators built into the statute reduces the political feasibility of cutting pollution.

False Assumption 2: "Air pollution is a local problem." Congress in 1970 assumed that unsafe levels of air pollution come primarily from nearby pollution sources. This assumption is false. A big part of the pollution that we breathe comes from factories and other sources hundreds or even thousands of miles away.[19]

The false assumption was, however, politically convenient for federal legislators. It enabled them to look to the states to require pollution sources within their borders to cut emissions sufficiently to achieve the mandatory air-quality goals the EPA had set. Members of Congress said this arrangement would give state officials the opportunity to allocate the cleanup burden among the wide variety of pollution sources in their jurisdiction. It has become clear today that this arrangement was nonsensical because a state on its own can do relatively little to reach the air-quality goals for the deadliest pollutants, fine particulates, and ozone, the bulk of which come from out of state.[20]

The Clean Air Act still requires the states to take the lead in cutting emissions, but in 1977 Congress added an embellishment. The statute now *tells* the EPA to *tell* the states to *tell* the pollution sources within their borders to protect downwind states from emissions. This circuitous response to a national problem has guaranteed complexity and years and years of delay. It is not good for anyone's health, pocketbook, or faith in the democratic process. Congress still looks to the states to solve a national problem so that its members can shift the blame to them for the costs of controlling pollution. According to a report from the eminent National Research Council, this roundabout way of controlling pollution consumes

> extensive amounts of local, state, and federal agency time and resources in a legalistic, and often frustrating, proposal and review process, which focuses primarily on compliance with intermediate process steps…and draws attention and resources away from the more germane issue of ensuring progress towards the goal of [protecting health].[21]

Members of Congress could get rid of the two false assumptions in the Clean Air Act by directly regulating the nationally important pollution sources. We know this because in 1990 Congress did directly regulate nationally important sources of one pollutant: acid rain.[22]

The acid rain came most prominently from sulfur and other pollutants emitted by power plants in the Midwest. In 1971, President Richard Nixon proposed placing a tax on sulfur emissions, which could have gone a long way in reducing acid rain. Groups as diverse as the National

Association of Manufacturers, the Sierra Club, and the National Academy of Sciences supported the sulfur tax, but the idea went nowhere in Congress.[23] And it's no wonder: Passing such a tax would have required members of Congress to shoulder the blame for the burdens of pollution control. So they left the problem to the EPA.

As the concern about acid rain mounted in the 1980s, eastern states bitterly complained that it damaged forests, lakes, crops, and lungs. These states asked the EPA to regulate the emissions, but the agency refused to set a mandatory air-quality goal for acid rain because achieving such a goal would be politically infeasible. Quite apart from acid rain, Congress had many urgent reasons to revise the Clean Air Act, but the acid rain issue got in the way. Legislators from Eastern states, faced with angry constituents, would not support any revision that failed to cut acid rain, while legislators from the Midwest feared that supporting cuts in acid rain would anger their constituents. The legislators could not dodge their constituents' anger by telling the EPA to impose the duties needed to control acid rain because (1) cutting emissions from Midwestern power plants was the chief way to cut acid rain, (2) cutting these emissions would impose costs on plant owners that would force the state utility commissions to increase electricity rates, and (3) the power plant owners and state commissions would tell consumers that it was Congress that had caused their electricity bills to jump. The impasse helped cause years of crisis in air pollution control.

To break the impasse and end the crisis, Congress eventually took a new tack in pollution control: Congress itself would decide *how much* to cut acid rain emissions but let the sources of pollution rather than the regulators decide *where* to cut acid rain emissions. This new approach reduced the cost of pollution control and so made it more palatable to Midwestern legislators. The administration of President George H. W. Bush recommended this approach and Democrats and Republicans in Congress joined in passing it.

Here, more specifically, is what Congress did: It prohibited any plant from emitting sulfur without an allowance to do so and kept the number of allowances within an annual cap that would decline to 50 percent from current levels of sulfur emissions. The allowances were distributed among power plants but could be bought and sold. Such trading meant that a plant that faced a high cost to cut emissions could save money by buying allowances from another plant that could make extra cuts in its emissions at a lower cost.

This cap-and-trade approach achieved the 50 percent cut in sulfur emissions that Congress promised on schedule and saved electricity consumers and plant owners billions of dollars, compared to traditional regulation. Moreover, cap and trade vastly simplified the government's job, reducing it to doing the bookkeeping needed to ensure that no plant's emissions exceed the allowances it holds. The entire program would now be run by fewer than fifty EPA staffers, compared to the many thousands of federal and state staffers required to regulate pollution the tricky way. Finally, because the program required that firms emitting more than their allowances must pay a steep automatic penalty, they have an almost-perfect record of compliance, far better than with traditional regulation. As a candidate for president in 2008, Barack Obama, stated: "A cap-and-trade system is a smarter way of controlling pollution" than traditional top-down regulation. With top-down regulation, as Mr. Obama explained, regulators dictate "every single rule that a company has to abide by, which creates a lot of bureaucracy and red tape and often-times is less efficient."[24]

With the acid rain program, Congress indulged in neither False Assumption 1 (that there is a completely safe level of emissions) nor False Assumption 2 (that pollution is a local problem) but instead used the "smarter way" to cut pollution.

The tax approach that President Nixon proposed in 1981 is like the cap-and-trade approach in these respects and also in requiring members of Congress to take a measure of responsibility for the burdens of pollution control. It took nineteen years of delay and a crisis for Congress to take that responsibility.

The failure in reducing lead in gasoline and the eventual success on limiting acid rain are only the beginning of the evidence that by leaving the hard choices to the EPA, Congress harms the public. Although Congress promised in 1970 that the agency would achieve health-based air-quality goals for the most widespread pollutants by the end of the 1970s, most Americans still breathed air that violated these supposedly mandatory goals into the 1990s. Congress also promised in 1970 that the EPA would promptly protect health from less widespread but especially hazardous pollutants. Yet, the EPA was unable to deal with the great bulk of these pollutants until Congress took some responsibility in 1990. The greatest gains in controlling pollution have come in those rare instances where Congress did take responsibility; examples include not just the acid rain program but also cutting emissions from new autos by more than 90 percent, requiring new cars to use lead-free gasoline, and totally eliminating chemicals that destroy stratospheric ozone.[25]

Given Congress's successes when it finally took responsibility for the hard choices required to solve environmental problems, it should also apply the cap-and-trade approach to other widespread pollutants. That is what the Breaking the Logjam project of New York Law School and New York University School of Law recommended.[26] The project brought together environmental experts, including me, from across the political spectrum to show how to reform the Clean Air Act and other obsolete environment statutes. One of the experts who worked with me on the air-pollution recommendations for the project was Ross Sandler, my litigation partner at the Natural Resources Defense Council and now my New York Law School colleague. The leaders of the project—Richard Stewart, former chairman of the Environmental Defense Fund; Katrina Wyman, his colleague on the NYU faculty; and I—wrote a book, similarly titled *Breaking the Logjam*, outlining our recommendations. The book received favorable endorsements from high environmental officials appointed by presidents of both parties.

When Richard Stewart and I met with people from both parties on Capitol Hill, they praised the project's recommendations and said they wished that Congress had already enacted them. After all, the recommendations would produce healthier air at less cost. Yet, they also doubted that they could get them enacted. Why? Updating the Clean Air Act to build upon the success of the acid rain program would require legislators to take responsibility for hard choices on how clean to make the air. On the other hand, if they left the act unchanged, they could continue to pin most of the blame for both the dirty air and the burdens that the Clean Air Act does impose on the EPA and the states.

In sum, leaving the Clean Air Act unchanged was good for legislators but bad for us, their constituents, because a something-for-nothing statute made them look good to us even as they harmed us. And so it remains that Congress last revised the Clean Air Act in 1990, more than a quarter century ago, although we have since learned much about smarter ways to control pollution.

★ ★ ★

Congress began down the road toward something-for-nothing legislation in pursuit of laudable ends. The passage of the Civil Rights Act helped build popular support for legislation to deal with other instances of unfairness in our society.[27] It was unfair that the poor had to rely for medical care upon the quirks of charity and local government, especially as the costs of care escalated. It was unfair that pollution increasingly poisoned us and our environment. Moreover, the American government undeniably had the capacity to do more to address these problems, as was evident from its outstanding successes. The government had, as already noted, gotten the people through the Great Depression, won World War II, invented the atomic bomb, built the interstate highway system, come to preside over the world's richest economy, and put humans on the Moon.

While these earlier successes had not come from using the Five Tricks, Congress would resort to them in dealing with the new challenges of health care and pollution. One reason is that whereas outlawing racial discrimination had required imposing burdens on a distinct subset of voters—bigots—with whom most other voters did not sympathize, financing health care for the poor and controlling pollution would require imposing burdens on most voters.

Another reason Congress resorted to the Five Tricks is that it had begun finding it tougher to make the hard choices needed to achieve compromise. Its Democratic and Republican contingents, once overlapping in ideology, were increasingly ideologically distinct, as political scientists have found. Moreover, as has also been found, while members of Congress had once communicated with their constituents primarily through broad-based organizations with ideologically diverse memberships, such as the Kiwanis or Elks, legislators were increasingly finding themselves dealing with organizations dedicated to fiercely advancing a particular agenda on a single issue, such as environmental protection, abortion rights, right to life, or lower taxes.[28]

Thus, members of Congress prefer to pass something-for-nothing legislation rather than make hard choices for which they would take heat. In writing the Medicaid and Medicare statutes in the late 1960s, Congress left to future Congresses and states the job of raising most of the money needed to pay for caring for the poor and aging in the future. In writing the Clean Air Act and other environmental statutes in the 1970s, Congress left it up to federal agencies and states to impose most of the duties needed to protect health.[29]

Congress could get away with something-for-nothing legislation because our government's past successes made it seem credible. Because our government presided over the world's richest economy, it could afford medical care for everyone, or so people thought. Because it had sent humans to the Moon, it could make the air absolutely healthy on Earth, or so people thought. Besides, to question such legislation was to coddle unfairness. Democrats and Republicans joined in passing these statutes.

Although something-for-nothing legislation takes many forms, they all share one essential feature: The current Congress and president leave to some other body—a federal agency, the states, or future Congresses and presidents—the task of defining the burdens needed to actually deliver the benefits. This shifts most of the blame for the burdens that come with delivering the benefits, or the failure to deliver them, away from the members of the current Congress.

Once federal legislators had gotten away with claiming the credit yet shifting the blame for Medicare, Medicaid, the 1970 Clean Air Act, and other early instances of something-for-nothing legislation, they resorted to such trickery throughout the entire gamut of federal activity (see chapters 4 and 7).

In designing Congress, the Constitution sought to put a *virtuous circle* at the center of our government (discussed in chapter 2). Subsequent eras brought many important changes in the structure of American government. In the late 1960s came the trickery and, with it, the illusion of legislation that could produce something for nothing. Judge (now Justice) Stephen Breyer has shown how something-for-nothing environmental statutes produce a "vicious circle," by telling the EPA to produce benefits by imposing burdens—burdens that the legislators failed to acknowledge in passing the statutes.[30]

When the EPA has attempted to implement the statutes and constituents voice objections to the burdens, legislators have pressured administrators not to impose those burdens. This, in turn, means that the agency has failed to deliver the promised environmental quality.

As a result, environmental advocates blast the agency and complain to members of Congress, and Congress responds by ordering the agency in yet-more-absolute statutes to protect the environment, still of course without taking responsibility for the required burdens. The result of this vicious circle, as Breyer showed, is that the EPA sometimes fails to stop major environmental harms for modest costs, and sometimes stops trivial environmental harms at huge costs.[31]

Not only in the environmental arena but in general, something-for-nothing legislation has turned the virtuous circle into a vicious circle, by promising benefits government fails to deliver and burdens legislators fail to forewarn us of. As a result, all sides feel cheated.

Voters, of course, know that the promises of something for nothing, or very little, are too good to be true, and so we sense that trickery is going on even though we don't quite understand how it works. The sense that cheating is going on negates the broad agreement on the fairness of a democratic system that is able to, in political economist and professor James M. Buchanan's thinking, maintain legitimacy despite rancorous politics (see chapter 2). With cheating in the air, people grab for what they can get.

By using the tricks, Congress fails to perform its function described in chapter 2—to set realistic expectations and thereby provide a context in which society can prosper and its members can individually pursue happiness. To the contrary, Congress tells everyone, in essence, that he or she is entitled to butt in at the head of the line, much as the corrupt officials in *The Hunger Games* tell each and every combatant, "May the odds be ever in your favor." The conflicting expectations that Congress creates set up our government to disappoint. No wonder we think our government is broken.

Moreover, by failing to face up to the inevitable trade-offs between benefits and burdens, Congress fails to educate voters about what makes sense and is fair. Legislators tell us what they are against rather than what they are for. Most legislators say they are against killing children with pollution. Most legislators say they are against killing jobs with regulation. What they say depends upon whom they are talking to. Such absolutism is possible in sound bites or tricky statutes, but not in deciding how much to cut emissions of a pollutant, where trade-offs between health and jobs are inevitable. Similarly, by using the Money Trick, legislators can position themselves as against cutting spending or raising taxes, yet avoid saying in concrete terms how they would restore balance. But only when government leaders focus on the concrete rather than the abstract can they tap into our shared sense of fairness.[32]

You might not remember all the ins and outs of the Clean Air Act when you finish reading this book, but please do remember the lesson that its story illustrates: The tricks let federal legislators avoid personal responsibility for hard choices. This helps them keep their jobs but prevents them from doing their duty—to forthrightly decide issues of legislative policy through open debate. The Constitution assigns them this duty in order to soothe divisions within society. When they fail to do their duty, these divisions get aggravated. Thus, a Congress that indulges in such tricks is antisocial, like a jerk who butts in line, but with far-greater destructive consequences because Congress has so much power.

★　★　★

CHAPTER 4

Four Tricks of the Legislative Trade— and How They Deceive Us

In enacting domestic legislation, members of Congress and presidents use four key tricks. This chapter will describe these tricks, how the nation prevented them for over a century and a half, and how Congress then came to get away with them.

The Money Trick

In the Money Trick, Congress enacts policies that will lead to such a huge gap between spending and revenue over the long run that it would not be possible for the government to borrow enough to make up the difference. So, future officials will have to close this fiscal gap with some combination of spending cuts and revenue increases. Nearly everyone will feel pain. Past and current officials have nonetheless used the Money Trick because it has let them get credit for enacting popular policies such as increases in benefits and cuts in taxes. Instead of closing the gap between total long-term spending and revenues that will be produced by continuing the current policies, Congress and the presidents leave the difficult choices needed to do so to their successors in office. As they put it, they "kick the can down the road." This is the Money Trick.

Using occasional deficit spending to stimulate a depressed economy is not part of the Money Trick, because, as I will show, deficits used solely for this purpose will not cause a painful fiscal gap over the long run.

How the Nation Once Prevented the Trick

To make members of Congress personally responsible for spending the people's money, the Constitution gave to Congress alone the powers to appropriate money and impose taxes.[1] The taxes would make clear to us that the money Congress spends comes from us.

Congress can, of course, raise less in taxes than it appropriates, leaving a deficit that it will have to finance by borrowing. The Constitution does not bar deficits. To the contrary, it authorizes borrowing to finance them. The country needed deficits and borrowing to win the Revolutionary War. Yet for more than a century after the Constitution was adopted, voters opposed deficits except in emergencies. The Constitution armed voters with the information needed to stop deficits that lacked popular support, requiring Congress to provide "a regular Statement and Account of the Receipts and Expenditures of all public Money." Such statements would show how much cash the government had received and spent in the year, thus revealing whether Congress had run a deficit or surplus. Reflecting popular concerns, Congress ran surpluses to pay down the debt incurred in fighting the Revolutionary War and the War of 1812, and eliminated the debt entirely in 1835.[2]

Since then, the government has had a debt, but its size was limited by opposition to deficit spending except in emergencies. This opposition lasted until the midtwentieth century. Indeed, as a candidate for president in 1932, Franklin Roosevelt criticized the deficits incurred under President Herbert Hoover and vowed to cut spending "to accomplish a saving of not less than 25% in the cost of the federal government." Under President Roosevelt, Congress did end up running large deficits, but the nation faced grave emergencies—the Great Depression and then World War II. After the war, Congress ran some surpluses to reduce the debt despite a rise in unemployment.[3]

The American government's first blunt rejection of the traditional concept of fiscal responsibility came when President John F. Kennedy, following John Maynard Keynes, urged Congress to cut tax rates to increase demand for goods and services and thereby stimulate a sluggish economy, even though there already was a budget deficit and the sluggishness was not severe. Many economists agreed with the president. Eventually, Congress went along with this call for tax cuts because they were popular and the Keynesian argument had convinced many people that nonemergency deficits can be provident rather than prodigal.[4]

Yet Lord Keynes's prescription for stimulating a sluggish economy need not necessarily lead to a fiscal gap—that is, spending exceeding revenues over the long term—because, in his view, the deficit would be temporary. Indeed, Keynes prescribed cooling an overheated economy by running a surplus,[5] which could readily offset a short-term deficit.

How Congress Came to Get Away with the Trick

Members of Congress ignored Lord Keynes's prescription for dealing with an overheated economy because it would have required them to take the blame for either increasing taxes or cutting spending. Meanwhile, President Lyndon Johnson argued that the government could afford not only the lower taxes but also the increased spending to fight the Vietnam War as well as fund his Great Society program.[6] Such "guns and butter" budgets helped overheat the economy under President Johnson, and then President Richard Nixon, leading to soaring inflation and later to a recession. Regardless of whether the economy was sluggish or overheated, whether the country was at war or at peace, deficits became routine for decades.

Thus, these deficits were not the result of Keynesian economics but of Congress and the presidents having scrapped the traditional norm limiting deficits—no deficit except in emergencies—and put nothing but political expediency in its place. These politicians offered a future with higher benefits and lower taxes, while leaving their successors to deal with the consequences.

Eventually, the ongoing deficits generated a popular backlash. Starting in 1985, Congress responded with a succession of statutes designed to force its members to control the deficit in the near term. These statutes, with the voter sentiment behind them and rising revenues from a surging economy, did cut deficits and eventually produce surpluses for the fiscal years from 1998 to 2001, although the surpluses were calculated with misleading accounting, as chapter 6 will show. The reports of budget surpluses together with the terrorist attacks of September 11, 2001, gave

Congress and President George W. Bush leeway to let the deficit-control scheme expire in 2002, with weakened forms reemerging intermittently thereafter.[7]

Congress currently pretends to show concern for the government's long-term fiscal health despite running high deficits by instructing the Congressional Budget Office to prepare an annual ten-year projection of the budget. Congress, however, then shapes its statutes to bring the good fiscal news onto the books for the next ten years and postpone the bad fiscal news until later. Political science professors Jacob Hacker and Paul Pierson described some of the sleights of hand used to misinform voters:

> Time and again, the GOP's tax initiatives were structured in ways that made sense only as a technique to mislead poorly informed voters. By employing phase-ins (gradually putting a provision in effect) and "sunsets" (declaring that a provision would be ended in the future, even if the chance of that happening was small), legislators could make the advertised cost of their proposals much lower than the actual cost was likely to be.

Such gimmicks are also used to increase spending and are used by both parties. The gimmick in the highway spending statute discussed in chapter 1 is but one of many examples.[8] As a result of such gimmicks, the deficits beyond the next ten years will be worse, but by pointing to the coming decade alone, Congress can claim to have government finances under control.

Not only does the ten-year time frame open the door to gimmickry but it ignores long-term trends that make the fiscal outlook much worse. "Our political system has focused exclusively on the 10-year cumulative budget deficit," wrote Professor Alan Blinder, a former member of President Bill Clinton's Council of Economic Advisors, yet "in truth, however, what happens over the next decade barely matters. Our deficit problem—and it is a whopper—is much longer-term than that."[9] In other words, the problem is not in the annual or ten-year deficit but in the deficits in decades to come.

Many economists recommend that Congress engage in deficit spending to stimulate demand when the economy is depressed. Nonetheless, the government cannot spend more in the long run than it receives. That is a fact that borrowing cannot change. Borrowing does bring in cash in the short run, but it requires more spending later to pay the principle and interest. Borrowing can't close the gap between spending and receipts over the long run any more than a dog with a short tail can catch it. The government can have a debt forever and still have no gap between long-term spending and revenue, but only if, throughout the years, it brings in sufficient revenue to both service its debt and meet other expenses. Under the current policies adopted by Congress, our government will lack the revenue needed to take care of these costs, as chapter 6 will show.

Although the government does report some data bearing on long-term spending and borrowing, the astronomically large numbers are abstractions with no more meaning to the average person than the distance to the Moon. What have obvious meaning to voters are the following questions:

- How much will it cost the public, either in spending cuts or tax increases, for the government to stay solvent over the long run?
- What is the average cost per family?
- How much has the current Congress increased or decreased that cost?

Answers to these questions would help voters hold legislators responsible for their fiscal decisions during the coming elections. Although the government could provide answers, both parties hide this politically significant information, as chapters 6 and 8 will show.

Freed from responsibility, Congress has played the Money Trick to the hilt. We have reason to be anxious about whether Social Security and Medicare will be there for us when we need it. We also have reason to be anxious that tax hikes will take away a substantial portion of the money that we have saved on our own for retirement. The trick yields job security for current legislators and social insecurity for us and our children.

With the Money Trick, legislators act like a car dealer who tells us that a vehicle we admire will cost us only $189 a month for the rest of the year but not that the payments in the following years will be much higher. The car dealer's conduct is dishonest, which is why Congress in the Truth in Lending Act made it a crime for firms to fail to reveal to prospective debtors how much they will have to pay in the long run.[10] Yet, Congress itself fails to reveal how much its current policies will cost us in the long run. Just as private borrowers need truth in lending, voters need truth in spending and taxing.

The Debt Guarantee Trick

In the Debt Guarantee Trick, Congress has the government insure the payment of private debts, but without charging a fee commensurate with the risk assumed. In contrast, when a private business guarantees a debt, it charges such a fee. The private debts that the government guarantees include the pensions that corporations promise their employees, as seen in chapter 1. Free or underpriced debt guarantees increase corporate profits, but if the debts are not paid, we the taxpayers are stuck with the bill.

Much worse still, such guarantees encourage too-big-to-fail banks to take on more debt and more risk in pursuit of speculative profits, and so become both bigger and more likely to fail. Indeed, free debt guarantees helped precipitate the financial crisis that began in 2007, as chapter 6 will show. The crisis caused, in turn, the Great Recession, in which millions of people lost their homes, jobs, or retirement savings. Before the fiscal crisis, the elected officials who supported these free debt guarantees reaped praise and campaign contributions from the executives of the financial giants, yet shifted the blame for the subsequent bad news to their successors in office. This is the Debt Guarantee Trick. With it, today's elected officials continue to take credit and shift blame despite the woes that began in 2007.

How the Nation Once Prevented the Trick

Americans learned during the 1800s that the government guaranteeing debts can lead to grief. At that time, corporations had told small towns that they could transform themselves into hubs of commerce by guaranteeing the bonds needed to build a railroad. In return, the railroad would be routed through their towns and stop in each. Many municipalities that fell for the deal found, however, that the corporation went bankrupt, never built the railroad, and left the municipality liable for the debt. People thus learned the hard way the lesson of Proverbs 11:15: "He that is surety for a stranger shall smart for it." In response to this lesson, many states have adopted constitutional prohibitions against the state or its subdivisions guaranteeing the payment of private debts.[11]

Congress and President Franklin Roosevelt drew on this lesson in setting up the Federal Deposit Insurance Corporation (FDIC) in response to a banking crisis in 1933. Panicked depositors, fearful that their banks would go bust, were withdrawing their money. Because such a run on banks can bring down even a financially sound bank, Congress and the president established the FDIC as a government entity to guarantee bank deposits and thus quell the panic. Wisely, however, the statute limited the guarantees to $2,500 per depositor. This way, the FDIC and thus the government would not guarantee the debts that banks owed big depositors and other large investors who lent money to the banks. Because these debts would still be at risk, these investors would demand higher interest rates from banks that took more risk and refuse to lend at all to those that took much-more risk. This approach protected little depositors without the means to gauge the riskiness of their bank yet gave banks a powerful incentive to control their appetite to take on too-much risk in pursuit of profit.[12]

How Congress Came to Get Away with the Trick

The original theory was that the government would guarantee only small deposits and was not out to subsidize the banks themselves. Fast-forward half a century to the 1980s and apply Yogi Berra's axiom that "in theory there is no difference between theory and practice. In practice there is." In practice, the government raised the limit on the amount of deposits insured when financial institutions grew shaky. It is now $250,000 and higher in some cases. Moreover, the government has often made good on deposits above the increased limit and on bank debts other than deposits even though the financial institutions paid no fee for the guarantee of these debts. Such departures from theory occurred when, for example,

- The Farm Credit System ran into difficulty in the 1980s.
- A large bank, Continental Illinois, failed in 1984.
- A third of the savings and loans failed in the 1980s and early 1990s.[13]

The government's actual practice sent a message far more credible than the theory, even though top officials vowed that they would stick with the theory in the future. Treasury Secretary Nicholas Brady stated in 1989, "*Never again.*" The same year, President George H. W. Bush vowed: "These problems will *never happen again.*" Despite such vows, the government bailed out many of the too-big-to-fail firms during the financial crisis of 2007–09. Later, President Barack Obama in signing the Dodd–Frank Wall Street Reform and Consumer Protection Act recycled the never-again vow: "Because of this law, the American people will *never again* be asked to foot the bill for Wall Street's mistakes."[14] Each of these self-congratulations was undeserved.

Under Dodd–Frank, the government charges fees far smaller than any private firm would charge to bear such risk, and in some cases charges no fee at all. So, Congress still has Jane Q. Public subsidize the profits of the financial giants. The debt guarantees still encourage firms to grow bigger and more likely to fail, meaning that we the taxpayers will likely have to foot the bill for the next severe financial crisis. All this is detailed in chapter 6. Moreover, even if we don't foot the bill as taxpayers, we will foot the bill as citizens living in an economy depressed by the financial crises that the debt guarantees promote. Meanwhile, the FDIC is still working out deals that save all deposits, not just those within the policy limits.[15]

Freed from responsibility, Congress continues to play the Debt Guarantee Trick. The government currently guarantees 61.0 percent of the debt of the financial sector, up from 44.8 percent in 1999 before the financial crisis.[16]

With the Debt Guarantee Trick, legislators act like a car dealer who says, "As long as you're in the showroom, do me the favor of signing this guarantee that my company will repay the money that it borrows from the car manufacturer to buy our inventory. There's no risk because the company has more in the bank than the $800,000 that it now owes. By the way, here's a free cup of coffee." You realize that the dealer wants your guarantee to help his company borrow more from the manufacturer. More debt would increase the chances that the company couldn't pay and, if that happened, the guarantee could cost you a fortune, and all for a free cup of coffee. That's so stupid, it's funny. Yet, we go along with Congress providing cheap or free debt guarantees to financial giants.

The Federal Mandate Trick

In the Federal Mandate Trick, members of Congress enact statutes that promise benefits to voters but coerce states, cities, villages, and other subdivisions of the state to deliver the benefits. To do so, state or local officials must raise taxes, cut spending on local priorities, or otherwise impose burdens on their constituents. Federal officials use the Federal Mandate Trick because it lets them take the credit for the benefits but leave to state and local officials the bill for the costs, and the blame that comes with it.

While the federal government should impose some mandates on states and localities, such as the requirements necessary to ensure compliance with constitutional rights, members of Congress have gone wild imposing mandates in order to take credit while shifting blame. This harms us by sabotaging the state and local government services that we depend upon everyday, such as schools, streets, and many other provisions. The mandates sabotage these services by wasting the limited funds of these governments. The former mayor of New York City Ed Koch explained why he, as a member of Congress, had voted for a wasteful mandate of this sort: "You'd be crazy to be against that. When you are a member of Congress and you are voting a mandate and not providing the funds for it, the sky's the limit."[17]

Congress also sabotages these services by making states and localities obey massive amounts of unwise instructions. Take an example discussed in chapter 3, fine particulates. This air pollution is a federal problem because the great bulk of it is transferred between states. Congress could deal with it efficiently and effectively through a simple federal scheme, but that would require its members to take a measure of responsibility. Instead, as previously noted, Congress now *tells* the EPA to *tell* the states to *tell* the sources within their own borders to protect downwind states from emissions. The result is hundreds of thousands of pages of federal instructions that produce a dysfunctional system. This particular use of the Federal Mandate Trick illustrates three ways that the trick, as used in many fields, harms us: First, to milk federal mandates for maximum political advantage, members of Congress control state and local government but fail to attend to matters within the exclusive control of Congress. Second, the mandates require state and local governments to follow detailed instructions from Washington rather than to respond to the wishes of their constituents. Third, tax dollars that could be used to serve us instead get spent on federal officials supervising state officials and state officials reporting to federal officials.[18]

How the Nation Once Prevented the Trick

The Constitution, as written in 1787, prevented the federal government from treating the states as branch offices. In England at the time, the central government in London had the power to fire key regional officials and thus maintained direct and intimate control over them. In contrast, the Constitution sought to ensure that voters in American states, rather than the government in Washington, DC, would select and control state officials. Moreover, the Constitution denied the federal government the power to order state officials to help with its work with only two narrow exceptions—Congress could order the states to implement congressionally ordained procedures for selecting its own members and the president could call forth the state militias, but only in response to congressionally ordained emergencies.[19] (As subdivisions of the state, local governments got the same protection. I include them in referring to "states.") Neither exception allowed Congress to play the Federal Mandate Trick.

Although it denies Congress the power to mandate the states to help with federal projects, the Constitution does contain many provisions prohibiting states from interfering with the work of the federal government or violating rights guaranteed by the Constitution, such as the right to be denied the vote on account of race.[20]

Honoring the Constitution, early Congresses abstained from ordering states to help with federal work. As Alexis de Tocqueville observed in the mid-1830s, the federal government did not use state government as an administrative apparatus to carry out congressional designs. "One sees," he asserted, "two governments completely separated and almost independent."[21]

How Congress Came to Get Away with the Trick

During the 1960s, Southern states actively resisted desegregation, and riots erupted in Northern cities. These developments put states and their subdivisions of both the South and the North in bad repute. This helped give Congress the political cover to coerce states and localities.[22]

To mandate the states, Congress had to find a way around the Constitution's prohibition on requiring the states to help with federal projects. The Supreme Court interprets the Constitution as barring Congress from requiring states to provide services or issue regulations. The Court reasoned that such requirements would undercut account-ability at both the federal and state levels:

> Where the Federal Government directs the States to regulate, it may be state officials who will bear the brunt of public disapproval, while the federal officials who devised the regulatory program may remain insu-lated from the electoral ramifications of their decision. Accountability is thus diminished when, due to federal coercion, elected state officials cannot regulate in accordance with the views of the local electorate.[23]

The Clean Air Act, discussed in chapter 3, illustrates how Congress sidestepped the Constitution and why it continues to do so. As enacted in 1970, the statute did not coerce states. Rather, it ordered a federal agency, the EPA, to set national air-quality goals and to regulate emis-sions from factories and other pollution sources to meet those goals by various deadlines in the late 1970s. The statute gave states the option of helping to regulate emissions but did not require them to do so. At first, most states opted to help, but when it became clear that meeting the federal air-quality goals would require draconian regulations (one example: barring most car travel in Southern California), many states left issuing the unpopular regulations to the federal EPA. Voters com-plained to their representatives in Congress about the harsh measures that the EPA might impose and also about its failure to deliver healthy air as promised.[24]

Members of Congress thus found themselves in a bind: They wanted to avoid the blame for backing away from their promise to protect peo-ple's health from pollution, yet if they had the federal EPA itself impose the duties needed to achieve those air-quality goals, they would get some blame. So, in 1977, to distance themselves from such blame, they amended the Clean Air Act to force the states rather than the federal EPA to take responsibility for imposing the duties. This shifted blame to state officials for both the burdens required to clean the air and the failures to achieve air-quality goals.[25]

Despite the constitutional bar on ordering states to help with federal projects, Congress in 1977 found clever ways to put the onus on state officials. For example, the statute now prohibits the construction of a major factory or the modification of one in states that fail to do the federal bidding to regulate pollution from all sources.[26] Such failure will leave state officials with the blame for freezing the state's economy and dashing the hope of new jobs. The prohibition could pass constitutional muster because it ostensibly has the federal government regulating the factory's air pollution rather than coercing the states. Yet, the prohibition's real purpose is to coerce states to regulate. So, state officials would have to do the federal bidding, but members of Congress, having used such an indirect method to get their way, could largely escape blame.

In another example of the statute coercing state officials to take the blame for the burdens of air-pollution control, it bars federal highway grants to states that fail to do the federal bidding. For state officials to allow their state to lose these highway grants would be political suicide. These federal grants are a massive part of state budgets; they are funded by federal taxes that voters of all states pay regardless of whether their state gets a grant; and the loss of the grant would harm voters by cutting off federally funded highway improvements, construction jobs, and lucrative construction contracts.

Yet the coercion has passed constitutional muster because Congress is ostensibly exercising its power to spend federal money rather than ordering the states to regulate. Under its spending power, Congress had previously offered states grants to help with federal projects such as building interstate highways. In so doing, Congress required the states to build the highways according to federal specifications so that the nation would get well-built roads. In denying highway funds to states that do not regulate air pollution as the federal government prescribes, Congress could claim that it was getting the roads it wanted to pay for, ones that not only move traffic but also do not result in excessive pollution. That, of course, was not Congress's real motive. Indeed, failing to build a new road can cause a traffic bottleneck in which cars pollute much and move little. Courts, however, ordinarily don't permit themselves to inquire into Congress's real motives and so uphold statutes if federal attorneys can conceive of some justifying motive that accords with the Constitution. Indeed, the courts have upheld the Clean Air Act's giving highway grants to states on the condition that they obey federal instructions on how to control pollution. Threatened with painful sanctions such as loss of highway funds, states must generally knuckle under.[27]

But how could members of Congress vote to threaten their own constituents with sanctions if their state failed to do the federal bidding? In the case of the Clean Air Act, the legislators didn't cast roll call votes to do so. They held forty-five roll call votes on the 1977 and 1990 Clean Air Act statutes, but none of those roll calls were specifically on the provisions that threatened harm to constituents as a means to coerce state officials.[28] They did, of course, vote for the statute as a whole, but that could be characterized as a vote for clean air rather than a vote to sanction their own constituents. Thus, our representatives left no fingerprints on the sanctions with which they threatened us.

The upshot is a politically optimal arrangement for members of Congress, but it makes the air dirtier, as discussed in chapter 3. The legislators get to stay in office longer; we get to die a bit sooner.

Congress had ample opportunity to use federal grants to impose mandates on states, as the number and size of grant programs grew explosively from the mid-1960s onward. Today, Congress mandates state and local governments to deliver congressionally announced benefits across the entire range of their activity, from education to community development to criminal justice. They are now branch offices of the federal government, but the courts can do little. They have no precise test to distinguish between Congress acting for the purpose of exercising its constitutional powers and Congress playing the Federal Mandate Trick. Indeed, the Supreme Court has struck down only one especially coercive mandate, and it is unclear whether that case will result in striking down other mandates.[29]

As the number of mandates grew, so did the resentment against them, which resulted in Congress passing the Unfunded Mandates Reform Act of 1995. In signing the bill, President Clinton stated, "Before 1964, the number of explicit mandates from the Congress on state and local governments was zero," but "on the day I took office [January 20, 1993] there were at least 172 separate pieces of legislation that impose requirements on state and local government."[30]

Although Republicans in Congress claimed the Unfunded Mandates Reform Act fulfilled a promise in their *Contract with America*, and

President Clinton praised the act as a "model for how we have to continue to change the way Washington does business," they engaged in more undeserved self-congratulations. The act calls for a study by a federal commission of mandates in old statutes, but Congress abolished the commission before it completed the study. To limit mandates in new statutes, the act empowers any member of Congress to raise a "point of order" against a mandate in a bill before the House or Senate passed it. The point of order supposedly would trigger a roll call vote and thus make members of Congress accountable for the mandate. However, the act exempts many types of bills from such points of order. As to other types of bills, the House and Senate typically use legislative maneuvers to limit the ability of legislators to raise points of order. No surprise here. In a span of twenty years, points of order were raised only fifty-nine times in the House and three times in the Senate.[31]

With the Federal Mandate Trick, federal legislators act like a car dealer who quotes a price for the car as "everything included," but leaves out the state and local taxes. The car dealer is dishonest. Just as are the federal legislators who evade responsibility for the burdens that their federal mandates impose on us.

The Regulation Trick

In the Regulation Trick, Congress enacts statutes that grant voters seemingly rock-solid rights to regulatory protection but orders agencies to impose the duties needed to fulfill those rights. With this trick, members of Congress get the credit for granting voters rights but shift to an agency much of the blame for the failures to fulfill those rights, as well as much of the blame for the burdens resulting from the duties the agency imposes.

With Congress playing the Regulation Trick with the Clean Air Act, as discussed in chapter 3, a timid agency did far less to protect us from lead in gasoline than an accountable Congress would have. Meanwhile, narrowly focused as they are on their assigned missions, bureaucrats often stop trivial environmental harms at huge costs.[32] As the discussion of the Clean Air Act also illustrates, the trick lets legislators avoid responsibility for revising obsolete statutes that no longer serve the public interest. We suffer such harms from the Regulation Trick not just in the field of environmental protection but also in the many other fields in which Congress uses the trick.

How the Nation Once Prevented the Trick

To fulfill the Revolutionary War cry of "No taxation without representation," the Founding Fathers gave Congress the power to impose the rules that require the payment of taxes. The Constitution also gave it the power to impose the rules regulating private conduct.[33] Over the decades, however, the Supreme Court increasingly let Congress openly delegate the power to write the regulatory rules to agencies. (For those who are interested, the discussion in the box that follows traces the changes in the Court's stance.)

How the Supreme Court Let Congress Outsource the Responsibility for Regulation

As an early Supreme Court decision stated, the power of Congress to regulate lies in its ability "to prescribe the rule" that governs the regulated conduct.[34] Because Congress would have to enact the rules of regulation, there would be no regulation without representation.

In attempting to uphold the principle that lawmakers in Congress should take responsibility for the rules, the Supreme Court in 1813 opined that they must state the rule to be imposed under the statute they are enacting, although executive and judicial officials would have a role in its interpretation and application. Yet, Congress frequently could not state the rules with precision. Often Congress could not readily get the information needed to do so, especially before the modern means of communication. Even more fundamentally, legislators could not anticipate every circumstance in which a rule might apply. So, for example, they made the statutes regulating steamboat safety as precise as they could, but that was often quite imprecise. Also, understandably, the Supreme Court kept changing its conception of Congress's responsibility. For instance, the Court opined in 1825 that legislators, if they dealt with the "important" issues in the statute, could leave others to supply the "details."[35]

In response to the Progressives' call for Congress to grant broad powers to agencies staffed by experts, the Supreme Court upheld such grants, partly because the justices viewed the work of experts as scientific and, so it was thought, unlike the political work of Congress. In 1928, the Supreme Court held that legislators could expressly delegate the power to write the rules to agencies so long as the statute stated an "intelligible principle" to guide the agency lawmakers. Yet, the Court gave no comprehensible definition of the intelligible principle test. It did, however, hold that even an instruction to protect "the public interest" was sufficiently intelligible to satisfy the intelligible principle test.[36]

In sum, the principle that legislators should take responsibility for the rules of private conduct became mush. Recently, the justices threw up their hands and admitted that they would leave it to members of Congress to decide how much responsibility they wished to shoulder.[37]

In the decades prior to 1970, Congress generally delegated the power to write the regulatory rules in vaguely worded statutes that gave agencies broad discretion to decide which regulatory rights to grant and which regulatory duties to impose. By giving such power to agencies, Congress also gave them much of the responsibility for the resulting regulatory protection and burdens. As a result, the agency rather than the legislators got much of the credit for granting rights to regulatory protection and much of the blame for the regulatory burdens. The Regulation Trick had not yet begun.

How Congress Came to Get Away with the Trick

The Regulation Trick began with statutes such as the Clean Air Act of 1970. Even though Congress granted rights to regulatory protection, it still delegated to an agency the job of imposing most of the duties on pollution sources needed to fulfill those rights. So the legislators got most of the credit for conferring regulatory protection, while avoiding much of the blame for the resulting burdens.

The Regulation Trick began around 1970, and not during the progressive era, because of four changes that were necessary for legislators to convince voters that agencies would actually deliver the regulatory protection promised. First, courts had to have procedures and standards with which to judge whether the administrative agencies had fulfilled their statutory duties. Congress first enacted a systematic set of such procedures and standards in the Administrative Procedure Act, passed in 1946.[38] Second, private citizens had to be able to go to court to defend the rights of the general public to regulatory protection—that is, to act as private attorneys general. The "private attorneys general" concept came to prominence during the civil rights litigation of the 1960s. Third, the agency imposing the duties on hundreds of thousands of sources concerning complex subjects like air pollution needed to have the appropriate technology to gather vast amounts of information and disseminate vast amounts of instructions. This work was impractical until such technological advances as the Xerox machine replaced carbon paper and the mimeograph machine in the 1960s. Fourth, and finally, Congress needed to have ostensibly stated the right to regulatory protection in terms that were sufficiently precise for courts to plausibly enforce the right. It would not be good enough, for example, for Congress to promise that the EPA would make the air "healthier," because courts could not enforce the right for the air to be made healthier to an unspecified extent. The federal government's impressive demonstrations of technological prowess culminating with landing men on the Moon in 1969 made it seem credible for Congress to grant an agency an ironclad right to healthy air. So, Congress ordered the EPA to make the air "healthy." It turned out, as already noted, that this order was gibberish.

Freed from the responsibility for the burdens and failures, Congress has paid little attention to the actual impact of regulatory statutes on constituents. Even though statutes like the Clean Air Act have done much good, they have done far-less good than Congress promised. To fulfill the act's legislative promises, the EPA would have had to impose far-greater burdens than legislators were willing to take responsibility for. Without the Regulation Trick, Congress would have done far-more good for us at a far-lower cost to us because the legislators would have had to bear responsibility for the consequences. Indeed, the Clean Air Act has done, by far, the most good in those few instances where legislators did take responsibility for the burdens, with expert advice from the agency, as seen in chapter 3. Congress can pair legislative responsibility with agency expertise, as chapter 8 will show.

With the Regulation Trick, legislators act like a car dealer who says to us as we admire a car in the showroom, "I can see that you have an eye for cars, but we have a team of experts who will select an even-better car for you. Just sign this contract to purchase the car they will select for you, and you will own a great car at a great price." You realize that this contract will give the dealer carte blanche to stick you with a bad car at a bad price. How absurd it would be to fall for this bait-and-switch. Yet, we put up with federal legislators baiting us with high-sounding statutory rights and leaving an agency to switch us to ineffective, inefficient regulations.

This chapter has focused on the federal legislators in Congress, but presidents function as legislators, too. In addition to members of Congress, presidents also use the Money Trick, the Debt Guarantee Trick, the Federal Mandate Trick, and the Regulation Trick to shield themselves from the blame for legislation.

In contrast to members of Congress, however, presidents must implement statutes. Yet, their responsibility for exercising executive power is no substitute for the responsibility that the tricks let members of Congress and the president dodge in their legislative work.[39] One reason is that the legislative power is more important than the executive power, because the president can exercise executive power in implementing statutes only within the confines that the statutes establish.

Moreover, the president who signs tricky legislation into law ends up shouldering little of the responsibility that the tricks allowed that president and Congress to duck in enacting it. The Money Trick and the Debt Guarantee Trick shift the blame to future presidents and members of Congress. The Federal Mandate Trick shifts the blame to state and local officials. That leaves the Regulation Trick. To the extent that it does shift the blame to the executive branch, the burdens often get announced after the president who signed the bill has left office. In any event, a president serving a second term escapes accountability at the polls for executive acts because the Constitution bars a third term.

Even a first-term president largely escapes the blame for the burdens imposed by agencies. While some agencies are independent of presidential control, most are subject to it, but presidents usually will personally announce the rules that they make only when the White House political advisors think that they would gain in popularity by doing so.[40] Otherwise, the president leaves the announcement to the head of the agency. The agency head can usually shift some of the blame to the statute or the court decisions that structured its decision making. Everyone is responsible, so no one is.

Moreover, few regulatory issues become important in a national presidential election because they are overshadowed by the president's work as commander in chief, diplomat in chief, economic strategist, and national leader. These roles generally let the president appear aloof from choices about regulation. In contrast, how representatives and senators would vote on such issues, if the Regulation Trick did not let them duck hard choices, would be important in many of their reelection campaigns.[41]

The tricks thus allow presidents as well as members of Congress to evade "the consent of the governed."

We tell pollsters that members of Congress are about as untrustworthy as car dealers.[42] Stopping there, however, lets us voters off the hook too easily. We are complicit in the trickery because many of us want to hear only good news. Returning to Tim Penny, the retired Democratic representative from Minnesota quoted in the introduction, "Voters routinely punish lawmakers who try to do unpopular things, who challenge them to face unpleasant truths about the budget, crime, Social Security, or tax policy." "Similarly," he continued, "voters reward politicians for giving them what they want—more spending for popular programs—even if it means wounding the nation in the long run by creating more debt."[43]

So we demand something for nothing, even though we know it is impossible—except by magic. Magicians on stage seem to work magic with smoke, mirrors, and sleights of hand. Federal legislators promise us popular benefits without unpopular consequences with their blame-shifting tricks.

We know why audiences of stage shows go along with tricks that appear to happen *abracadabra*, such as a magician pulling an animal from a seemingly empty box. As Penn Jillette, of the stage-magic team Penn & Teller, pointed out, the audience "wants to see that box empty with its own eyes, but the audience also knows that it has to follow the unwritten rules or the tricks just won't work. You can see that the box is empty from your seat, but you can't get up out of your seat, walk on stage and stick your hand in the 'empty' box. You would ruin the trick."[44]

So why do voters go along with the blame-shifting tricks? After all, these tricks harm us rather than entertain us. Partly because we don't yet see the sleights of hand that enable the tricks to deceive us. Politicians have veiled them with complication, silence, and phony corrective action. Federal legislators have every reason to avoid pointing them out once they begin using them. Because both parties use tricks, each of them blames the ills that come from them more on the other party than on the tricks themselves. Over the decades, the tricks have become routine and so seem natural. They go largely unremarked in day-to-day press coverage. Yes, there is talk of the current budget deficit or the national debt, but those things are not at the core of what makes the Money Trick work. Our failure to see the tricks means that Congress can use them again and again, as evidenced by its continuance of the cheap debt guarantees for the too-big-to-fail financial giants after the 2007–09 financial crisis.

However, it's not just that we don't understand the tricks. We also don't want to see them. In Penn's words, "We know somewhere in our hearts that our political saviors are not really magic, but we so want them to be." The Wizard of Oz blamed his trickery on those who expected him to work magic: "How can I help being a humbug when all these people make me do things that everybody knows can't be done?"[45] Car dealers no doubt blame their trickery on customers who want the car they want rather than the car they can afford. Likewise, members of Congress and the presidents enable us to hope for something for nothing (or very little) because that's what we want, and so we enable them to trick us. Long-promised something for nothing, we voters have evolved into a species that demands it.

We and our officials must wake up to the reality that we are codependent parties in a fantasy that produces a broken government.

The trickery is even more pervasive than I have already shown. The tricks in Congress have infected the American government from top to bottom. Emulating their federal counterparts, state legislators use the Money Trick, the Regulation Trick, and a variant on the Federal Mandate Trick in which they shift the blame for tax increases and spending cuts to local officials. City governments use the Money Trick and the Regulation Trick. It's tricks all the way down.

This book focuses primarily on trickery at the federal level because this is where it is the most rampant and if it is seen for what it is there, it can be seen for what it is everywhere.

In sum, the Money Trick, the Debt Guarantee Trick, the Federal Mandate Trick, and the Regulation Trick allow legislators to get the credit for promising us benefits without taking the blame for the burdens and the disappointments. Whom they shift the blame to varies with the trick:

- In the Money Trick and the Debt Guarantee Trick, legislators shift the blame to their successors in office.
- In the Federal Mandate Trick, they shift the blame to state and local officials.
- In the Regulation Trick, they shift the blame to bureaucrats.

Legislators' shifting the blame means they don't have to consider whether the benefits for us are worth the burdens or how to provide the most benefit for the least burden. They focus instead on how to get the most credit for the least blame.

Congress also uses a fifth trick, the War Trick, to avoid responsibility for controversial decisions to go to war, as chapter 7 will show. I deal with this trick in a separate chapter because by using it, members of Congress avoid responsibility altogether, instead of the usual course of taking responsibility for the good and shifting responsibility for the bad, and the president ends up shouldering responsibility.

Chapters 8 and 9 will show how to stop the tricks. By putting an end to them, we can get up out of our seats, "walk on stage and stick [our hands] in the 'empty' box," and make government work for us.

CHAPTER 5

The Tricks Harm Us Now

We've all had quite enough of your clever tricks.

—ROALD DAHL[1]

Decades ago, Congress gave us the seemingly good news that we don't have to pay income tax on health care insurance that employers provide. That's an exception to the general rule under which we must pay income tax on the valuables we receive from employers, whether in kind or cash. This exception cut the tax bill for the average family with employer-provided health insurance by a whopping $6,000 a year in 2008.[2] Yet, the tax break actually costs families far more than it provides. Worse still, it has long sickened the health care system upon which our lives depend. We suffer, but it remains in force because the tricks make it politically profitable for legislators to harm us, their constituents.

How this tax break does such harm is tough to see because it began before most of us were born, yet a thought experiment can help to see how it has made life worse for us. Follow along with me as I imagine what would happen if Congress were to decide today that we don't have to pay income tax on any *home* insurance that employers provide.

Employers generally do not provide home insurance, and, if they did, we would have to pay income tax on it.[3] But were it, like health insurance, excluded from taxable income, we would want our employers to divert some of our salary to pay for the home insurance. Doing so would cost employers nothing but let us shield from tax the money that we now spend both to buy the homeowners' policies protecting against fires and other catastrophes and to pay plumbers and other workers making routine repairs. In other words, we would want our employer-provided home insurance to be comprehensive—that is, to cover routine as well as catastrophic costs, just like our "comprehensive" health insurance does.

Excluding the cost of employer-provided home insurance from taxable income would seem at first to have done nothing other than make home maintenance more affordable. The plumber would fix a clogged drain, charge the traditional fee, and the insurer would pay. In time, however, the maintenance workers would realize that they could charge the insurer more than they could charge a homeowner. The plumber might raise the hourly rate, exaggerate the time the job took, or do a bigger repair than needed. We wouldn't much care because the insurer would pay.

Paying out more for these services would force the insurer to raise the premiums for the insurance, which would likely prompt the employer to renegotiate the insurance contract to cut costs. The new contract might do things like cap the fees paid to plumbers, require preapproval for repairs, and limit plumbing to a list of plumbers that charge cut rates and likely cut corners. Employers and insurers would thus end up making the decisions about the maintenance of our homes that we and our families had previously made ourselves.

The insurer would hopefully aim to pay the necessary claims and reject the rest, but no written guidelines could definitively distinguish between the two because of the wide variety of conditions requiring home repair and the many factors that influence how to do them in a particular location. Moreover, unlike a home owner, an insurer would have to decide whether a repair is necessary over the telephone or Internet. So the insurer would sometimes refuse to pay necessary claims (forcing the homeowners to pay for them themselves or forgo the needed repairs) and sometimes pay unnecessary or excessive claims (in turn increasing the insurance premiums ultimately coming out of take-home pay).

The tax break would also increase the cost of home repair because of the insurers' elaborate systems for controlling home repair costs. Producing the paperwork required by the insurers would be a hassle and a cost for the maintenance workers. Processing the paperwork would be a cost for the insurer. These costs would increase the insurance premium.

Computer-based billing systems would cut the maintenance workers' cost of dealing with the insurers, but many individual maintenance workers couldn't afford such systems, while large home-repair corporations could. So, when needing a repair, we would more frequently find ourselves calling a corporation rather than our plumber or electrician. Yet, these large corporations, with their technology, office staffs, executives, and shareholders demanding dividends would add still-more overhead to the cost of paying a plumber to repair the pipe.

Even though the tax break would benefit the average family by reducing their income tax bill, this benefit would come at an even-bigger cost. Not only would employer-provided home-repair insurance increase the cost and hassle of maintaining our homes but Congress would eventually have to replace the revenue being lost by raising taxes or cutting spending. But the Money Trick would let legislators shift the blame for the bad news to their successors in office so that Congress would continue the tax break once it began.

The tax break for employer-provided home-repair insurance is a thought experiment, but the tax break for employer-provided health insurance is all too real. I use the tax break for health insurance to illustrate how the tricks harm us. My focus is on this tax break rather than the Affordable Care Act passed in 2009 because both before and after that statute was passed, the tax break has made the country's health care problems much worse, not because abolishing the tax break would in itself be a sufficient remedy for those problems.

The tax break began during World War II. Before the war, health care worked much as home repair does today. Some people had insurance coverage for hospitalization, which, as medicine was practiced then, was the medical equivalent of coverage for the catastrophes that current homeowners' policies protect against. Few people had comprehensive health insurance covering out-of-hospital medical expenses. Most physicians worked alone or with a few others, not in large organizations.[4]

The tax break for health insurance came in the fog of war. The War Labor Board, which limited wages to curb wartime inflation, decided to ignore employer-provided health insurance in determining whether employers paid wages in excess of the limits. At the time, employers did not generally provide health care insurance, but the board's decision prompted some to start doing so. This would allow them to attract employees by offering them something valuable in addition to the maximum permitted wage. The Internal Revenue Service followed the lead of the War Labor Board by excluding the cost of health care insurance from employees' taxable income.[5] The Money Trick had little to do with the start of this tax break, because in the early years relatively few people had employer-provided health insurance, and so the impact on federal revenues was small.

Although the wage limits ended shortly after the war, the tax law continued to exclude employer-provided health care insurance from taxable income. With the top marginal tax rate exceeding 90 percent in most years from 1944 to 1963, the tax break massively subsidized the health care of those with employer-provided insurance. Unions got employers to use some of the money that would otherwise have gone into salary increases to buy health care insurance for employees. This insurance covered routine care as well as catastrophic costs such as hospitalization. That is why it was called "comprehensive." In the decades following World War II, Americans increasingly had various kinds of insurance, with individuals generally buying homeowners' insurance and automobile insurance on their own and getting health care insurance from their employers.[6]

At first, employer-provided health care insurance had little discernible effect on the relations between patients and physicians. Physicians, still working for themselves or in very small practices, had the latitude to vary fees with the income of the patient or to donate their time to clinics for the poor. This was done by physicians who were friends of my parents when I was a child. Here was society at work, however imperfectly. Physicians showed concern for many things, money, health, and fellow feeling included.[7] There was some room here for the fair side of human nature.

The tax break for employees with employer-provided health care insurance gradually changed health care for the worse. The insurer's deep pocket, notwithstanding the patients' limited means, became the determining factor in doctors setting fees and selecting procedures. Some physicians not firmly socialized in the old ways upped their income by raising fees and performing unnecessary procedures. After all, the insurer would pay. This practice accelerated with the advent of Medicare in 1965, which vastly increased the number of insured patients and added to the government subsidy for health care, particularly because Medicare initially did not cap fees. Medicine became more lucrative relative to other professions. As cardiologist and *New York Times* contributor Dr. Sandeep Jauhar concluded, physicians started focusing more on making money and less on patient care. New medical technologies added to the cost of medical care, but the tax break and the changes it wrought also added to the cost. In his book *Doctored: The Disillusionment of an American Physician*, Dr. Jauhar wrote, "Premiums for insurers like Blue Cross, whose reimbursement rates were determined by doctors, increased 25 to 50 percent annually."[8] Thus, the revenue lost to the government through the tax break started to skyrocket at about the time that Congress began to play the Money Trick in the 1960s. The tax break was beginning to bring out the selfish side of human nature.

Paying out more to doctors forced insurers to raise the premiums they charged employers. Ultimately, employers and insurers negotiated insurance contracts to try to slow the increase in premiums by doing things like capping fees paid to physicians, requiring preapproval for many procedures, and limiting reimbursement to physicians willing to work on the insurers' terms. Dr. Jauhar reported that "by the early 2000s, 95 percent of insured workers were in some sort of managed care plan."[9]

Like my hypothetical example of insurer control of home repair, insurer control of health care was intended to pay for the necessary claims and reject the rest. In practice, it has created hassles, required paperwork, and made mistakes for the same reasons that comprehensive home repair insurance would.

The insurers' control of health care drove most physicians out of individual practice. Dr. Rita Mariotti, for example, practiced medicine for thirty-seven years in an office in her home in a small New Jersey town, making house calls on a motor scooter. As she wrote,

> As managed care invaded my limited private practice, the logistics of competing to stay in medicine became impractical because the system required so much more wrangling with insurance companies. It would have been impossible to hire two other employees to do all the added paperwork.

I finally sold my practice to the community hospital, and a family-practice resident was placed in [my] office temporarily while a huge family-practice center was built in a nearby town. The patient load dropped precipitously, while the staff increased to three employees, plus a "practice management team" in control of all operations; office hours were theoretically expanded, but the doctor was available less and less of the time.[10]

She had previously thrived in her practice, she reported, because of the "very personal involvement with my patients," while the new regime increased costs, turned patients into statistics, and eliminated house calls.[11]

My own physician, Dr. David Zimmerman, is one of those rare doctors who continued to practice without submitting to insurer control. I first went to Dr. Zimmerman in the early 1970s and have stayed with him because he is scrupulously careful, keeps current on medical research, listens to my concerns without ever making me feel rushed, answers my questions, and lays out choices for me to make.

As insurer control put pressure on his practice, he realized, as had Dr. Mariotti, that a sole practitioner could not afford the staff needed to deal with the insurance companies. He told his patients other than those on Medicare or Medicaid that they would have to pay him directly. He would provide patients with completed insurance forms, and it would be up to us to get what reimbursement we could. Seeing him on these terms is more expensive than seeing a doctor who submits to insurer control. Because patients would end up paying more, Dr. Zimmerman feared that his caseload would dwindle to the point where he would have to close his office. His physician friends, most having given up their solo practices and joined group practices, warned him that he had better join a group before it was too late. The groups contract with hospitals, other groups of physicians, and insurers to form a network of medical providers. If my doctor had joined a group, he would practice medicine as, in essence, an employee of the network. However, he decided to stay on his own. That decision nevertheless made him nervous.

Why did Dr. Zimmerman risk going it alone? The issue was not money. As he explained his choice: "What would go out the window is enjoyment, practicing medicine is how I define myself, [and] I like the way I practice medicine. Maybe it's ego, but I like to think it's a matter of conscience."[12] He would rather work under a system that pays only modestly but leaves it up to him and his patients to make their health care decisions than work under a system that pays handsomely but restricts how he practices. This reflects his own preference, stated more than fifteen years ago, not a prediction of how a government system would work in the future.

When I asked the doctor how joining a network would have changed his practice, he rattled off quite a list. The network, he said, would have reduced his income if he didn't prescribe unnecessary procedures, required him to squeeze six patients into each hour, prevented him from taking extra time with new patients, and pressured him to gather patient histories through written questionnaires rather than in person. Moreover, the network would require him to send patients to its own specialists rather than the ones he believed would provide the best care. Dr. Zimmerman noted that nowadays "my physician friends who told me in the 1990s that I would be foolish not to join a network tell me, 'you were right.'"[13]

Despite all the harmful effects felt by many people, the exclusion of employer-provided private health insurance looks good to many voters, largely because it is a massive tax break. Yet, the tax break will cost us in the end because the government's loss of revenue will add to the tax increases and spending cuts that future Congresses will inevitably have to impose to make up for it. Moreover, by making patients largely indifferent to how much gets spent on their individual health care, the tax break inevitably led to insurer control, with all its limits on how much time doctors can devote to our care, what they can do for us, and how much they are paid. Furthermore, by subsidizing health care, the tax break increases health care costs.[14]

Not only is the tax break bad for patients, it is also bad for physicians. General practitioners work longer hours and have twice the patient caseload. In addition, their average inflation-adjusted income went from $185,000 in 1970 to $161,000 in 2010. So, although in recent years the nation has spent much more on health care, in part because of the tax break, the money does not end up in the pockets of physicians. Much of the money goes to administrating the insurance system. The salaries of health care administrators have in fact surpassed those of the physicians who provide the care. Then there are the overhead and profits of the insurance companies themselves as well as the costs to physicians of complying with the bureaucratic requirements of insurance companies, which average $83,000 per doctor annually. In the United States, about a third of the health care dollar goes to administration, six times more than in other OECD countries. Insurer control accounts for half of that administrative cost. In urging Congress to pass the Affordable Care Act, President Obama called for controlling the upsurge in health care costs.[15] He didn't have to call for controlling the upsurge in home repair costs.

The longer hours, lower pay, and bureaucratization of medicine discourages young people from becoming physicians. According to polls, the majority of physicians have gone from rejoicing in their profession in the 1970s to now discouraging others from going to medical school. We now have a shortage of physicians. As Dr. Jauhar put it, "Try getting a timely appointment with your family doctor. In some parts of the country today, it is next to impossible." As he pointed out, with the much-higher caseloads and bureaucratization of doctors, for many people "it is rare to find a primary physician who can remember us from visit to visit, let alone come to know us in depth." Summing it all up, he remarked: "Unhappy doctors make for unhappy patients."[16]

All health insurance brings with it some degree of insurer control, and almost everyone wants to have health insurance in place for catastrophic costs, but the tax break interfered with our control of our health care far more than that. The tax break subsidized insurance to cover all health expenses rather than just catastrophic ones, and so broadened insurer control. The tax break also gave employers power over what sort of insurance people would have, rather than leaving us in charge individually. According to a 2003 Joint Economic Committee staff report, four out of ten employers offered their employees only one choice of insurance plan.[17]

The sickening consequences of the tax exclusion raise the question, Why has Congress failed to end it? The answer is, in short: the Money Trick. The tax break relieves us of having to pay tax on the dollars that employers use to buy our health care insurance. This savings reduced our federal income taxes by a total of $226 billion in 2008. (I use the 2008 figure to make it clear that I am talking about the tax break rather than the Affordable Care Act.) Together with the accompanying reduction in state income taxes, this worked out to an annual reduction in income taxes of roughly $6,000 per family of four covered by employer-provided insurance.[18] Yet, the government must eventually replace the lost revenue by taking money from us through tax increases or spending cuts.

The richest families get by far the biggest benefit from the tax break. In 2008, it was worth far more than $6,000 per year to families in a high-income tax bracket with expensive insurance plans, far less to families in a low-income tax bracket with bare-bones insurance plans, and nothing to families without employer-provided insurance.[19] Further, families who buy health care out of pocket or through individually purchased insurance must bear the higher prices that the tax break causes.

Prominent policy makers from the left and the right have noted the perverse consequences of the tax break, but Congress has failed to phase it out, even though it has had many opportunities to do so. It enacted sweeping statutes on health care under both Democratic and Republican presidents—creating Medicare and Medicaid in 1965 and adding Medicare drug benefits in 2003. Nonetheless, it continued the tax break. In 2007, Senator Ron Wyden, a liberal Democrat known for his mastery of policy and willingness to work with Republicans, joined by nineteen Democratic and Republican senators, introduced a bill to eliminate it.[20] The bill went nowhere in Congress.

The Affordable Care Act perpetuated the tax break, even though the tax break had caused or exacerbated many of the very problems that President Obama identified as reasons to enact his health care proposal. These problems include escalating costs, the loss of insurance when an employee leaves a job, and bias against the needs of lower-income people. While the statute as passed does not end the tax break, it does place an excise tax on so-called Cadillac health care plans. This arrangement recoups only a small fraction of the revenue lost, leaves higher-income employees with a much-bigger benefit, and does not reliably end the insurer control of health care that comes from the tax break. The Republican caucus, for its part, failed to propose an alternative to the Affordable Care Act that would have gotten rid of the tax break.[21]

Keeping the tax break in force has paid political dividends to members of Congress and presidents of both parties due to the Money Trick.

With it, politicians have been able to continue to take credit for the good news (the tax break now saves many families much more than $6,000 a year)[22] but hide the corresponding bad news (the taxes will have to be increased or the spending cut to offset this loss in revenue). Without this trick, voters would have started asking questions about who benefits from the tax break, and come to see that by far the largest benefits go to the rich, the smallest go to the working poor, and nothing goes to families without employer-provided insurance. If legislators had to justify such a grossly unfair scheme, they would lose votes in the next election.

Moreover, by keeping the tax break in force, legislators and presidents have pleased the special interests that profit from it—the health insurers, hospitals, medical-provider networks, and drug companies. Also benefitting are those labor-union officials who administer health care plans. They lobbied fiercely to keep the tax break.[23] All of these special interests are, of course, an important source of campaign contributions and other reelection support for elected officials. With the Money Trick, legislators could accommodate the special interests involved in health care without losing votes.

So, even though the tax break continues to increase the cost of health care, decrease its quality, and add to the hassles of being a patient or health care provider, members of Congress can escape blame for these things. The blame instead goes to the insurance company that increases the premium, the employer that holds down our salary to pay for the increase or opts for skimpier coverage, or the insurance company that consequently forces us to jump through hoops to get treatment or refuses to pay for it at all.

Unfortunately, however, ending the tax break alone would not cure all of America's health care problems. My focus so far in this chapter has been on showing that the Money Trick helps perpetuate a tax break that harms us, and not on offering a way to cure all these health care problems.

Using health care as an example, the balance of this chapter identifies three reasons that not only the Money Trick but also the Debt Guarantee Trick, the Federal Mandate Trick, and the Regulation Trick harm the general public.

Reason 1: The tricks allow legislators to escape blame for the harm that they do to us. Because legislators are able to escape blame, they tolerate not only the tax break for health care insurance but also the financing of highways through gimmicks (see chapter 1); a Clean Air Act that fails to save lives but does impose unnecessary economic burdens (see chapter 3); and the harm that many other perversely designed statutes inflict upon us.

Insulated from blame, members of Congress don't have to spend time investigating how their statutes will actually affect us.[24] As the widely respected former congressman Lee Hamilton explained, "The truth is that the House has developed atrocious habits. One is that [its] members spend only two or three days a week in Washington."[25]

Even when they are in Washington, legislators spend little of their time paying attention to legislation. In 2012, the Democratic Congressional Campaign Committee advised newly elected representatives to allocate their days in Washington as follows:

- **four hours:** call time (telephone solicitations for campaign contributions)
- **one to two hours:** constituent visits
- **two hours:** committee/floor time
- **one hour:** strategic outreach: breakfasts, meet and greets, press
- **one hour:** recharge time[26]

This schedule calls for only two hours devoted to "committee/floor time," even though committees are where legislators are supposed to evaluate the impact of legislation on us and the floor of the House is where representatives are supposed to debate and act upon legislation. Freshmen Republicans get the same sort of advice on how to allocate their time. Two hours per day for two to three days per week spent paying attention to the impact of legislation on constituents is less time than many weekend golfers spend golfing.

Members of Congress spend more hours a day telephoning for campaign contributions than they do in committee or on the floor because contributions are more important to their reelection than is the impact of legislation upon us. They will spend more time on legislation once we force them to stop the tricks and therefore bear responsibility. After hearing my proposal to stop the tricks, a senior Capitol Hill staffer commented, "They would have to start paying attention."[27]

Contrast the slapdash work habits of our modern designers of statutes with the care that designers of arches in ancient Rome lavished on their work. Many Roman arches built two thousand years ago still stand. Some say that Roman architects were so careful because when the scaffolding holding up the arch during construction was removed, they had to stand beneath the arch, meaning that if it collapsed, they died.[28] The tricks allow our modern legislators to avoid standing behind their work, let alone under it.

Reason 2: The tricks skew legislation to favor the rich and connected at the expense of the general public. The tax break for health care insurance disproportionately allocates several hundred billion dollars per year to the rich and also boosts the revenues of insurance companies, drug makers, and other entities with political connections. This is but an illustration of how the tricks enrich the wealthy and empower the connected. Scholars from across the ideological spectrum point to many ways that Congress favors the wealthy at the expense of the general public.[29] Ever since the tricks took hold in the early 1970s, the government's actions have raised the incomes of the top 1 percent shockingly faster than those of the rest of the population. In contrast, in many previous decades, the share of income that went to the top 1 percent held steady.[30]

In their book *Winner-Take-All Politics*, political science professors Hacker and Pierson explained the shift of income in favor of the top 1 percent as follows: Having suffered a series of setbacks during the early 1970s in the wake of the enactment of aggressive environmental, occupational-safety, and consumer-protection statutes, big businesses set out to increase their power in Washington. They, for example, moved the headquarters of the National Association of Manufacturers from New York to Washington and ramped up spending on lobbying and campaign contributions.[31]

Meanwhile, the middle and lower class were losing much of their organized influence on bread-and-butter issues. Previously, unions had spoken in Washington not only for their own memberships on work-related issues but also for the less affluent generally on a broad array of economic issues. So, too, did membership-based service clubs such as

Rotary, Lions, and Kiwanis speak for the less affluent on such issues. Such clubs and unions representing workers in the private sector eventually lost membership and therefore clout. Organizations concerned with environmental protection, civil liberties, women's rights, religious fundamentalism, or other ideological issues would subsequently gain power in Washington, and often opposed big business on ideological issues, but as Hacker and Pierson pointed out, not on bread-and-butter ones.[32] Big business used its organizational superiority on bread-and-butter issues to press for favorable decisions on "laws governing unions; the minimum wage; regulations of corporate governance; rules for financial markets, including the management of risk for high-stakes economic ventures" and much more, like tax cuts for the wealthy.[33] As a result, the rich grew richer.

Hacker and Pierson also addressed the question of how big business gets elected officials to make decisions that disproportionately benefit the 1 percent at the expense of the general public when these officials are answerable to the general public at the polls. Their answer was that business interests tell legislators "to substitute symbolic actions for real ones, for example, or manipulate complex policy designs to produce more favorable yet opaque distributional outcomes." Here Hacker and Pierson were alluding to what I call tricks, although they did not say much about the different forms that the tricks take or the sleights of hand that make them work. Because of the tricks, "discrete, atomized voters," as they termed interests without organized representation, lack the ability to know they are getting the shaft.[34] In contrast, organized interests have the expertise, information-processing capability, and follow-through to get legislators to favor them.

From this analysis, one might get the impression that we can stop the harm from the tricks if we could somehow reduce the influence of big business to the level of the early 1970s. Hacker and Pierson never made this claim and, in any event, the claim would be wrong. The tricks began to take hold in the 1960s, before big business increased its organized presence in Washington (see chapter 4). The tricks worked in favor of the rich from the start. For example, the debt guarantees for too-big-to-fail financial institutions began before 1970, as chapter 6 shows.

Moreover, big business is but one of the interest groups that has the organization needed to get Congress to use the tricks to advance their agendas at the expense of "discrete, atomized voters." As Hacker and Pierson noted, ideological organizations wield power in Washington. Their staffs are generally not super rich, but they are connected. They, like big business, have seats at the table of power in Washington. As Brookings Institute scholar Jonathan Rauch argued, while almost everyone has some interest represented by some organization in Washington, whether it be an ideological organization or AARP, the job of their professional staffs is to advance the goals of their organization rather than the broad public interest. The broad public interest goes unrepresented.[35]

As participants in the legislative process, Congress as a whole and the president do have the duty to represent the broad public interest, but they use the tricks to avoid blame for shirking this duty. To take advantage of the tricks, Congress actually harms the broad public interest.[36] For example, Congress often fails to adopt smarter statutory designs for environmental regulations that would produce a better environment, better public health, and a more robust economy. That hurts everyone, the rich included, but legislators do not opt for win-win solutions because smarter designs would get in the way of their using tricks to shift the blame for regulatory burdens. Because those hurt in the process are so numerous and have such diverse interests, no powerful organization has arisen to take legislators to task for failing to serve the broader public interest. Besides, in the ridiculously complicated and expensive regulatory system that Congress leaves in place, the professionals who advise big business, staff environmental organizations, and fill the ranks of government agencies derive their sense of purpose from waging combat against one another, rather than from revealing the foibles of our tricky Congress.

The remainder of this chapter and chapters 6 and 7 highlight other ways in which the tricks hurt us without necessarily benefiting the rich.

In sum, we suffer from "legislators-get-tricky politics," of which the the-rich-get-richer politics is only one of the harmful manifestations.

Reason 3: The tricks promote polarization and gridlock. In 1989, the Democratic chairman of the House Ways and Means Committee, Dan Rostenskowski, helped enact a statute that provided for prescription drugs for Medicare recipients with the cost paid by a surcharge on higher-income seniors. Having grown accustomed to something for nothing, some seniors resented the surcharge. Back in his district, Rostenskowski found himself pursued by a mob of angry elderly constituents. Congress soon repealed the surcharge and, with it, Medicare drug coverage. When Congress and President George W. Bush reinstated Medicare drug coverage in 2003, they financed it mostly by adding its cost to the deficit.[37] That meant that elected officials left most of the bill for the medicines taken by today's seniors to the grandchildren and great grandchildren of those seniors. Had seniors been given this information, which the Money Trick hides, many would have opted for a compromise that put less burden on their grandchildren. As chapter 2 discusses, political science professors Benjamin Page and Robert Shapiro have shown that voters tend to be fair and rational unless politicians mislead them about what they are doing. That's where the tricks come in.

In misleading voters, the tricks foster polarization. Polarization is a plant that has many possible roots and can be described in many ways.[38] Regardless, the tricks fertilize the plant. They turn the virtuous circle that the Constitution sought to establish (chapter 2) into a vicious circle (chapter 3). As a result, our sense of fairness gets lost in the scramble for gain.

Moreover, we hear politicians talking about highfalutin absolutes rather than actually facing the inevitable trade-offs. They spew platitudes and vitriol, which spread to talk radio and political discourse generally. So the politicians are less capable of compromise. According to Professors Hacker and Pierson, "Polarization primarily reflects not the growing polarization of voters, but the declining responsiveness of American politicians to the electoral middle."[39]

Polarization, in turn, promotes gridlock.

By forcing politicians to face trade-offs, stopping the tricks would help to alleviate polarization and gridlock.

Stopping these tricks would help in other ways, too. Restoring accountability for the consequences of legislation would give members of Congress a strong incentive to spend more time in Washington attending to their legislative business. That would induce more of them to bring their families to Washington, as was the practice until recent decades. According to the celebrated congressional scholars Thomas Mann and Norman Ornstein, when legislators and their families spent most of the year in Washington, their children became friends at school, their spouses became friends in the community, and the legislators themselves had time to socialize. The network of friendships crossed party and ideological lines. Democrats and Republicans lunched together on Capitol Hill. All this discouraged the mean-spirited partisan tactics that typify Congress today. Nowadays, Democrats and Republicans lunch in separate rooms when they are at the Capitol and their families don't know one another. Mann and Ornstein argued forcefully that the Republicans bear more of the blame for the polarization. Even so, both parties bear blame.[40]

The authors also argued that a full-time Congress with families in Washington would help reduce the polarization that now gets in the way of Congress reaching sensible compromises. Experts in psychology agree. So does former senator Evan Bayh, who wrote that it would be "much harder to demonize someone when you know his family or have visited his home." What we have now, instead, is, in Representative Lee Hamilton's words, "a breakdown in the deliberative process that guarantees that all legislation is carefully scrutinized, and all voices heard."[41]

That the tricks harm us for the three reasons described in this chapter does not in itself prove that we should stop these tricks. A majority of political insiders say that they distrust voters,[42] and stopping the tricks would make the government more accountable to voters. Such insiders might worry that stopping the tricks could be worse than the tricks themselves.

I don't trust voters to be angels or philosopher-kings. Yet, despite the tricks, voters still wield great power. They still elect members of Congress and the presidents, and these officials are anxious to please voters. Put another way, our most important foible is that we are addicted to the tricks. As the legal philosopher and professor Jeremy Waldron wrote, political scientists, referring to ones quite different in viewpoint from Page and Shapiro, "have done democracy a great disservice" by portraying the public's seeming lack of understanding as an inevitable fact rather than as "the consequence of something comparable to malfeasance in office or corruption or electoral fraud"[43]—in other words, the tricks. So, yes, voters are sometimes unreasonable, but that is partly an understandable reaction to a deceitful government.

So, we find ourselves with political insiders distrusting voters and voters distrusting insiders in Congress. I personally have heard about this cycle of distrust for seventy years, as my grandfathers debated about it

Photograph by Robert Schoenbrod.

FIGURE 6. My grandfathers—affectionate debaters and avid card players.

with the greatest of affection at our regular family gatherings when I was a little boy. From Grandfather Marschak's perspective, people should rule themselves (as discussed in chapter 2), whereas Grandfather Schoenbrod argued that people were too selfish and ignorant to do so (as discussed in chapter 3).

What changed from Sunday to Sunday were the anecdotes and quotations that the debaters invoked. Today, seventy years later, I have a scrap of paper on which Grandfather Marschak had penciled one of those quotations. It was from a letter that Thomas Jefferson had written to an elitist friend: "We both consider the people as our children, and love them with parental affection. But you love them as infants whom you are afraid to trust without nurses; and I as adults whom I freely leave to self-government."[44]

In suggesting that we can get good government only if we let elected officials in the capital city deceive us with tricks, the political insiders are like the citizens of the Land of Oz in *The Wonderful Wizard of Oz*. They tell Dorothy and her friends that they can get what they want only if they put themselves in the hands of the great magic-working expert, the all-powerful Wizard of Oz in his Emerald City. Dorothy, the little girl who has been swept away from her farm family in Kansas to this strange land, is no member of the elite. Nor are her allies in her quest to go home,

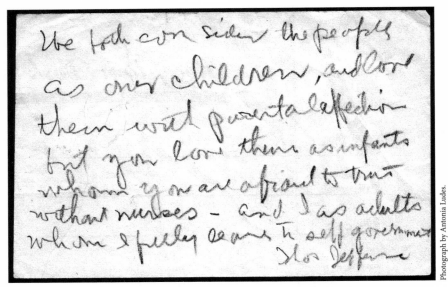

FIGURE 7. Grandfather Marschak invokes Jefferson in support of self-rule.

the Scarecrow (who wants a brain) and the Tin Woodman (who wants a heart). The Scarecrow depicts farmers and the Tin Woodman, laborers. The qualities that the Scarecrow and the Tin Woodman think they lack correspond to the faults Progressives ascribed to voters in Baum's time[45] and—ignorance and selfishness. Elitists today ascribe the same faults to voters.

L. Frank Baum, who wrote *The Wonderful Wizard of Oz* about the same time that Grandfather Schoenbrod rolled cigars and J. P. Morgan ran business empires, sided with ordinary people against the elitists. According to Michael Patrick Hearn, a leading authority on the Oz books, "Baum considered the cultured classes to be snobby, deceitful, superficial." The Wizard turns out to be a humbug, and Dorothy and her friends discover that they always had within themselves what they thought they lacked. The Scarecrow can think, the Tin Woodman can love, and the Cowardly Lion can be brave. Dorothy herself has had the power to return home from the very first day she arrived in the Land of Oz. In contrast, in the film version produced during the New Deal, Dorothy lacks that power. Glinda the Good Witch—that is, an expert—"arrives like a good fairy," wrote Hearn, "to conveniently solve Dorothy's dilemma for her, whereas in the book she does it for herself."[46]

It is in response to *our* concerns that Congress legislates good intentions to take care of those who need protection. Yet, Congress often mouths good intentions but fails to deliver. We don't need the tricks to give us good intentions any more than the Tin Woodman needed the Wizard of Oz to give him a heart.

If all the legislators had to stop the tricks, individual politicians would not have to worry about being upstaged by other politicians who could still use the tricks. Although they might not be profiles in courage, legislators would have more capacity to face hard choices rather than run scared. The tricks are humbug.

To complete my argument that we should stop the tricks, I show in the next chapter that, through the tricks, our political "nurses" are actually leading us to ruin. For that reason, we will eventually have to stop the tricks one way or another.[47] We should realize that we will pay a terrible price unless we act sooner. In chapter 8, I will show that there are practical ways to stop the tricks.

It doesn't have to be this way.

CHAPTER 6

The Tricks Will Ruin Us Later

Mother, should I trust the government?

—PINK FLOYD ("Mother")[1]

In *The Honeymooners*, a classic sitcom from the early days of television, Ralph and Alice Kramden are a long-wedded couple who live in a run-down apartment in Brooklyn. As the episodes typically begin, they don't seem like honeymooners. Ralph proudly tells Alice of some scheme to get rich quick or boost his pride, she predicts that the scheme will fail, and he flares. Each exasperated, they seem to think, "We can't go on like this." Then, after Ralph's scheme does fail, as it invariably does, they realize that despite their arguments, they do love and respect each other. Ralph and Alice will go on like this forever. They really are honeymooners.

The American people and Congress don't respect each other. Voters think that Congress does a terrible job and is unaccountable to them. Meanwhile, "political insiders," epitomized by members of Congress, think that voters don't "know enough about the issues facing Washington to form wise opinions."[2] Yet, despite voters and their representatives having had low opinions of each other for decades, we have managed to get this far.

Yet, we can't go on like this. As this chapter will show, unless stopped,

- the Money Trick will bring a crisis in federal finances;
- the Federal Mandate Trick will bring a crisis in state and local finances;

- the Debt Guarantee Trick will bring a crisis in the private financial system;
- the tricks will collectively sap strength from the economy and thus make us more vulnerable to crises; and
- these risks will exacerbate one another.

Federal Finances

One reason to dismiss concerns of the federal government running short of money is that despite fiscal fundamentalists having long warned that budget deficits and debt will destroy the nation, the federal government still pays its bills. Another reason is that John Maynard Keynes prescribed deficit spending to stimulate the economy when it is depressed. This book takes no issue with Lord Keynes's prescription, but rather builds upon a fact that chapter 4 shows is consistent with it: *Even by borrowing, a government cannot spend more in the long run than it receives.* The government can have a debt forever and still stay solvent only if there is no gap between total long-term spending and revenue.

The question is whether the spending and revenues that would result from continuing our current policies meet that requirement. In 2011, Federal Reserve Board Chair Ben Bernanke answered that it would not: "The unsustainable trajectories of deficits and debt [under current policies] cannot actually happen, because creditors would never be willing to lend to a government whose debt, relative to national income, is rising without limit." In 2014, the current chair of the Federal Reserve, Janet Yellen, gave a similar answer. Top politicians from both the Democratic and Republican parties also admit that our current fiscal policies are unsustainable. They talk, however, as if they could readily make them sustainable, yet perpetually leave the task of doing so until later.[3]

Arithmetic can help test the truth of this politically convenient talk, and the Constitution requires Congress to do the calculations and show them to the public, as discussed in chapter 4. From early on, it published an annual accounting of the cash received and cash spent each year. Such cash accounting was how most businesses kept books back then. They also used quill pens. Today, large businesses keep books that look beyond cash received and cash spent in the current year. They count as expenses future financial obligations incurred in the present year. For example, businesses count as a current expense the pensions payable in future years that employees now earn. In contrast, the federal government, in calculating the budget deficit, still generally sticks with the quill pen method: It counts only the cash it actually received and spent in the current year.[4] It ignores the many liabilities presently incurred, including the pensions payable in future years that millions of military and civilian government employees earned in the current year.

In the early years of the Constitution, cash accounting functioned well enough because Congress did not promise to pay large amounts of money in the future. Strapped as it was, the government could not credibly make big promises.[5] Today, however, our government still uses the equivalent of a quill pen to keep its accounts even as it undertakes huge legal and moral commitments that people of the quill pen era could never have imagined.

Consider, for example, the storage of nuclear waste. During the 1970s, the nuclear power industry had no answer to the question of how the public would be protected from the dangerously radioactive wastes coming from its power plants. The wastes were being stored at the plants on an interim basis, but that was no long-term solution. The industry got Congress to provide a seemingly definitive answer in the Nuclear Waste Policy Act of 1982. That statute required electric-utility companies to charge consumers a fee that would go to the government, in return for which it would build a facility in which to safeguard the waste forever. The fee brought the government $43 billion over the years, of which it spent $12 billion to build a storage facility at Yucca Mountain in Nevada. Faced with opposition from Nevada, however, the government later abandoned the Yucca Mountain plan. As a result, the courts held the federal government (that is, us) liable for the expense of nuclear plant operators in continuing to store the waste until the government chooses and pays for some way to store the waste permanently.[6] We paid as electricity consumers and will have to pay again as taxpayers, both for the interim and permanent storage of the waste.

Cash accounting contributed to this fiasco. By counting revenues and expenses on a cash basis, the government's books from 1982 showed the $43 billion in consumer fees as revenue and the $12 billion in building the facility as expenses. This made it seem that the program had cut total budget deficits for the period by $31 billion. Nowhere in this politically convenient way of bookkeeping did the cost of safeguarding the waste in the future appear, even though this is a cost that the government must pay, as we've just seen. As a result Congress ended up helping the nuclear power industry by agreeing to store the radioactive waste, hid from taxpayers the cost of that promise, and made it instead seem that Congress had cut the deficit. The legislators scored points in the short run, but left us with a large liability for a radioactively hot potato in the long run. That's the Money Trick in action.

Congress did not play the Money Trick in 1935 when it passed the Social Security Act and took responsibility for raising sufficient money to make the future payments it promised. Congress could and did tell people that the contributions they made to Social Security and those employers made on their behalf were sufficient to pay the cost of the benefits promised in the long run, much as if they had purchased the same benefits from a private insurance company. Indeed, the statute called for the program to be run in accordance with the accepted actuarial principles—that is, the way a private insurance company would administer such a program. President Franklin Roosevelt insisted that the Social Security payments be called contributions rather than taxes in order "to give the contributors a legal, moral, and political right to collect their pensions and their unemployment benefits." Recipients of government largesse financed by taxes have no such rights. To underscore our rights, Congress soon put people's contributions into "trust funds."[7] In this way, members of Congress presented themselves as biblical Josephs, requiring us to save money in the "fat years" so that we would not starve in the lean ones. It would be our money, not the government's money.

Decades later, however, Congress started to treat this money as the government's money. President Richard Nixon convinced Congress to increase benefits for Social Security recipients two months before the 1972 elections under a new formula in which payments have risen far faster than the cost of living. Here, the modern Josephs have used the money that workers were saving for their future retirement to increase payments to retirees in the present.[8] With Medicare, Congress does much the same.[9]

As things now stand, Congress uses the money that today's younger workers must pay to receive a Social Security pension and Medicare in their old age to pay for the current pensions and Medicare of older, mostly retired people. The idea is that each generation of workers will get its benefits paid for by the next generation or two.

To know whether this idea works in practice requires doing some serious accounting—accounting that looks at whether the government will actually be able to provide the promised benefits to people who retire many decades in the future. It requires looking beyond cash flows in the current year or the current decade or even the near decades. Here is why. Social Security, Medicare, pension insurance, crop insurance, flood insurance, and dozens of other congressionally created insurance programs have, as Undersecretary of the Treasury Peter R. Fisher put it, made our government into "a gigantic insurance company (with a sideline business in national defense and homeland security)." To Fisher, an insurance company with cash accounting "is an accident waiting to happen."[10] That is especially true for an insurance company run by elected officials because politicians are prone to ease their reelection by promising big insurance benefits in the future and charging current voters too little to pay for the future benefits, and so shifting the blame for the shortfall to their successors in office. Cash accounting is essential to the sleight of hand in the Money Trick.

Congress does feign concern for the government's long-term fiscal health by having the Congressional Budget Office prepare projections of the budget for the coming decade, but as chapter 4 noted, this time frame is too short to include the government's more-serious fiscal problems. Indeed, as illustrated by the Nuclear Waste Policy Act, Congress designs statutes to make the ten-year projection look good by using techniques that worsen the government's long-term fiscal outlook.

In another effort to appear concerned about the long-term fiscal sustainability of the federal government, Congress mandates that the Department of the Treasury prepare a financial report of the US government each year. As shown by the chart in figure 8, based upon the projection in the Treasury's *Financial Report of the United States Government: Fiscal Year 2015*, the continuing of current policies will result in the deficit growing far larger in the future, not just in absolute terms but also as a percentage of the national economy, or gross domestic product (GDP).[11]

Because of the ongoing deficits, the national debt will grow under current policies, as shown in the chart in figure 9, which is also based

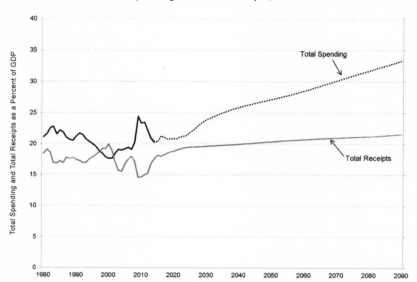

FIGURE 8. Totals are a percentage of Gross Domestic Product.

on the projection in the Treasury's 2015 financial report. The debt grows rapidly not only because the deficit grows bigger and adds to the amount owed but also because the growth in the debt increases the interest that the government must pay and so further increases future deficits.

We cannot let current policies continue. As the 2015 financial report confirms, "A sustainable policy is one where the ratio of debt held by the public to Gross Domestic Product (GDP) (the debt-to-GDP ratio) is stable or declining over the long term."[12] Figure 9 shows that, on the contrary, this ratio is increasing. It has gone from around 25 percent in 1980 to 74 percent in 2015, a three-fold increase. Moreover, the report projects that under current policies, the ratio would grow to 223 percent in 2090, about a nine-fold increase.

According to the comptroller general of the United States, even the current ratio of 74 percent is worrisome, because "debt held by the public at these high levels could limit the federal government's flexibility to address emerging issues and unforeseen challenges, such as another economic downturn or large-scale disaster."[13]

Debt Held by the Public, 1980–2090

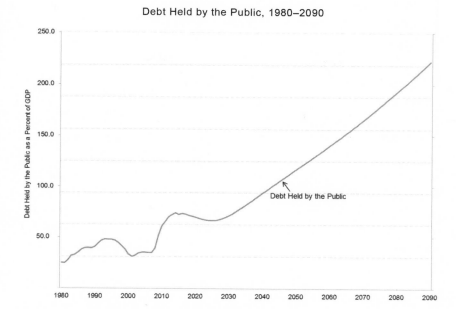

FIGURE 9. Debt is a percentage of gross domestic product.

Although the financial reports for 2015 and previous years do acknowledge that current US policies are unsustainable, they nonetheless themselves participate in the Money Trick. The Department of the Treasury under both Democratic and Republican presidents, for example, successfully avoids press coverage. This happened under former president George W. Bush when the department released its 2005 financial report just before Christmas without a press conference or even a press release, and under President Barack Obama when the department did the same with its 2012 financial report.[14]

Because of this evasiveness, and also because the reports feature vague reassurances and hide specifics that could arouse anxiety, they have had scant impact on public opinion. The 2015 financial report opens with "A Message from the Secretary of the Treasury" in which Treasury Secretary Jacob Lew claims that the nation is "on the path of long-term fiscal sustainability," continuing with the vague assertion that "I am confident that we can lay the foundation for durable economic growth and broadly shared prosperity."[15]

Such bland assurance fails to equip voters with the information they need to play a responsible role. To take responsibility, voters need data on how much current practices will have to change to close the gap between long-term spending and receipts. This data must be *balanced, produced with a transparent methodology*, and *presented in a form whose relevance to their lives voters can readily understand*. The financial reports meet none of these requirements.

First, the financial reports are not balanced. They lowball the size of the change needed to close the gap between long-term spending and receipts. For example, they ignore everything that will happen later than seventy-five years from now. While they count the contributions that children born in the coming decades will make to Social Security, Medicare, and other benefit programs over the next seventy-five years, they leave out any benefits that will need to be paid to them beyond those years.[16] Ignoring future generations' expectations to receive benefits in their old age is downright shameful.

Then, the financial reports are not produced with a transparent methodology. For example, one would look in vain for a succinct statement of why the 2015 financial report projects a much-smaller gap between spending and receipts for the coming seventy-five-year period than the 2014 report did. The smaller gap is significant in that the projected seventy-five-year debt-to-GDP ratio is greatly reduced from the 321 percent increase predicted in 2014 to a 223 percent increase predicted in the 2015 report. And, despite going on for hundreds of pages and discussing dozens of topics, the report does not clearly address the question of why the gap is so much smaller. In all likelihood, a key reason is that the 2015 report projects smaller increases in health care costs than the 2014 report did. The projection is nevertheless controversial. In explaining why the General Accounting Office refused to render an audit opinion on the 2015 report, the comptroller general cited "significant uncertainties . . . primarily related to the achievement of projected reductions in Medicare cost growth." He went to explain that that GAO's concerns about health care costs were shared by "the Trustees of the Medicare trust funds, the Centers for Medicare & Medicaid Services' (CMS) Chief Actuary, the Congressional Budget Office, and others."[17] The lengthy 2015 financial report also fails to explain why it resolves the uncertainties about health care costs as it does.

Finally, the financial reports are not presented in a form whose relevance to their lives voters can readily understand. The "Citizen's Guide" section in the 2015 financial report claims that increasing revenues or decreasing spending in the current policy by 1.2 percent of GDP would completely close the gap between long-term spending and long-term revenues.[18] The report highlights this seemingly small adjustment—a 1.2 percent change appears to be a near neighbor of a 0 percent change—but conveniently fails to bring home the scale of the spending cuts or tax increases needed to produce that much money.

So I went in search of experts who could provide better information for voters on the scale of the measures needed to match revenues with spending in the long run. Two economists, Dr. Jagadeesh Gokhale and Dr. Kent Smetters, each with prestigious publication records of their own, had together made such calculations as of 2002.[19] Dr. Gokhale wanted to update these old calculations to provide a current estimate, but could not readily do so because he now lacked access to the data that he needed. The researchers had based their calculations on a model that the Office of Management and Budget (OMB), a component of the Executive Office of the President, uses to project the future spending and revenues that would result from continuing current policy. The OMB revises the model each year to reflect changes in current policy. Under President George W. Bush, the office had made its model available to them on the condition that it be kept secret from other researchers. In early 2009, under the new presidential administration, Dr. Gokhale asked for the updated version of the old model, but the OMB refused. He felt stuck.

Yet, President Obama had announced, as his first official act in office, a policy of "transparency and open government." In so doing, the president said that "my Administration is committed to creating an unprecedented level of openness in Government."[20] It so happened that the White House staffer in charge of this new open government project was a friend and colleague of mine at the New York Law School, Professor Beth Noveck. I asked her if she could get the current budget model for me, and her immediate response was "Piece of cake." So I told Dr. Gokhale that I could get the model, he said that he didn't believe it, and we made a bet, agreeing that the loser would pay for lunch.

Professor Noveck and I were going on hope. Our hope was disappointed. She couldn't get the model. So, invoking the president's claim of commitment to open government, Dr. Gokhale and I formally requested the information from the OMB director. In reply came an e-mail blandly stating that the information "[was] not available to the general public"—this from the administration of a president who had recently said, "Information maintained by the Federal Government is a national asset."[21] Dr. Gokhale and I then sought help from various members of Congress of both parties. Many legislators could have gotten the information for us. One influential Republican promised me that he would try to get it, but then did nothing. One of his staff members later wrote that the congressman was "not interested." Apparently, neither the Obama administration nor the legislators want voters to know whether they are actually increasing or decreasing the gap between spending and receipts. While Democrats and Republicans claim to be breaking records in sprinting toward fiscal responsibility, they each insist on using their own personal stopwatches to measure their performance. I ended up filing a request to obtain the model under the Freedom of Information Act, but that was similarly rebuffed. I paid for lunch.

Dr. Gokhale decided to use the Congressional Budget Office's budget model for the current year of 2012 as the next-best way to estimate how much the government would have to cut spending or raise revenues in the long run. Adapting this model to the purpose was a big job, but he did it. What he found is that continuing current policies over the long run would result in a $91 trillion gap between the present value of future expenses and future revenues. To close the gap, he estimated, would require changes in current policies that increase revenues or decrease spending by 9 percent of GDP.[22]

The financial report for the same year, 2012, finds that a much-smaller adjustment would be necessary—2.7 percent, rather than the 9 percent predicted by Dr. Gokhale. One reason for this discrepancy is that, as noted a few pages ago, the financial reports shamefully ignore Social Security and Medicare payments due more than seventy-five years from now.

Also differing from the financial report were Dr. Gokhale's calculations of the scale of the spending cuts or tax increases needed to close the fiscal gap. He found that Congress would have to

- cut total government spending, including Social Security, Medicare, military, and all the rest, by 35 percent;
- increase revenues from personal income taxes by 86 percent;
- increase revenue from other sources in an equivalent amount; or
- some combination of the above.[23]

Making changes on this scale would necessarily have a widespread impact. Cutting military spending by well over 35 percent, even if wise, would not be nearly enough to significantly offset the cuts otherwise needed in Social Security, Medicare, and other benefits, because the lion's share of future spending is for such benefits. Nor would increasing taxes only on the rich be nearly enough to cover these costs. Besides, modern Congresses under Democrats and Republicans have done the opposite of soaking the rich, according to some progressive and conservative analysts.[24]

However Congress chooses to close the gap—whether by increasing the taxes on individuals or businesses or by cutting the spending that benefit individuals, businesses, state and local governments, or other organizations—in the end the burdens will fall on individuals, not only as taxpayers and beneficiaries of entitlements but also as employees, shareholders, beneficiaries of pension plans, and the like.

If spread evenly across the population, the required tax increases or spending cuts, I calculate, would have cost an average family of four $17,988 in 2012 *plus* similarly large sums in each and every year thereafter. By comparison, when Congress claimed to have taken a big stride toward fiscal responsibility by passing a bipartisan budget deal in December 2013 that supposedly would have cut the deficit by $23 billion over the next ten years, the projected savings were only $25 out of the $17,988-plus cost per average family needed every year.[25]

Given the scope of the problem that Dr. Gokhale described, there is a temptation to try to try to dismiss it by indulging in the ad hominem argument that he came up with the figures while he was on the staff of the Cato Institute, an organization dedicated to small government. But a joint project of the Century Fund and the Urban Institute, two organizations with quite a different perspective from the Cato Institute, reached fundamentally the same conclusion—that Congress has charted a course that would put our government in such a deep fiscal hole that we wouldn't possibly be able to grow out of it. Similarly, Dr. Alice Rivlin, the director of the Office of Management and Budget under President Bill Clinton, told Congress's Joint Economic Committee in 2016, "Faster growth alone will not reduce the debt to GDP ratio in a society that has already committed itself to benefits for a growing older population— benefits that will increase more rapidly than revenues even at hoped-for higher rates of GDP growth."[26]

We can, however, avoid a crisis, but only if we stop the Money Trick soon. Policy analysts from across the political spectrum have pointed out ways in which Congress could achieve its stated policy objectives with less spending.[27] Yet, Congress does not take such advice because the tricks encourage its members to design statutes to make them look good in the short term, rather than to serve us over the long term.

Members of Congress know that by failing to do their duty, they imperil themselves, their families, and their constituents. Erskine Bowles and Alan Simpson, whom President Obama appointed in 2010 to chair the bipartisan National Commission on Fiscal Responsibility and Reform, reported that "members of Congress would constantly come up to us and say 'save us from ourselves.'"[28] Congress and the president failed to pursue the commission's recommendations.

On the contrary, they kick the can down the road and that can gets bigger. The 2015 financial report estimates that a ten-year delay in taking action to stop the growth of the debt-to-GDP ratio would increase the annual cost by 25 percent and a twenty-year delay would increase the annual cost by 60 percent.[29] Based on Dr. Gokhale's calculation that the fiscal gap in 2012 will be $91 trillion, my guestimate is that in 2017 it will be roughly $100 trillion.

This kicking of the can cannot continue indefinitely because, as Ben Bernanke warned, creditors will eventually refuse to lend to the United States. Before that happens, creditors would condition further lending on the government drastically cutting spending and raising taxes. They would also condition it on the government paying them a higher rate of interest on the debt. With lenders getting more interest, there would be even-less money to spend to meet the needs of the people. Meanwhile, the spending cuts and tax increases would depress the economy, thereby increasing people's needs. For many, the government's cupboard would be bare.

Nonetheless, the Money Trick allows Congress to avoid changing current policies to avoid the coming crisis in federal finances.

State and Local Finances

Starting in the 1960s, Congress took credit for providing health care for the poor through Medicaid, but shifted much of the costs to states. As a result, Medicaid has surpassed education as the single-biggest expense at the state level.[30] Shifting the costs of Medicaid to states didn't reduce these costs, but did shift the blame for the painful measures needed to pay the bill from members of Congress and the presidents to state officials.

Federal statutes coerce state and local governments to provide federally specified benefits not only in health care but also in education, transportation, and many other areas. Where the Money Trick lets members of Congress and the presidents take credit for expensive promises yet shift the blame for the costs to their successors in federal office, the Federal Mandate Trick lets members of Congress and presidents take credit for expensive promises yet shift the blame for the costs to state and local officials.

Meanwhile, states and their subdivisions, like the federal government, have a bad fiscal prognosis. The bankruptcy of Detroit is the forerunner of a coming crisis among the states, according to the State Budget Crisis Task Force's 2014 report. The taskforce is cochaired by Richard Ravitch and Paul Volcker, both of whom have high standing on the left. The taskforce pointed out that many states engage in a state-level version of the Money Trick. Meanwhile, they fail to maintain infrastructure, thus doing the opposite of investing for the future.[31]

While Congress looks to the states to fund its promises, the states look to the federal government for grants. In fact, states now receive about a third of their budgets from the federal government. Yet, according to Richard Ravitch, as the federal government gets into greater fiscal difficulty, Congress will likely cut grants to the states.[32]

The federal government and the states are increasingly like two drowning men, each trying to push down on the other to keep his own head above water.

The Private Financial System

The Debt Guarantee Trick has allowed Congress and the presidents to irresponsibly guarantee the debts of too-big-to-fail banks and other giant financial giants. These irresponsible guarantees have done grave damage to the private financial system and the entire economy, yet they continue. To understand the peril, consider the stories of Fannie Mae and Freddie Mac.

The federal government established Fannie Mae as a government agency in 1938. At that time, deep in the Great Depression, mortgage lenders had little cash on hand to grant loans to home buyers. Fannie's initial job was to buy mortgages from the mortgage lenders in order to provide them with cash that they could use to grant more mortgages, and thus stimulate home construction, home ownership, and the economy generally.

To get the money to purchase the mortgages, Fannie borrowed. Because it was a federal agency, it was the government itself that owed the debt. So Fannie's borrowing arguably contributed to the national debt. Confronted with concern about growth in the debt during the Vietnam War, President Lyndon Johnson and Congress parried arguments that Fannie's debt and spending should be put on the government books by selling Fannie to private shareholders in 1968. That way, its debt would not be a debt of the government, as the statute authorizing the sale stated.[33]

Yet, if Fannie was no longer backed by the government, it could no longer borrow at the same low interest rate as the government. To enable Fannie to continue pumping inexpensively borrowed money into the housing market, Congress assured investors, without actually saying so, that the government still stood behind Fannie's debts by giving this supposedly private corporation governmental trappings. The statute authorizing the sale of Fannie immunized it from state and local taxes, exempted it from Securities and Exchange Commission regulation, gave it a line of credit at the US Treasury, and empowered the president of the United States to appoint one-third of its board of directors. After this implicit guarantee of Fannie's debt, federal bank regulations put its safety on a par with that of the government's own debt.[34] So the now-supposedly-private Fannie could borrow at practically the same low interest rate as the government yet get the debt guarantee for free.

At first, Fannie continued to operate much like the federal agency that it had been before 1968. It paid modest salaries and bought only safe mortgages by insisting that the banks it bought mortgages from provide documentation that the homes that had been carefully appraised and bought with significant down payments by people with good credit histories and sufficient income to make the mortgage payments. Fannie profited because it usually could borrow at a much-lower interest rate than it got on the mortgages. Yet, the limited supply of mortgages that met Fannie's rigorous standards limited growth in its profits.[35] In 1970, Congress created Freddie Mac, practically a clone of Fannie Mae, to focus on buying mortgages originated by savings-and-loan firms.[36]

Later, however, Fannie and Freddie began to buy much-riskier mortgages. In 1992, Congress passed legislation that required them to buy more mortgages financing purchases by families of low and moderate income and in inner-city areas. The administrations of the first president Bush, President Clinton, and the second president Bush implemented, with increasing vigor, the statute requiring the companies to buy riskier mortgages.[37] Whether the purpose of Fannie and Freddie buying riskier mortgages was to increase their profits or to meet affordable housing goals, they could not have bought such risky mortgages without the debt guarantees. Here's why.

In order to purchase more mortgages, Fannie cultivated close relationships with disreputable mortgage lenders such as Countrywide Financial, which cared more about maximizing the amount of money it lent than about whether home buyers could make the payments. Such lenders shifted the risk of nonpayment to Fannie or Freddie by selling them the mortgages. This risk wouldn't do any great harm to Fannie and Freddie so long as home prices kept rising, as they did each and every month from mid-1995 through mid-2006.[38] Most home buyers who couldn't make their payments could still sell their homes for enough to pay off the mortgages. There was, of course, no certainty that home prices would continue to rise, but that was of no concern to investors who lent to Fannie and Freddie because the government had implicitly guaranteed that the investors would get repaid with interest.

The debt guarantees that Fannie and Freddie got for free allowed them to borrow money at interest rates appropriate for low-risk investments. The guarantees saved them huge amounts of interest expenses, between $122 and $182 billion, according to a 2005 study by the Federal Reserve. Much of the savings was paid in dividends to the companies' shareholders, rather than passed on to home purchasers, according to the same study. Additional bits of the bonanza went to providing the firms' managers with big salaries, bonuses, and stock options. The managers also got opulent offices. The CEO of Fannie met visitors "perched in a wingback chair near a fireplace in his office suite, featuring a silky oriental rug. Liveried doormen, resembling those in posh hotels, ushered guests to and fro." A senior official at the Department of Housing and Urban Development quipped that Fannie's headquarters are "what Versailles would have looked like if the French king had more money."[39]

Because the firms needed the goodwill of members of Congress and the presidents to keep the free debt guarantees that were boosting their profits, Fannie and Freddie could not resist demands to meet affordable-housing goals. Meeting affordable housing goals in Fannie's view would provide "enormous political cover for its growth plans," according to a book coauthored by *New York Times* reporter Gretchen Morgenson and Joshua Rosner.[40]

Fannie and Freddie did indeed grow rapidly. In 1970, these two companies accounted for only 4 percent of the mortgage market, but by 2008 they accounted for 41 percent.[41] These percentages included not only the mortgages they purchased but also mortgages they guaranteed and were purchased by others. For making these guarantees, Fannie and Freddie received a fee.

With the rapid growth in the amount of mortgages the companies held or guaranteed came an increased risk that home buyers would fail to make payments. As Morgenson and Rosner pointed out, "Fannie Mae led the way in relaxing underwriting loan standards...a shift that was quickly followed by private lenders." For example, in 1989, only 1 in 230 home buyers could purchase a home with little or no down payment (3 percent of the purchase price or less). By 2007, however, 1 in 3 home buyers were doing so.[42] A scanty or nonexistent down payment meant that, with even a slight drop in the housing market, home buyers would have a debt greater than the value of their home—that is, left "underwater." This could readily translate into the buyers being unwilling or unable to pay. If enough of them failed to pay their mortgages, Fannie and Freddie would lack the income needed to pay the debts they had incurred in buying their own mortgages or to honor the guarantees they gave to other buyers of mortgages. Without sufficient income, these corporations would have to draw upon their own capital to meet their obligations.

Indeed, Fannie and Freddie lacked sufficient capital to pay their debts should they be unable to collect payments on many of the mortgages they held. Regulations required them to have only $2.50 of shareholder capital for every $100 of mortgages that they bought. They would borrow the remaining $97.50. In essence, their shareholders needed to make a down payment of only $2.50 per $100 of mortgages issued to home buyers, many of whom had made no significant down payment.[43] So, if large numbers of home buyers failed to make their mortgage payments, Fannie and Freddie would lack a sufficient cushion of capital with which to pay their own debts.

Congress and the presidents had We the People guarantee the whole house of cards. Fannie and Freddie thus gambled, but for them, it was "heads our shareholders win, tails the people lose," or at least take most of the loss.

The managers of Fannie and Freddie had an even-better bet. Because the companies had adopted a high-growth, high-risk business model, their managers would get Wall Street–style bonuses and stock options if they met targets for increasing profits. Those managers who exited in the glory days got to keep their bonanzas.[44]

Then, reality set in. The spectacular surge in housing prices reversed in 2006, and by 2008 Fannie and Freddie could not pay their own debts. Given the debt guarantees the government had implicitly given the two corporations, the government now had to pay their debts or take a hit on its own ability to borrow. As then-secretary of the Treasury Henry Paulson later explained: "Foreign investors held more than $1 trillion of the debt issued or guaranteed by [Fannie or Freddie]." To these investors, if the government

> let Fannie or Freddie fail and their investments [get] wiped out, that would be no different from expropriation. They had bought these securities in the belief that [Fannie and Freddie] were backed by the U.S. government. They wanted to know if the U.S. would stand behind this implicit guarantee—and what this would imply for other U.S. obligations, such as Treasury bonds.[45]

In 2011, the cost for the government of honoring its guarantee of Fannie and Freddie's debts was estimated to be $130 billion. In addition, because Fannie and Freddie could not honor their own guarantees of other investors' mortgages, there was an additional cost for the government of backing up those guarantees that was estimated to be another $187 billion. The total cost was thus an estimated to be $317 billion, more than $1000 for every adult and child in the United States. The government now claims that it is recovering much of this money.[46] Nonetheless, the debt guarantees put our money at risk.

With the Debt Guarantee Trick, members of Congress and the presidents pursued the popular objective of easing home ownership in ways that would be better for them and disastrous for us. The free debt guarantees were supposed to let Fannie and Freddie borrow money at low interest rates from investors who had no taste for lending directly to home buyers and to buy mortgages from firms that did lend directly to home buyers, and thus to pass the savings on to home buyers in the form of lower interest on their mortgages. This arrangement pleased diverse and politically connected constituencies—the home finance industry, the home construction industry, the real estate brokerage industry, and the organizations dedicated to affordable housing. To help legislators take credit, Fannie provided them with data on the mortgages it had helped underwrite in their districts.[47]

Congress and the presidents could have eased home ownership in many other ways than by endowing private corporations with free debt guarantees. It could have left Fannie as a federal agency and made Freddie one, too. Or it could have turned Fannie into a truly private company and separately appropriated funds to subsidize home purchases, especially for low-income buyers. Either alternative would, however, have meant that more spending and debt would appear on the government's books. While the Money Trick would have allowed elected officials to shift most of the blame for these burdens to their successors in office, the politicians preferred instead to shift all the blame. As someone who interviewed one of the key aides involved in making Fannie into a shareholder-owned corporation under the Johnson administration in 1968 summarized the conversation: "[Fannie's] new incarnation was seen as a way to attract private funds that otherwise wouldn't have gone into housing.... We thought this was brilliantly leveraging federal power to draw more money into housing without increasing the budget." According to Viral Acharya, Matthew Richardson, Stijn van Nieuwerburgh, and Lawrence White, four New York University business school professors, as the guarantees were "nowhere to be found on the government's books, [they] appeared to be a free lunch—until they weren't."[48]

Members of Congress and the presidents chose the Debt Guarantee Trick as a way to ease home ownership since it allowed them to claim the credit for the full benefits and avoid the blame for the burdens altogether.

The elected officials who privatized Fannie in 1968 took no blame because the firm was then so small and safely run. Besides, they gave the debt guarantee with a sly statutory wink.

The free debt guarantees together with pressure from Congress and the White House to meet affordable housing goals prompted Fannie and Freddie to borrow more money to buy riskier mortgages. Doing so increased the amount of their debt and the risk that they could not pay it and further increased the value to them of the free debt guarantees. Thus Fannie and Freddie could vastly increase what they got from us, the people, without elected officials having to take responsibility.

The elected officials' free lunch, however, failed to do much to make home ownership more affordable. Little of the savings in interest trickled down to home buyers, at least according to the 2005 Federal Reserve study, which finds that the debt guarantees reduced the interest rate on home buyers' mortgages by only *seven-hundredths of one percent*. Whatever the savings, most of the benefit went to the well-to-do rather than to the poor.[49] That should be no surprise. The rich spend a lot more on housing than do the poor. If Congress had provided subsidies through appropriations that appeared on the government's books, it could have directed the money to low-income home purchasers in particular, but that would have required the legislators to take some responsibility for the burdens.

According to Edward DeMarco, former acting director of the Federal Housing Finance Agency under President Obama, "Homeownership rates in the U.S. today are the same as they were 50 years ago, despite all the government efforts to promote affordable housing. 'Let's say it was a failed effort.'"[50]

Still worse, the free debt guarantees helped to trigger the Great Recession that began in 2008. This recession began with a financial crisis, which had in turn sprung from the meltdown in housing finance. By making risk largely irrelevant to those who lent to Fannie and Freddie, the free debt guarantees helped inflate the bubble in housing prices whose bursting caused the financial crisis. Christopher DeMuth concluded that next to housing finance, there is "no remotely comparable instance in a private credit market (commercial real estate, credit cards, automobiles) of such a massive degradation of lending standards and explosive growth of extreme-high-risk debt."[51]

The meltdown in housing finance, the fiscal crisis, and the Great Recession were not entirely the fault of Fannie and Freddie. Far from it.

Greed on Wall Street, as so graphically portrayed in the film *The Big Short*, played a big part, too. Indeed, the greed produced political support for the debt guarantees, but the guarantees enabled the greedy to take bigger risks with other people's money, as I will explain.

The debt guarantees were given not only to Fannie and Freddie but also to large commercial banks and other large private financial firms, which, for simplicity's sake, I will call "Wall Street." While Congress had in 1933 restricted the explicit guarantees of the debts of commercial banks to those owed on small deposits, it later condoned the government implicitly guaranteeing the debts of the too-big-to-fail Wall Street firms, no matter how large the debt on the theory that one of them going over the brink would freeze the financial system and thus imperil the entire economy, as discussed in chapter 4. Because these implicit debt guarantees allowed the Wall Street titans to borrow at lower interest rates and Congress to charge no fee for the guarantees, these firms earned much-higher profits. This welfare for Wall Street subsidized the too-big-to-fail firms to take on more debt and more risk, and so made them both bigger and more likely to fail.

In particular, the implicit free debt guarantees encouraged Wall Street to imitate the risky business model of Fannie and Freddie. Mortgage lenders like Countrywide found that they could make money by selling risky mortgages not only to Fannie or Freddie but to Wall Street as well. Wall Street found that it could make money by selling investors securities whose value came from the payments due under these mortgages. In selling these mortgage-backed securities, Wall Street was emulating Fannie, Freddie, and other government-sponsored enterprises that had done so first. Many of these securities and the mortgages themselves were owned by Wall Street firms when the housing bubble burst.[52]

The mortgages' loss in value threatened the financial viability of some of the Wall Street firms selling mortgage-backed securities, because these firms, as did Fannie and Freddie, had little capital to provide a cushion in case the value of their assets fell. In the nineteenth century, commercial banks had to have $25 of shareholders' capital for every $100 of assets the bank owned. That meant that a bank could borrow at most $75 for every $100 of loans it made. So, to make $100 million in loans, it would have had to possess $25 million of shareholders' capital and could borrow the remaining $75 million. If the bank could collect only $80 million of the $100 million, it could pay the $75 million that it had borrowed, but only because the shareholders' capital of $25 million provided a cushion. Currently, weaker regulations have greatly reduced the capital requirement for commercial banks and thus reduced the cushion.[53] Therefore, if the bank in my example had $10 million of shareholders' capital rather than $25 million, it would go broke—that is, unless the government provided a bailout.

The implicit free debt guarantees provided by the government allowed Wall Street to borrow at lower interest rates than those they would otherwise been required to borrow at based on their thin capital cushion and risky business activities. If Wall Street had to pay the government the interest expense they saved because of the guarantees, they would have had a profit-based incentive to borrow less and limit the risks they took. With the free debt guarantees, however, for Wall Street, it was "heads our shareholders win, tails the people lose." Thus, according to Professor Charles Calomiris, the guarantees helped to induce "excessive risk-taking and systematic bank collapses."[54] The government in fact bailed out most of the too-big-to-fail firms that ran into difficulty.

Some argue that the deregulation of Wall Street deserves greater blame than Fannie and Freddie for the meltdown in housing finance; others disagree. I myself do not apportion blame because my point is that the free debt guarantees along with greed promoted the dangerous activity of Wall Street as well as that of Fannie and Freddie. The four NYU business school professors I quoted previously agree. They concluded that how Fannie and Freddie and Wall Street did business was "quite similar—a highly leveraged bet on the mortgage market by firms that were implicitly backed by the government with artificially low funding rates."[55] The free debt guarantees made risk less relevant to the key participants.

Fannie and Freddie and Wall Street fought hard against regulation that would have kept them from maximizing the profits they got from the free debt guarantees. According to Morgenson and Rosner, using "bare knuckle" tactics Fannie's CEO was the "financial industry's leader in buying off Congress, manipulating regulators, and neutralizing critics." The authors also pointed out that Fannie set up political action committees to make "huge campaign contributions to supporters in Congress" and buy influence in other ways.[56]

When the financial crisis struck, three-quarters of the subprime and other low-quality mortgages were on the books of Fannie, Freddie, and government agencies. Two years later, in 2010, Representative Barney Frank, previously a defender of the corporations stated, "I hope by next year we'll have abolished Fannie and Freddie. It was a great mistake to push lower-income people into housing they couldn't afford and couldn't really handle once they had it."[57]

By then, the elected officials who began the debt guarantees in 1968 had long since left office. The legislators in office after the financial crisis tried to distance themselves from blame for the bailouts by passing a statute intended to demonstrate to voters that they had taken strong action to prevent future bailouts. Barney Frank, then-chairman of the House Financial Services Committee, and Chris Dodd, his counterpart in the Senate, were in charge of writing the legislation. The resulting statute is called the Wall Street Reform and Consumer Protection Act of 2010, or Dodd–Frank for short.[58]

Proponents of Dodd–Frank promised that taxpayers' money wouldn't be used to pay the debts of too-big-to-fail firms. Yet, as Professor Peter Conti-Brown found, this promise is not credible to a "wide consensus among legal scholars, economists, and even, perhaps surprising, members of the President's own administration."[59]

Dodd–Frank is the Debt Guarantee Trick in new clothing. Read carefully, it does not end the debt guarantees of too-big-to-fail firms. Rather, it promises to stop using taxpayers' money for this purpose. This promise is far-fetched for many reasons.[60] Here is one of them.

If a too-big-to-fail firm goes bust, the statute requires that the money used to cover its debts must come from other too-big-to-fail firms, rather than from taxpayers. To buttress this claim, the statute creates a so-called Orderly Liquidation Fund that would pay creditors of insolvent firms by taking cash from other firms. Yet, in a systemic financial crisis, the Orderly Liquidation Fund will probably not work. The statute provides that the other too-big-to-fail firms must contribute to the fund in proportion to the size and riskiness of their debts. Thus, the debts of a dead firm will be paid by taking the flesh off of those firms that are still alive, with those closest to death having to pay more. In a systemic crisis, such contributions would likely kill off some of the nearly dead firms and thus require taking even-more cash from the firms still alive, likely killing off still more of the firms struggling to survive. It sounds like a script for a bad horror film. To avoid such horror, as experts have warned, officials will do as they have done in the past: use taxpayer funds.[61]

One of those experts is Neel Kashkari, president of the Federal Reserve Bank of Minneapolis, who in 2016 warned of what would happen if more than one large bank ran into trouble in the midst of an economic downturn:

> Given the massive externalities on Main Street of large bank failures in terms of lost jobs, lost income and lost wealth, no rational policymaker would risk restructuring large firms and forcing losses on creditors and counterparties using the [Dodd–Frank] tools in a risky environment, let alone in a crisis environment like we experienced in 2008. They will be forced to bail out failing institutions—as we were. We were even forced to support large bank mergers, which helped stabilize the immediate crisis, but that we knew would make too-big-to-fail firms worse in the long term. The risks to the U.S. economy and the American people were simply too great not to do whatever we could to prevent a financial collapse.... The financial sector has lobbied hard to preserve its current structure and thrown up endless objections to fundamental change.... The time has come to move past parochial interests and solve this problem. The risks of not doing so are just too great.[62]

Much more important than the risk to taxpayers' money is the likelihood that Dodd–Frank will someday precipitate another financial crisis by failing to charge too-big-to-fail firms fees that reflect the riskiness of their debt. Firms whose debts are riskier should have to pay higher fees, but the statute fails to impose higher fees on such firms and thereby subsidizes behavior that imposes more risk on the financial system and economy on which we depend. No surprise here. After all, their top executives are major contributors to politicians and political organizations of both parties. Under Dodd–Frank, as before, debt guarantees still subsidize the profits of financial giants.[63] The welfare being paid to Wall Street goes on, continuing to make the too-big-to-fail firms both bigger and more likely to fail.[64] According to Morgenson, writing in the *New York Times*, the statute increases the likelihood of another financial crisis.[65]

Dodd–Frank is even worse when it comes to Fannie and Freddie. The statute calls for a study of how Congress might reform them, but still gives these firms free debt guarantees in the meantime. They now provide the financing for half of the new mortgages written in the United States, even more than before the financial crisis.[66]

Congress promises us that government regulators will stop Wall Street and Fannie and Freddie from running excessive risks in the future, but this promise is also far-fetched. Experience shows that regulation tends to get weaker as memories of financial failures grow dimmer.[67] Indeed, one can depend on the regulation of finance being undependable. As Professor John Cochrane put it, "Guaranteeing debts creates perverse incentives, so our government tries to regulate the banks from taking excessive risks: 'OK, cousin Louie, I'll cosign the loan for your Las Vegas trip, but no poker this time, and be in bed by 10.'" Professor Calomiris had data to back up this observation:

> The regulatory system that was developed over the past several decades, in the U.S. and in many other countries, has failed repeatedly to provide effective, prudential regulations that limit taxpayer financing of bank losses. The recent financial crisis of 2007–2009 is just the latest (and most severe) in a long line of episodes that demonstrate the terrible costs of continuing government protection of banks with ineffectual regulation. Since 1980, more than 100 countries have experienced banking crises [defined as bank debts exceeding bank assets by more than 1 percent of the country's economy].... Such frequency and severity of bank loss are historically unprecedented, and are clearly consequences of the brave new world of government protection of bank debts. Consider that, a century earlier, from 1874 to 1913 ... [there were found to be] only four episodes of bank-insolvency crises worldwide.[68]

In sum, unless curbed, the Debt Guarantee Trick will put us at grave risk of another financial crisis like that of 2007–09 and the Great Recession that came in its wake.

The Sapping of the Economy

While the Money Trick, the Federal Mandate Trick, and the Debt Guarantee Trick each threaten the economy with a sudden crisis at an uncertain time, the Regulation Trick saps the economy all of the time.

The problem is not the goals of regulation, which are generally good but the unnecessary harm that comes from the tricks inducing Congress and the presidents to choose wasteful, ineffective means to pursue the goals.

Much as members of Congress and the presidents use the Money Trick to finesse the gap between the future spending they promise and the taxes they impose, they use the Regulation Trick to finesse the gap between the regulatory benefits they promise and the regulatory burdens they take responsibility for. They do the same thing when they use the Federal Mandate Trick to force states and localities to regulate.

The sleights of hand used to mask these tricks work by giving agencies as well as state and local governments excruciatingly detailed instructions on how they should go about delivering the promised benefits. Complication is hardwired into these tricks. Philip Howard showed that about the same time that Congress started the tricks, it began to pass statutes that exert control over society in extravagant detail, leaving little room for individual judgment. The statutory rules apply to every aspect of society, from the private sector to state and local governments and federal executive officials. The statutes further order these executive officials to issue their own detailed rules through regulations binding the private sector, state and local governments, and the federal government itself.

One consequence of all this micromanagement is that despite the hope that the stimulus funds appropriated in 2009, near the beginning of the recession, would be used to fix our broken transportation infrastructure such as the South Park Bridge, only 3.6 percent could be used for this purpose (see chapter 1). Howard argued persuasively that we would be far better off if the statutes allowed more flexibility, but he provided that those subject to them would be accountable for how they used that flexibility.[69]

Illustrative of the amazing complexity that Howard described is the Clean Air Act:

- The statute contains enough words to fill approximately 450 pages as densely worded as those in this book.[70]
- The EPA regulations imposing duties required to implement the statute contain enough words to fill approximately twenty-three thousand pages.

- The EPA documents explaining how to implement the regulations are—incredible as this may seem—about fifty times longer than the regulations themselves.
- Moreover, the Clean Air Act forces each of the fifty states to impose the duties through additional statutes, regulations, and documents of its own.

This mountain of instructions makes controlling pollution incredibly complicated and actually gets in the way of achieving clean air. Yet, to switch to a simpler, more effective, and less expensive way of achieving clean air, members of Congress and the presidents would have to take responsibility for imposing the burdens themselves (see chapter 3). Instead, in their legislative capacities they hide behind the Regulation Trick and the Federal Mandate Trick. In implementing statutes as well as enacting them, presidents aren't accountable either (see chapter 4). Nor are agency officials because they are not elected. With scant accountability for bad consequences, the course of least resistance is to leave what doesn't work in place. As Philip Howard neatly explained in his book *The Rule of Nobody*:

> American democracy is basically run by dead people—by past generations of legislators and regulators who wrote the laws and regulations that dictate today's public policy, allocate most of annual budgets, and micromanage public choices. It's not surprising that Washington works so badly. Imagine if you had to run a business by following every idea that any former manager ever had.[71]

All these old statutes and regulations, backed up by the force of law, accumulate over time like plaque on a sclerotic artery. Even though Howard embraces popular objectives such as clean air, as I do, he objects to how Congress goes about achieving them. As law professors who favor strong environmental protection acknowledge, even big, sophisticated firms can't keep themselves in consistent compliance with the regulations. The chief difficulty is not the cost of compliance but understanding the regulations and coping with their complexity. The problem is even worse for small firms and individual practitioners. Even your dentist, no matter how well intentioned, stands not a chance of staying in compliance with the letter of the regulations.[72]

Scholars from the left and the right call for simpler regulation,[73] but the agencies can do little to simplify the regulatory system on their own and the legislators won't relent so long as they can get away with the Regulation Trick and the Federal Mandate Trick.

Unless curbed, these tricks will continue to sap the economy.

The Compounding of the Crises

A single crisis brought on by the Money Trick, the Federal Mandate Trick, or the Debt Guarantee Trick can trigger multiple crises. Here is one of many scenarios.

A financial crisis brought on by the Debt Guarantee Trick could lead to crises in both federal and state and local finances that would exacerbate the financial crisis. Consider that the top officials in Congress and the administration dealing with the financial crisis that began in 2007 feared at the time that they would fail to contain it.[74] They did contain it, but if they had failed we would have suffered an economic downturn far more serious than the Great Recession that began in 2008. Such a downturn would have decreased government revenues; increased the need for government spending; and excited anxiety about the creditworthiness of governments at the federal, state, and local levels. To preserve their ability to borrow, governments might well have found that they must raise taxes and cut spending, even though doing so would have made the economic downturn even worse. All this would have compounded the financial crisis in the private sector. As a result, the crises would spread and feed upon each other.

A strong private sector would help us weather crises, but the Regulation Trick and the Federal Mandate Trick continue to sap the economy.

Moreover, to cope with crises, societies need both trust between the people and the government and trust among the people—trust that people, especially the leaders, will act ethically in the main. "The most important principle for designing an ethical society," the behavioral psychologist Jonathan Haidt wrote, "is to *make sure that everyone's reputation is on the line all the time*, so that bad behavior will always bring bad consequences."[75] In other words, for a society to be ethical, its members must be accountable to one another. For that reason, the Constitution envisioned accountable legislators in charge of enacting statutes that make people accountable for bad behavior.

As it is, the tricks not only allow members of Congress to themselves evade accountability but allow their lack of accountability to spread through the rest of society like an infection that goes epidemic. For example, as this chapter has already shown:

- The Debt Guarantee Trick allowed members of Congress to evade accountability through issuing free or cheap debt guarantees; in turn allowing
- Fannie, Freddie, and the too-big-to-fail firms to borrow money to buy risky mortgages from disreputable mortgage lenders without being accountable for their questionable ability to repay the borrowed money; in turn allowing
- the disreputable mortgage lenders to grant mortgages without being accountable for whether the home buyers could pay them back; in turn allowing
- the home buyers to lie on mortgage applications.

Thus did the evasion of responsibility in Congress result in "liar loan" becoming a term of common parlance. The health care insurance tax break is another of the many other instances in which Congress sows discord rather than fulfilling its function, which, as discussed in chapter 2, is to be a "conductor" that enables people to live in society harmoniously even as they pursue happiness individually.

Because the tricks promote distrust, we will find it hard to cope with the next crisis.

The marriage of Congress and the people survived the last financial crisis because the government got away with blaming the misery on Wall Street, even though Congress and its Debt Guarantee Trick also deserved a big share of the blame. Yet, the marriage will not so readily survive the next crisis. If the crisis begins with federal or state finances, the blame will fall directly on the government. Even if it begins in private credit markets, the government will likely not be able to pin all the blame on Wall Street this time because Congress already told us that it dealt with the problem through Dodd–Frank.

The polls show that the public already distrusts the federal government in general and Congress in particular. Former Indiana governor Mitch Daniels, now the president of Purdue University, warned that democracy itself is at risk:

> A record 1 in 4 young people say that democracy is a "bad way" to run the country, and an even larger fraction of the citizenry would prefer an authoritarian leader who did not have to deal with the nuisance of elections.... If national leadership continues to allow our drift toward a Niagara of debt, until solemn promises are broken as they would then inevitably be, today's sense of betrayal will seem tame. When today's young Americans learn the extent of the debt burden we have left them, they may question the premises of our self government, with good reason. When tomorrow's older Americans finally understand how they have been actively misled about the nature and the reliability of our fundamental social welfare programs, it may be the last straw breaking the public confidence on which democracy itself depends.[76]

No, we can't go on like this.

CHAPTER 7

★ ★ ★

A Trick Even for War—and How It Deceives Us

This chapter explains the War Trick, the fifth and final of the Five Tricks. The Five Tricks are not the only ways that elected officials blunt their accountability to voters. Consider gerrymandering, which is the drawing of legislative districts in convoluted ways so as to produce a desired outcome, such as giving incumbents of both parties districts loaded with voters of their own party. Such gerrymandering corrupts democracy by letting the representatives pick their constituents, rather than the other way around. The term *gerrymander* dates back to 1812, but its use has intensified in the past half-century.

There is also constituent service, a process in which members of Congress get credit from voters for helping deal with federal agencies. People do need such help, but Congress could provide it by funding what are called citizen-advocate offices. Instead, members of Congress prefer to fund offices in their districts that have their name on the door and are devoted almost exclusively to constituent service. Over the past half-century, Congress has multiplied the funding for these offices many times over. The government paying incumbents to provide constituent service is a form of campaign financing that helps insulate them from accountability at the polls for their legislative work.

Other ways that Congress blunts the government's responsiveness to voters include the corruptive influence of campaign contributions, the increased use of the filibuster in the Senate, and an innovation in the House called the Hastert Rule that can prevent votes on bills that have majority support.[1]

I focus on the Five Tricks but overlook Congress's other flaws for several reasons. If we were to fix all the flaws except the Five Tricks, the tricks would continue to do us grave harm. Indeed, they would ruin us (see chapter 6).

Another reason is that fixing many of these other flaws, although important, is difficult and complicated. For example, even advocates of campaign finance reform from the left disagree on how to structure it. Meanwhile, the Right complains that the Left's campaign finance proposals fail to adequately limit the influence of powerful interests such as government employee unions. Both the Left and the Right want to limit the amount given by sources likely to fund the other side.[2] In contrast, voters from the left, the right, and in between agree that Congress is tricky and fails to serve us.

Focusing on stopping the Five Tricks will consequently reduce the harm that results from some of these other flaws and will ultimately make it easier to fix them. For example, the first four tricks let elected officials do favors for their campaign contributors while avoiding responsibility for the bad consequences, and so enable them to please those donating to their campaigns without losing votes. By forcing elected officials to take more responsibility, stopping the tricks will reduce the extent to which money talks. In addition, campaign contributions will become less valuable to incumbents and so make them more amenable to reform.[3]

My final reason for focusing on the Five Tricks is that while other flaws, such as the corruptive influence of big campaign contributions, have received extensive attention, there has been much-less work focusing on stopping the tricks.

The War Trick

With the War Trick, members of Congress duck responsibility for wars that might later prove controversial. The president alone gets to decide whether to enter such wars and thus takes the credit and blame for the consequences. It's war without responsibility for members of Congress.

With the other tricks, in contrast, Congress and the president signing the statute take most of the credit for the popular consequences but shift most of the blame for the unpopular ones. The War Trick is a bit different. I include it in the book because going to war is the most solemn and weighty of the government's decisions.

How the Nation Once Prevented the Trick

Under the Constitution, only Congress may declare war,[4] but Congress has declared only five wars, the last being World War II.[5] Presidents wishing to launch a war have usually asked Congress to authorize it by statute rather than by (itself) declaring war. For example, only a decade after the ratification of the Constitution, President John Adams got Congress to pass a statute authorizing a little-known war against France, known variously as the Undeclared War with France and the Quasi War, which lasted from 1798 to 1800. The practice of authorizing war by statute rather than declaring it would have come as no surprise to those who drafted the Constitution. During discussion of the Constitution's ratification, Alexander Hamilton wrote that in Europe, "The ceremony of a formal denunciation of war has of late fallen into disuse."[6]

The Constitution says nothing explicit about whether presidents must get authorization from Congress for undeclared wars. Until 1950, however, the general practice was for presidents to refrain from waging wars, whether big or small, unless (1) Congress had declared war; (2) Congress had explicitly approved the combat by statute; or (3) the president needed to repel an enemy attack, in which case he would simultaneously seek a vote of authorization in Congress.[7]

In the rare case that a president deviated from the general practice of asking for Congress's authorization, he usually paid lip service to it and tried to cover up the deviation. For example, Congressman Abraham Lincoln and other legislators vehemently criticized President James Polk for manipulating Congress to declare war against Mexico by covertly provoking the country to attack our troops. President Polk denied the charge, but not the principle that the president alone cannot launch a war. The House passed a resolution condemning the president and rejected requests for funds to continue fighting the war. The main issue in the next presidential election was abuse of presidential authority, and President Polk's party lost.[8]

How Congress Came to Get Away with the Trick

Breaking with a century and a half of tradition, President Harry Truman openly put combat troops into Korea in 1950 with neither a declaration of war nor specific statutory authorization from Congress. His rationale was that American forces were conducting a United Nations–approved "police action." Some police action! During the Korean War, American forces suffered more than thirty-three thousand deaths in battle. At the signing of the armistice, General Mark Clark said he had "the unenviable distinction of being the first US Army commander to sign an armistice without victory."[9]

Before 1950, presidents generally could not duck going to Congress for approval and members of Congress could not shirk responsibility for war because the United States would largely disband its forces when a war ended. So a president who wanted to wage a war had to ask Congress for funds to muster forces. Congress not only authorized the Quasi War with France in 1798 but funded a navy to fight it.[10] In contrast, after World War II, the Cold War required the United States to maintain a powerful military. So President Truman had troops to deploy in Korea without the leave of Congress.

Congress willingly went along with the president's launching of the unauthorized war in Korea. As the historian and professor Arthur Schlesinger put it, "It was as much a matter of congressional abdication as of presidential usurpation." The constitutional scholar and professor John Hart Ely agreed: "The legislative surrender was a self-interested one: Accountability is pretty frightening stuff." Or as Robert Gates, who served as defense secretary under presidents George W. Bush and Barack Obama, put it, "In matters of national security, Congress absolutely hates to challenge the president directly in a way that would saddle them with clear and full responsibility if things went to hell."[11]

After Korea, presidents continued to unleash the lethal power of our armed forces without seeking authorization from Congress and Congress acquiesced. By doing this, its members could avoid voting for or against a war before knowing how their constituents would end up feeling about it after the dust settled, which can be difficult to predict. In the words of Winston Churchill, "The statesman who yields to war fever must realize that once the signal is given, he is no longer the master of policy but the slave of unforeseeable and uncontrollable events."[12]

Since Korea, however, presidents have asked Congress to authorize military campaigns when they are confident that legislators will do so. This way, the president doesn't have to shoulder the entire responsibility. President Lyndon Johnson asked Congress in 1964 to authorize what became known as the Vietnam War. Reporting to Congress that North Vietnamese ships had attacked our navy in the Gulf of Tonkin, he requested authorization to take military action to stop the "aggression" by North Vietnam. The reports of the attacks were exaggerated and the attacks themselves may have been provoked. But Congress failed to look behind the reports before granting the authority. It also failed to get solid information on whether the administration planned military action on a little or big scale. Instead it gave President Johnson carte blanche to proceed. By the time he left office, there were 536,000 Americans in uniform in Vietnam.[13] Regardless of whether Congress chose rightly in authorizing the Vietnam War, it chose sloppily.

We waged war in Vietnam for more than eight years after Congress authorized it and then withdrew in 1975. Along the way, we failed to accomplish the stated goal of stopping North Vietnamese aggression and lost credibility around the world. Millions of young Americans went to a war reviled by many of their fellow citizens. Of the troops, 58,220 were killed and 303,644 wounded. War protestors spat on returning soldiers. War supporters sneered at draft dodgers. The country was in agony. It also spent a fortune, throwing the economy into rampant inflation.

As the Vietnam War grew increasingly unpopular, many legislators tried to wash their hands of it. As President Johnson remarked:

> I said early in my Presidency that if I wanted Congress with me on the landing of Vietnam, I'd have to have them with me on the takeoff. And I did just that. But I failed to reckon with one thing: the parachute. I got them on the takeoff, but a lot of them bailed out before the end of the flight.

Yet, Johnson had used dubious tactics to get congressional authorization. In addition, neither he nor President Richard Nixon ever asked Congress to authorize the closely related military campaigns in Laos from 1962 to 1969 and in Cambodia from 1969 to 1970. Nevertheless, Congress kept voting money for the military operations in Southeast Asia and extensions of the military draft. Yet, many of the legislators denied that their votes signified approval of the war. They played both sides down the middle.[14]

Although American voters disagreed about the wars in Southeast Asia, the majority agreed that presidents should get approval for military campaigns from Congress. Passing a statute to that effect would give members of Congress a chance to please the public. Many of them believed themselves honor-bound to decide whether to authorize military campaigns in the future. To do so, they had to overcome two obstacles. First was their own propensity to avoid responsibility. Second was the propensity of presidents to cut Congress out of the decision to launch controversial military campaigns, including those not only in Laos and Cambodia but also in the invasion of the Dominican Republic in 1965.[15]

To force presidents to lay out the goals and risks of war and ask for approval, members of Congress passed the 1973 War Powers Act. President Richard Nixon vetoed it, but Democrats and Republicans in Congress joined in overriding the veto. The key provision requires the president, within forty-eight hours of introducing forces into areas of ongoing or impending hostilities, to report to Congress in writing the "circumstances necessitating" the campaign and its "estimated scope and duration." The report was intended to prevent the kind of half-truths that led to the Tonkin Gulf Resolution. According to the statute, unless Congress explicitly approves the president's action within sixty days of receiving the report, the president must end the use of force, subject to some limited exceptions. The deadline was designed to force Congress to decide whether to authorize military campaigns so that it could no longer avoid making formal decisions about going to war.[16]

Since the War Powers Act, presidents of both parties have sought authority from Congress to go to war, when they think legislators will provide political cover for military campaigns, as President George W. Bush did in the case of Iraq and Afghanistan. When presidents are unsure whether they will get Congress's approval, however, they have violated the requirement in the War Powers Act that they submit the report that forces Congress to decide in sixty days. Examples include the disastrous deployment of the marines in Lebanon in 1982–83, the invasion of Grenada in

1983, the bombing of Tripoli in 1986, the start of the Persian Gulf naval war with Iran in 1987–88, the invasion of Panama in 1989, Black Hawk Down and related events in Somalia in 1992–95, and the deployment of forces in Bosnia in 1993–96 and Kosovo in 1999.[17]

When he was running for office in 2008, Barack Obama insisted that presidents must seek authority for combat from Congress, but in 2011, as president, he decided not to seek authorization to intervene in Libya to help the rebellion to overthrow Muammar Gaddafi. Congressional leaders from both parties privately urged him to intervene but not to make Congress vote. He did as they urged. One of the president's excuses: The United Nations has sanctioned the military activities (shades of Korea). Another excuse: The United States has not deployed ground forces. (In other words, because the United States did not deploy ground forces in Libya, it was not engaging in hostilities, as if killing Libyans with planes and missiles was not engaging in hostilities.) Still another excuse: The combat will likely be over before sixty days has elapsed. Yet, the War Powers Act requires the president to start the sixty-day clock regardless of how long the combat is likely to last. President Obama's own secretary of defense, Robert Gates, called the intervention "an act of war." Gates also noted in his book *Duty: A Memoir of a Secretary at War* that although members of Congress in private urged the president to intervene without giving them the responsibility, they had the gall to criticize him in public for not complying with the War Powers Act.[18]

Overall, the War Powers Act is flawed: it provides no effective response to presidents who refuse to start the sixty-day clock. So, to *stop* the president from continuing unauthorized combat, Congress would be required to enact a new statute cutting off funding for the war. Given the inevitable presidential veto such a statute would receive, it would need to get affirmative action by two-thirds of the House and the Senate.[19] In contrast, under the pre-1950 practice, a simple majority of either the House or the Senate could block combat.

Although Congress does indeed know how to fix the War Powers Act to bar wars that it did not authorize, as chapter 8 will show, it has done nothing. The damning lesson learned from Vietnam, once so compelling, is now convenient for legislators to ignore: There is, according to John Hart Ely, "a tacit deal" between presidents and Congress that "the president will take the responsibility (well, most of it) so long as he can make the decisions, and Congress will forego actual policy-making authority so long as it doesn't have to be held accountable (and can scold the president when things go wrong)." In 1995, then-senator Joseph Biden stated that legislators have failed to fix the War Powers Act because "they do not have the political courage to take a stand on whether or not we should go to war."[20]

Nonetheless, the principle that legislators should be responsible for war remains popular with voters. They agreed with it by a margin of three to one when President Obama ordered acts of war in Libya in 2011 and by five to one when he contemplated intervening in Syria in 2013.[21]

In short, members of Congress fail to fix the War Powers Act because its present broken state lets them strike the popular pose that they wish to take responsibility for war, but don't actually have to take responsibility for controversial wars. So, they can march in the parade if a war proves popular but put the entire blame on the president if it does not.

What's good for legislators is bad for us, their constituents. We end up in unwise military campaigns that a vote in Congress might well have prevented through early airing of the goals and risks. According to foreign policy specialists Leslie H. Gelb and Anne-Marie Slaughter:

> Time and again in recent decades the United States has made military commitments after little real debate, with hazy goals and no appetite for their inevitable setbacks. Bill Clinton, having inherited a mission in Somalia to feed the starving, ended up hunting tribal leaders, and trying to nation-build. Ronald Reagan dispatched the Marines to Lebanon saying stability there was a "vital interest," only to yank them out sixteen months later, soon after a deadly terrorist attack on the Marine barracks.[22]

Congress's evasion of responsibility for war also makes achieving success in war unnecessarily difficult since public support never got crystallized with affirmative votes in the House and Senate. That encourages enemies to hope to defeat us on our home front even if they are losing on the battlefront. Requiring the president to get authorization from Congress would help close the gap of distrust between the public and the president as commander in chief. We need to reestablish that trust. Speaking shortly after President Reagan ordered the withdrawal from Lebanon, then–secretary of defense Caspar W. Weinberger stated:

Before the US commits combat forces abroad, there must be some reasonable assurance we will have the support of the American people and their elected representatives in Congress. This support cannot be achieved unless we are candid in making clear the threats we face; the support cannot be sustained without continuing and close consultation. We cannot fight a battle with the Congress at home while asking our troops to win a war overseas.

Similarly, as a presidential candidate, Barack Obama stated, "History has shown us time and again . . . that military action is most successful when it is authorized and supported by the Legislative branch."[23]

Despite all the reasons for requiring congressional approval, our government is divided on who has the power to decide to go to war. In the War Powers Act, Congress says one thing. In their actions, members of Congress and the presidents say the opposite.

A clear assignment of responsibility to Congress would also clarify the president's role in decisions to go to war: to lead within our democracy rather than to dictate. Such clarity is vital. Consider what happened after President Obama announced in 2012 that President Bashar al-Assad of Syria would cross a "red line" if he used chemical weapons in that country's civil war: When Assad proceeded to cross that red line repeatedly in 2013, President Obama claimed that he, acting alone, could authorize acts of war against Syria, but decided not to do so in the face of public opposition. Poof, the red line disappeared. Had the War Powers Act been fixed, President Obama would have known that he should not lay down his red line in the first place without securing the support of congressional leaders. Had he gotten that support, his threat to Assad might have had more credibility. As Obama himself said in 2014, "We are strongest as a nation when the president and Congress work together."[24]

On December 1, 2015, in the midst of terrorists killing 130 people in Paris and 14 people in San Bernardino, Secretary of Defense Ash Carter stated, "We're at [w]ar" with ISIS. That evening, *PBS NewsHour* aired an essay by Phil Klay titled "What I'll Tell My Son about Fighting in the Iraq War." Klay served in Iraq from 2007 to 2008 and won the National Book Award for a volume of short stories about the horrors experienced by both American soldiers and Iraqi civilians in Anbar province, the later success of efforts to pacify the province, the subsequent withdrawal of American forces, and the return of the horror with the invasion of ISIS. Klay's point: We should not blame the military for "the failure." As he put it, "In a democracy, everyone shares responsibility. Troops don't issue themselves orders. War is paid for by our tax dollars and ordered by politicians we as a people need to hold accountable."[25]

In the next chapter, I show how we can make these politicians accountable.

CHAPTER 8

The Honest Deal Act

America! America!
God mend thine every flaw,
Confirm thy soul in self-control,
Thy liberty in law!
　　　—Katharine Lee Bates ("America the Beautiful")[1]

By empowering legislators to be responsible to voters for both benefits and burdens, the Constitution sought to bring self-control. Yet, by allowing legislators to dodge responsibility for unpopular consequences, the Five Tricks produce a government that is dangerously out of control, as seen in chapters 5 and 6. In this book, I propose that Congress pass a statute that will stop these tricks. The present chapter explains the statute, which I call the "Honest Deal Act." Appendix A concisely outlines its terms.

The Money Trick

Were I a candidate for Congress, I would feel honor-bound to disclose how I would keep the government solvent. As a constituent rather than a candidate, I demand that the government disclose how much it will cost us in the long run to maintain solvency and how the current Congress and president have increased or decreased that cost. This requires of the government the same thing that it does of private lenders under the Truth in Lending Act: to provide a crystal-clear statement of the costs people will have to bear in the future. Instead the government provides us with false information shrouded in fine print. "A false balance is abomination to the Lord," states Proverbs 11:1. A false balance sheet from the government is abomination to the people.

The Honest Deal Act would require the government to disclose how much we would have to pay in tax increases or spending cuts to make ends meet in the long run but not that Congress has to increase taxes or cut spending now. How to respond to this disclosure would be up to members of Congress, who could no longer keep us in the dark.

It is possible to provide reasonable estimates of the costs we will ultimately have to bear despite uncertainty about the future:

- We don't know how large the national debt can grow without imperiling the government's credit but we do know that the debt cannot grow infinitely large. For this reason, the government's spending (including interest on the debt) cannot exceed its revenue in the long run, as discussed in chapter 4.
- To determine the size of change in current policy needed to bring spending in line with revenues in the long run, we can use a budget model that estimates how much Congress would need to permanently cut annual spending or increase annual revenue if it acted now. Such estimates are surprisingly not too sensitive to changes in assumptions about the rate at which the economy grows.[2]
- We don't know whether Congress will cut spending or increase taxes to close the gap or how it will do so. What we do know is that in the end the impacts will be felt primarily by individuals, whether as taxpayers, beneficiaries of entitlements, employees, consumers, shareholders, local taxpayers, or the like, and we can calculate the average annual impact on a family of four.
- We don't know on which families the impacts of increased taxes or spending cuts will fall most heavily. What is clear is that if the tricks remain unstopped, lower- and middle-income families will likely suffer an even-greater cost than the average family because the trickery tends to especially benefit the rich and connected, as seen in chapter 5. As a point of comparison we can estimate the average cost per family.

A calculation of the average cost per family would be better than an estimate but, realistically, the choice is between an estimate and flying blind.[3] For a similar reason, responsible people produce estimates as to whether they can afford a long-term expense such as a mortgage. The irresponsible rely on wishful thinking.

The key thing is that the estimate should be apolitical. The Congressional Budget Office could do the job. When it began operation in 1975, the office's first director, Dr. Alice Rivlin, set out to make it independent and nonpartisan. It has stayed that way.[4] What the office needs to do the job of estimating the average cost per family is a mandate from Congress, a completely free hand in how to do it, and the means to get its analysis sent to every voter. This will give the CBO support from many in the electorate and so help insulate it from tampering.

As it has done before, the CBO would provide information rather than recommend policy, let alone tie the hands of Congress. The CBO's work would not impose so-called fiscal cliffs or sequesters. Elected officials would get to decide how to react, but would be responsible for the consequences.

Under the Honest Deal Act, at the conclusion of each Congress and before each general election, the Congressional Budget Office would send citizens an easily understood letter explaining the size of the changes needed for the government to make ends meet. The letter might look something like this:

"The Honest Deal Act requires the Congressional Budget Office to provide citizens with forthright information on the state of the government's finances over the long run.

The Congressional Budget Office calculates that the government will not be able to pay its bills in the long run if it continues its current practices of taxing and spending.

If Congress and the president act now to close the gap between spending and taxation by increasing income taxes on individuals and corporations, revenues from such taxes will have to be increased permanently by _____ %. If they instead act to close the gap by cutting government expenditures (including Social Security, Medicaid, Medicare, military, and all the other programs), total expenditures will have to be cut permanently by _____%.

Congresses and the presidents now and in the future will have to choose the extent to which they increase taxes or cut spending, and how to do so, but in the end the impacts will be felt largely by individuals. Assuming that the cost is spread equally among the population, the average tax increase or spending cut to a family of four in the current year will be $_____, with similar amounts cut each subsequent year.

During the most recent Congress, which began in _____ and ended in _____ [(or in the case of a letter sent before a general election) the current Congress, which began in _____ and will end in _____], legislators have taken actions that increased [or decreased as the case may be] this amount $_____ per family.[5]

The size of the tax increases or spending cuts required to make ends meet will grow larger the longer Congress and the president delay action. If they delay ten years, the size of the required tax increase or spending cut will grow _____% larger.

Current spending and taxing policies will not only leave the federal government with insufficient funds to make ends meet but will take funds from future generations to benefit current voters. For more information on the actual impact that the current actions will have on an average person born in a particular year (such as someone born the same year as you, your children, or your grandchildren), see the Congressional Budget Office's Web site at _____."

The CBO shall, to the greatest extent possible, have a copy of this letter delivered to each individual of voting age. The Honest Deal Act should also require the Social Security Administration, any other agencies that provide information on benefits, and the Internal Revenue Service to enclose the CBO's letters along with their own mass communications they send to the public.

To fill in the blanks in the letter, the CBO would adopt its own budget model that projects future spending and revenues under current policies. The model would be based upon actual current policy rather than the tax increases or spending cuts that current statutes suggest will happen in the future but for which elected officials have not taken responsibility.

Because the public needs information on how the votes of their own senators and representatives have affected the cost per family, the CBO should be required to make its budget model public. Analysts of every stripe could then use the model on their own to assess the fiscal impact of these politicians' positions on various legislative proposals. Such analysts could also critique the budget model.

Overall, the letter and model would provide us with a common language to discuss the government's fiscal future. Because we now lack such a language, politicians can get away with talking past one another and confusing us. Depending on what is politically convenient to them, they now choose to talk about either the national debt or the deficit for the current year, the next ten years, or the next seventy-five years. Current politicians can also speak about how much their proposals would cut any of these amounts from many different baselines, each of which they choose on the basis of political convenience. In contrast to this babel, the information produced by the Congressional Budget Office would prompt our politicians to tell us what they propose to do, if anything, to make ends meet. The CBO's information would also help Standard & Poor's, Moody's, and other companies that rate the creditworthiness of government bonds to be more precise. Bond buyers would in turn pay attention, and that would reverberate back into politics.

Given the salience of such information, isn't it likely that Congress would want to amend the Honest Deal Act to suppress it? Yes, but changed conditions will provide no cover to amend the statute, even though changed conditions did provide cover for gutting the balanced budget statutes of the 1990s. Back then, the statutes controlled the budget, so that changed circumstances provided an argument for changing that control. Under the Honest Deal Act, the CBO would control nothing; its only job would be to provide information.[6] Changed circumstances would provide a reason for Congress to react differently to the information rather than to amend the Honest Deal Act. If Congress can be made to order the CBO to put such information into the hands of voters, it will have to live with that order.

As it is, the Money Trick hides not only the long-term cost of the Congress's current policies but also the fact that current policies enrich current voters at the expense of their children and grandchildren.[7] And the longer Congress waits to close the fiscal gap, the worse the deal will be for future generations. As people who want to be fair to those who come after us, we should know the burdens that we are imposing on them. For that reason, the CBO should also compute how much programs with intergenerational consequences will enrich or impoverish a person born in any particular year.

We cannot excuse leaving a larger bill to succeeding generations on the basis that they will benefit from investments that their forebears made. Yes, we who came before them have built roads and other government-owned infrastructure and fought wars to defend the country. But the great bulk of the growing shortfall comes from money going to older people. Moreover, if members of the older generations such as me get credited for having invested in government-owned infrastructure, we should also get debited for failing to maintain that infrastructure adequately and selling off government-owned oil, gas, and other nonrenewable resources. Congress has, in Christopher DeMuth's words, erased "the distinction between investing in the future and borrowing from the future." Nor can Congress excuse its current policies by claiming that they are necessary to take care of the poor. As the mildly conservative John Micklethwait and his coauthor Adrian Wooldridge put it: "For all the worries about 'benefit scroungers' and 'welfare queens,' most [government] spending is sucked up by the middle classes, many of them conservatives."[8]

That is why the proposed letter from the Congressional Budget Office should include language of the following sort:

> "Current spending and taxing policies will not only leave the federal government with insufficient funds to make ends meet but will take funds from future generations to benefit current voters. For more information on the actual impact that the current actions will have on an average person born in a particular year (such as someone born the same year as you, your children, or your grandchildren), see the Congressional Budget Office's Web site at _____."

Better Rather Than Best

To provide a strong basis for concluding that the proposals in the Honest Deal Act would make the government better, I have limited them to methods that can clearly work. By limiting myself to such methods, I aim to propose an Honest Deal Act that delivers the better but not necessarily the best.

We can accept the better rather than the best when we understand that improvements can come incrementally. Once we have experience with the implementation of the reforms in the Honest Deal Act, we will have information that is useful in considering further reforms. In so suggesting, I am following the advice of the famous political science professor Charles Lindblom, who pointed out that we seldom have the information and consensus needed to agree on objectives and identify the very best policies to achieve them in designing reforms.[9] Instead, we usually make policy by considering whether an obvious change in current practice would make things better.

Frustration with Congress's inability to control the deficit has generated some support for amending the Constitution to restrict its spending, but I do not propose such an amendment requiring Congress to produce a balanced budget. Whether such an amendment is good economics, it is unlikely to succeed. An amendment of this type has never gotten the two-thirds approval in both houses of Congress needed to submit it to the states for ratification. Even if it did get this approval, it would not be likely to then be ratified by three-quarters of the states as is necessary to amend the Constitution. Besides, as happened in the last years of the twentieth century, Congress can produce a seemingly balanced budget for the current year while also having current policies that will produce a huge gap between spending and revenues in future decades. And if a balanced budget requirement were to be proposed, Congress would likely find ways to skirt it, just as some state legislatures have found ways to skirt the balanced budget requirements in state constitutions.[10]

What the perpetually unsuccessful balanced budget amendment does accomplish is to let some elected officials strike a pose in favor of fiscal responsibility without actually having to take the blame for raising taxes or cutting spending. Stopping the Money Trick, on the other hand, would make legislators pay a political price for leaving a big fiscal gap and make us, the voters, be honest with ourselves.

The Debt Guarantee Trick

Many financial analysts and market participants think that no matter what Congress says, the government will not let the debts of the financial giants go unpaid in a crisis. Otherwise, as the government sees it, the crisis would grow even bigger.[11] It also cannot hand off guaranteeing the debts of financial giants to private firms because these firms lack sufficient capital to back up these massive debts. So, as long as the government guarantees the debts of these firms, it should charge them market-based fees for what they get.

The market should determine these fees because otherwise the government will set them too low. Government officials tend to overlook politically inconvenient risks. Consider this statement by the director of the agency regulating Fannie and Freddie only six months before they collapsed: "Let me be clear—both [Fannie and Freddie] have prudent cushions above [my agency's] capital requirements." Two months before the collapse, Senate Banking Committee Chairman Chris Dodd stated, "What's important are facts—and the facts are that Fannie and Freddie are in sound situation."[12]

To set a market-based fee, the government should require each financial giant to buy a guarantee from private guarantors for a portion of its debt that is small enough to ensure that the guarantors will be good for it. The guarantors would charge higher fees to the riskier financial giants. The government would then guarantee the balance of the debt, basing its fee on that charged by private guarantors. For example, if private guarantors guaranteed 10 percent of a financial giant's debt at a certain fee, the government would provide the remaining 90 percent at a fee nine times higher than that charged by the private guarantors.[13]

The market-based fee would end the welfare for Wall Street that comes from free or cheap debt guarantees. The fee would also give the financial giants a profit-based incentive to limit the risk that their debts inflict upon the economy and thus on our livelihoods. Moreover, the private guarantors would lobby regulators to limit the riskiness of the firms whose debts they guaranteed, thus helping to offset the influence over regulators of too-big-to-fail firms.

How to go about charging market-based fees for debt guarantees is, however, complicated. One reason is that such fees for financial giants may need to be phased in. As these firms are now structured, they would have to pay very high fees because their debts are large and far from risk-free. To reduce the risk, they will need to raise capital and that will take time. A phase-in period may be necessary to avoid a tightening of credit.[14]

Another reason that charging market-based fees would be complicated is that the government now guarantees many sorts of private debts. Examples include commercial loans to alternative-energy manufacturers such as Solyndra (which famously went bankrupt) and the pensions owed by private corporations. In many cases, the government charges no fee for the guarantees or a fee not fully reflective of the risk that it assumes in backing up the debt. For example, Congress sets the fees that the Pension Benefit Guaranty Corporation (PBGC) charges corporations too low for it to cover the risks, as chapter 1 discussed.

To help decide how to initiate market-based fees, I propose that

Congress should create a "Debt Guarantee Honesty Commission." At the end of year one, the commission would produce an exhaustive list of existing debt guarantees, explicit and implicit. The commission would then divide the debt guarantees into three groups to be the subject of proposals at the end of years two, three, and four. At the close of these years, the commission would recommend whether each kind of debt guarantee could and should be eliminated and, if not, how to set a market-based fee for it.[15] The commission would also recommend whether there should be a phase-in period for the elimination. Congress would vote on each year's recommendations as a package on a fast-track basis that permits no amendments or filibusters.

I modeled this process on one that Congress established to eliminate redundant military bases. Congress tasked the Defense Base Closure and Realignment Commission to propose which bases to eliminate and set up a process in which the legislators voted on the commission's proposals on a fast-track basis.[16] The reason for the commission was that Congress alone could not come to grips with getting rid of redundant bases despite their huge cost to the public. The legislators fiercely defended the bases in their own districts, redundant or not. Similarly, members of Congress would likely defend debt guarantees that benefit their campaign contributors. These beneficiaries are smart enough to give heavily to both parties. The base closure commission is widely viewed as a great success.

Charging a market-based fee would, of course, end the subsidies that Congress covertly grants through free or underpriced guarantees. If Congress wishes to subsidize an activity, it should have to do so openly by appropriating the money through the discretionary budget on which it votes annually. This would effectively prevent beneficiaries of the guarantees from growing the subsidy, as Fannie, Freddie, and the too-big-to-fail firms did, without the legislators having to take responsibility.

While the Debt Guarantee Honesty Commission would provide a short-term process to deal with the backlog of free or underpriced debt guarantees that currently exist, another process would be needed to deal with any free or underpriced debt guarantees that may creep into existence in the future. This could happen through a firm growing to the point where it becomes too big to fail. It could also happen if Congress were to enact a new statute providing a free or underpriced debt guarantee. Either occurrence is likely to be infrequent, so it makes sense that the

Debt Guarantee Honesty Commission would end after four years and the job of dealing with the occasional new problems be assigned to another entity. I suggest the Federal Reserve Board.

Better Rather Than Best

Federal officials have long understood the popular appeal of making firms whose debts are guaranteed pay a market-based price for the guarantees—private businesses have long used this method to deal with debt guarantees—and have sometimes tried to make it seem as if they have applied it.

Some observers contend that the very best way to deal with the systemic risk from the collapse of financial giants is to break them up or to radically change their internal structure.[17] They may be correct, but I stick with advocating a market-based fee because it is simpler to understand and therefore has a better chance of bringing home to voters the injustice of financial giants continuing to get a hidden subsidy from taxpayers. Until voters understand this injustice, no change is possible. Ending the subsidy for being big would both reduce these firms' incentive to swell their size and reduce their resistance to solutions that may be even "better."

The Federal Mandate Trick

Ideally, members of Congress should cast a roll call vote on all of the statutory provisions that would harm constituents if states or localities fail to do the federal bidding. This ideal would be, however, impossible to implement because statutes include large numbers of such provisions, often on issues as noncontroversial as denying federal highway grants to states unless they build the highways with concrete that meets federal specifications. Voting on each and every such provision would take too much time.

To prompt votes on the most controversial provisions without requiring votes on all of them, the Honest Deal Act would adopt a method similar to that used to challenge the most controversial rulings by National Football League officials. The act would amend the standing rules of the House and Senate to allow legislators to challenge provisions in a bill that threaten to do harm to states or localities if they fail to do the federal bidding. The challenges would be made when the bill comes up for passage on the floor of the House or Senate. Each legislator would be entitled to make one such challenge during each Congress, which lasts two years. The challenge would take the form of a point of order and state how to amend the bill to avoid the harm. The House or the Senate would resolve the challenge by roll call vote. There would be no debate. Each successful challenge would result in the bill being amended and the legislator being yielded a chance to make another challenge.[18] So smart legislators could make many challenges. In response, smart bill sponsors would strip their bills of mandates for which legislators would not take responsibility. While nothing would require legislators to actually issue challenges, their ability to do so would tend to make them responsible for controversial mandates.

Limiting each legislator to only one unsuccessful challenge and blocking debate on any of them would prevent these challenges from becoming a routine way to kill bills. In contrast, the Unfunded Mandates Reform Act, discussed in chapter 4, imposes no limit on the number of challenges, and as a result it has given the leadership of the House and Senate an excuse to use legislative maneuvers to prevent challenges against mandates. To make sure that they don't do so, we should ask candidates for Congress to sign my proposed "Honest Deal Pledge" (see appendix B), which includes a promise to oppose any maneuver to prevent challenges to mandates under the Honest Deal Act.

Better Rather Than Best

The Honest Deal Act's proposal to stop the Federal Mandate Trick employs the method that Congress actually adopted in the Unfunded Mandates Reform Act but failed to design in a practical form.

My proposal to stop the Federal Mandate Trick would not apply to mandates arising under statutes that antedate the Honest Deal Act. However, my proposal to stop the Regulation Trick, which I outline later in this chapter, would require Congress to vote on major new regulations, including those that impose new mandates under both new and old statutes.

It is ideal for Congress to take responsibility for old mandates because those that that were once popular can become unpopular in time. For example, state and local officials have supported some mandates because Congress promised states money to implement them, only for Congress to then fail to produce the money. Implementation of the Honest Deal

Act will suggest some process by which elected officials can reconsider old mandates.

Retired senator and judge James Buckley argued that Congress should replace all federal grants to states and localities (and the mandates that they impose) with federal grants that these states and localities can spend as they wish.[19] Because my focus is on making Congress accountable for its decisions rather than dictating what decisions it should make, I take no position on his proposal. If, however, the Money Trick and the Mandate Trick were stopped, members of Congress could consider this proposal without a blatant conflict between their own interests and those of their constituents.

The Regulation Trick

We can't stop the Regulation Trick by insisting that Congress make all the rules of conduct without the help of agencies. To produce rules on complex subjects, Congress needs their expertise. We can, however, marry the expertise of agencies with accountability for Congress. James Landis, the New Deal's sage of administrative law, showed how. In 1938, as the dean of Harvard Law School, he wrote that for administrative officials, "it is an act of political wisdom to put back upon the shoulders of Congress" responsibility for "controversial choices." Congress, he urged, should vote on agencies' important decisions. The votes could be on whether (1) to ratify or (2) to veto the choices. In this way, the agency would be, in Landis's words, "the technical agent in the initiation of rules of conduct, yet at the same time . . . [the elected lawmakers would] share in the responsibility for their adoption."[20]

Congress built Landis's second alternative into dozens of statutes by providing that the House and the Senate (or in some statutes, either of them acting alone) could veto an agency action regardless of whether the president agreed. In 1983, however, the Supreme Court held that Landis's legislative veto violates the Constitution because it cuts the president out of the legislative process. The Constitution, the Court reasoned, provides that legislation receive the support of majorities of both the House and the Senate and then be presented to the president to sign or veto. The Court so held despite legislators of both parties arguing that the legislative veto is good public policy.[21]

Responding to the Supreme Court's decision in a law review article, then-judge Stephen Breyer argued that Congress could achieve the effect of a legislative veto by, in essence, adopting Landis's first alternative. In other words, Congress could, consistent with the Constitution, provide that agency actions would not go into effect until Congress approved them by roll call vote and presented the bill to the president, thus going through the Constitution's full legislative process. Breyer went further, suggesting a fast-track legislative process that would force legislators to take responsibility by a deadline without the possibility of amendment or filibuster.[22] His design is similar to the process for closing redundant defense bases I previously discussed in my proposal to stop the Debt Guarantee Trick.

In 1995, some members of Congress asked for my help in designing a bill to stop Congress from passing the buck on regulation. I suggested a bill based upon Landis's first alternative and Breyer's fast-track design. The bill, titled the Congressional Responsibility Act, would have barred agency regulations unless approved through the Constitution's legislative process, which includes presenting the bill to the president.[23] After the bill began to gain traction, Congress pulled a switcheroo. It passed a sound-alike called the Congressional Review Act. Signed by President Clinton, it gave legislators the option of voting on agency regulations. The Congressional Responsibility Act, in contrast, would have required them to do so. Not that it's any surprise but, as it turns out, legislators hardly ever opt to take responsibility under the Congressional Review Act.[24]

Starting in 2009, after the failure of the Congressional Review Act had become apparent, members of the House have regularly introduced bills modeled on my original Congressional Responsibility Act. Yet the sponsors of the new versions of the original bill have done a grave disservice to it by casting their bill as antiregulatory instead of proaccountability. This is apparent from the newest bill's title, Regulations from the Executive in Need of Scrutiny Act, or REINS. Not only did these legislators stake out the low rather than the high ground in titling the bill, they have put into it poison pills that make it unlikely that it will ever become law. For example, the version passed by the House of Representatives in 2015 requires that any and all Affordable Care Act regulations, no matter how trivial, get congressional approval.[25] This provision will make the Affordable Care Act unworkable and therefore prevent REINS from getting enacted unless Republicans already have the votes to repeal the Affordable Care Act.

Such poison pills allow supporters of REINS to strike a proaccountability pose while shielding themselves from accountability. That's convenient because voting against regulations with broad public support can cost votes in the next election. In the mid-1990s, as Howard Dean related, "Voters started to blanch when Republicans went after the Endangered Species Act and a host of other basic environmental, health and safety measures."[26] Fear of accountability helps us to understand why some legislators turned the Congressional Responsibility Act into the toothless Congressional Review Act in 1996 and today put poison pills into REINS to prevent it becoming law. That way, they can continue to surreptitiously pressure agencies to go easy on campaign contributors but avoid having to cast roll call votes that could cost them votes at the next election.

Legislative responsibility for agencies' decisions is even more imperative now than when Landis wrote in 1938. Since then, as Professor Bruce Ackerman has shown, presidents have come to exert tight political control of the once supposedly expert and apolitical agencies.[27] We need a new version of REINS suitable for lawmakers who are actually willing to be responsible for the laws that benefit and burden the people. The new version would omit the poison pills and instead require Congress to vote on regulatory actions to make regulation both *less* and *more* protective.

Also unlike REINS, the new version would provide that a petition signed by a majority in either house would add an extra thirty days to the deadline for a final roll call vote in order to allow time for a hearing on the promulgated rule. The extra time would not usually be necessary, however, because the Honest Deal Act would come with the expectation that both houses hold hearings when an agency *proposes* a rule that would trigger votes in Congress. Proposed regulations usually come months if not years before the agency finalizes them. At these hearings, the time should be devoted to committee counsel carefully questioning witnesses, especially agency officials, rather than to members of the committee putting on a show for constituents and campaign contributors. The hearings on the proposed rule would launch a conversation between swing legislators and the agency.

The Honest Deal Act's provision on regulation would apply only to regulations that are "major," as defined by the White House's Office of Management and Budget.[28] This limit accords with Dean Landis's proposal, which calls for Congress to vote on only the important decisions, and would ensure that Congress has sufficient time to do the job. Voting on a major regulation would not take much time in Congress because the agencies would have already drafted the regulation, solicited comments from the public, revised the proposal in light of those comments, and estimated the impacts. Debate would be strictly limited in order to prevent filibusters and conserve time. During the two years of the 111th Congress, agencies promulgated 126 major regulations. Congress could make the time to vote on major regulations. During the same Congress, it voted on 112 symbolic public laws, such as those naming post offices.[29] The bills assigning names are one of the numerous ways in which legislators devote time to striking poses rather than taking responsibility for the actual consequences that will be felt by their constituents. Voting on major regulations would require legislators to shoulder much-more responsibility than they do with laws that name post offices, but shouldering responsibility is their job.

To further ensure that Congress does not kill major regulations by failing to vote by the Honest Deal Act's deadline, such failure should automatically cut off appropriations (including those for their salaries, travel expenses, staffs, and office expenses) for members of whichever house fails to vote until such time as that house ends the failure.

This response to the Regulation Trick would carry risks for both the Left and the Right. Regardless of which side the president is on, agencies would often have to appeal to swing legislators to get their major regulations through Congress. The Left and the Right are both sure that they can produce the kind of regulation that is correct and reflects the people's values. But they both can't be correct. They are, in fact, both incorrect for two reasons. First, they will not always have the kind of president that they want. Second, to repeat the words of Professor Ackerman in chapter 1, "It makes good sense to require the president to gain the support of Congress even when [the president's] vision is morally compelling."[30]

I am not predicting that Congress would always approve the regulatory decisions that I favor. Yet, courts do not always approve regulations, and agencies' fear of losing in court often results in them delaying needed regulations for years. Congressional approval of an agency's regulation would markedly improve its chances of passing judicial review and therefore allow the agency to promulgate it more quickly.

Besides, small-*d* democrats worthy of the name cannot limit democracy to instances in which it produces decisions that accord with their individual preferences. We must resist what Professor Jeremy Waldron called the "dangerous temptation to treat an opposing view as something which is 'beneath notice,'...by assuming that it is necessarily ignorant or prejudiced or self-interested or based on insufficient contemplation of moral reality."[31]

What about Climate Change?

"How," people concerned about climate change, as I am, might ask, "can you have scruples about democracy when greenhouse gases alter the climate of the planet?" Here's how.

During the administration of President Obama, the EPA had eight years to promulgate regulations limiting greenhouse gas emissions, yet its regulations were inadequate. They directly addressed mainly auto makers and power plant operators. Deeper cuts could be achieved through reducing the combustion of fossil fuels and other greenhouse-gas-producing activities by businesses of all sizes and sorts, farmers, governments, universities, and ordinary citizens. For example, we citizens might be made to change how we insulate, heat, and cool our houses; where we live relative to where we work; and how we commute to work. The EPA knows deeper cuts in emissions require society-wide changes in behavior, and so it issues regulations that coerce power plant operators to encourage customers to use less electricity. This roundabout way of cutting electricity consumption is messy and will do nothing to promote less use of fossil fuels for purposes other than generating electricity or to change other activities that produce greenhouse gases. The EPA takes this backhanded, halfhearted approach because the Clean Air Act does not provide an efficient way to achieve society-wide changes and in order to fool voters into thinking that the burdens that it imposes fall on giant corporations rather than ordinary people.

To get deeper cuts, we need a far-more-honest, comprehensive, and efficient approach than the current Clean Air Act allows. We need new legislation of the sort that Richard Stewart, Katrina Wyman, and I proposed in *Breaking the Logjam*. The legislation would establish market-based incentives that influence the conduct of everyone. Were this done by taxing greenhouse gas emissions and using the proceeds to reduce other taxes, we could cut greenhouse gas emissions without significant loss in our standard of living. That is the finding from the deeply respected nonpartisan think tank Resources for the Future. It is a plausible conclusion when one considers that a tax on income discourages the work and investment that brings prosperity, while a tax on emissions discourages the emission of greenhouse gases. We should tax what we don't want and reduce the tax on what we do want. Many conservatives, as well as liberals, are open to such an approach. We can implement it without making taxes less progressive.[32] The EPA, however, lacks the power under the current Clean Air Act to opt for this win-win solution, and the tricks make Congress much less likely to make the necessary legislative changes.

With the Honest Deal Act in place, I don't know what choices Congress would ultimately make, but the representatives would have to account to constituents no longer misled by the tricks. That is how government in a democracy should work. Meanwhile, without the Honest Deal Act, the EPA under the new presidential administration could, without the approval of Congress, weaken the existing regulations limiting greenhouse gas emissions.

Nonetheless, some on the left may oppose requiring Congress to take responsibility for major regulations because they fear that legislators on the right would reflexively block popular regulations. I disagree because they would pay a price for that at the polls. Yet, if such fear on its own would block the Honest Deal Act, a fallback position is available—make Congress vote on only those major regulations promulgated under newly enacted or amended statutory authority. That way, the sponsors of new legislation would have the option of including agency-drafted rules in the bill rather than having the agency promulgate the rules in regulations after the statute is enacted. Either way, Congress would have to take responsibility for the major regulations promulgated under the new statutory authority.

I strongly prefer, however, that Congress commit itself to voting on major regulations promulgated under both its new and old statutory authority. Because legislators escape responsibility for the consequences of old regulatory statutes, we continue to live under obsolete statutes such as the Clean Air Act that fail to deliver the protection we need and impose wasteful burdens on us. Or, as Philip Howard argued, we continue to live under regulations made by dead people.[33] The fallback position would, however, be better than nothing, in that Congress would recognize the principle that its members should take responsibility for the major regulations, although not fully vindicating that principle. Should experience with the fallback ease fears, Congress could extend the requirement to major regulations promulgated under old statutes.

Better Rather Than Best

The Honest Deal Act's proposal to stop the Regulation Trick employs the method that James Landis proposed in 1938 and a variant of which was used by Congress from then until 1983. Gaining experience with the Honest Deal Act could then help induce Congress to adopt ways to accept responsibility for major regulations that antedate the act.[34]

The War Trick

The Constitution states that the "President shall be Commander in Chief" of the military. That means Congress cannot interfere with *how* the president conducts combat. But *whether* the president can commit the United States to combat without congressional approval is quite another question. President Dwight Eisenhower's answer was that the Constitution requires the president to get approval from Congress. Professor John Hart Ely argued that the Constitution requires congressional approval whether the war is "big or small, 'declared' in so many words or not." Others answer that presidents can wage undeclared wars without congressional authorization.[35]

Yet even those who claim that presidents can start undeclared wars without congressional approval concede that Congress can stop a war by cutting off funding. After all, the Constitution allows the government to spend only the money that Congress has appropriated.[36]

Congress can use its power over the federal budget to require congressional approval for war. In his book *War and Responsibility*, John Hart Ely proposed a statute that would do so.[37] Relying heavily on Ely's proposal, the Honest Deal Act would work as follows:

1. In the absence of a declaration of war, a president shall submit a report before or, in the case of an emergency, simultaneously with the introduction of the military into an area of ongoing or impending hostilities. The report must detail the reasons for the mission and its estimated scope.

2. In the event that the president does not submit a report, any member of the armed forces ordered into the area may bring a lawsuit. The court shall declare if the president should have submitted a report but issue no order to the president. The court's decision can be directly appealed to the Supreme Court. This is the kind of case, Ely contended, that courts should and would decide.[38]

3. Within twenty days of when a president submits a report or a final court decision declares that the president should have submitted such a report, whichever is earlier, no funds otherwise appropriated may be used for the military action except for the purpose of withdrawing the military unless Congress has declared or otherwise explicitly authorized the war.[39]

If the Honest Deal Act had been in place, President Obama would have, for example, been required to submit a report triggering a vote in Congress on the bombing of Libya in 2011, and members of Congress would have had to take responsibility rather than just kibitz.

Even if Ely was wrong that courts would decide cases against the president for failing to file the report, as described in the second point, his statute could still work. The president could file a report without being sued, which would cut off funding in twenty days unless Congress authorized the war. The president would file such a report if enough voters wanted candidates for president to commit to doing so. In other words, voters would need to demand that officials act in a way that makes the government accountable. Enacting the new statute would help by eliminating provisions in the War Powers Act that are arguably unconstitutional and so give presidents political cover for not filing reports that trigger votes in Congress. A new statute would also embody a political commitment to accountability and, in particular, a demand that presidential candidates take the Honest Deal Pledge to obey the Honest Deal Act on war and everything else.[40]

There are those who believe that presidents need the power to enter wars without the approval of Congress. For example, John Yoo, an assistant attorney general under President George W. Bush, argued that the current War Powers Act, if obeyed, would constrict the president's flexibility too much. Professor Yoo warned that requiring congressional authorization "can have a steep cost—congressional delay can keep the United States out of wars that are in the national interest."[41] Delay is a real concern, but Ely's statute does not require delay. Under the statute, the president can in an emergency launch a military campaign without prior approval so long as Congress is notified simultaneously. Congress then has twenty days to decide whether to authorize the campaign. Meanwhile, it can continue.

Professor Yoo also warned that requiring congressional approval would keep us out of needed wars: "If Congress had held the upper constitutional hand in war and had refused to send troops to Korea and Vietnam, the Cold War may have ended very differently." Although he acknowledged that we don't really know what the outcome would have been, he went too far in suggesting that requiring congressional approval would give Congress "the upper...hand." The president can use the office's unique ability to speak to the public and frame the issue. In addition, the president as commander in chief and diplomat in chief can shape events to make congressional approval more likely. Meanwhile, even now, presidents must reckon with how Congress will react. As strategic studies expert Eliot Cohen explained, "The powers of investigation, legislation, and authorization to spend money give Congress the ability to oversee and influence a war for good or ill."[42] My conclusion: Ely's proposal would not shift the upper hand from the president to Congress but rather work a marginal adjustment in the balance of power between them.

The major change would be in accountability rather than power. A marginal shift in the balance of power and a major shift in accountability is the right mix. There is no exact allocation of power that could ensure that the nation always makes wise decisions about whether to go to war. Indeed, it is hard to say in the abstract what is the best allocation. Professor Yoo and Jide Nzelibe argued that congressional approval of military campaigns does not always mean that Congress deliberates carefully. That is so, but recent experience suggests that confining authority to the president and those under the president's thumb often leads to narrow-minded groupthink in decisions about war.[43] In the absence of a clearly optimal allocation of power, we should opt for making both the president and Congress accountable.

Professor Yoo's argument that the president should have the power to wage war without congressional approval parallels the argument of some on the left that the president and the president's appointees should have the power to impose major regulations without congressional approval. They, like Yoo, argue for cutting Congress out of the process since the president is more apt to make the right decision. I respond to Yoo, as I do to those on the left, by invoking Professor Ackerman's admonition that "it makes good sense to require the president to gain the support of Congress even when [the president's] vision is morally compelling."[44] This principle should be applied with special force to decisions to go to war because we risk so much in war. Moreover, with presidents often justifying wars as fought to protect democracy abroad, democratically accountable legislators at home should feel a heightened duty to shoulder responsibility.

Better Rather Than Best

The Honest Deal Act's proposal to stop the War Trick employs the rule generally used from the beginnings of the republic until 1950—no combat without a declaration of war or specific authorization by statute.

Leslie H. Gelb and Professor Anne-Marie Slaughter argued that authorization of combat by statute is not good enough; the president should have to get Congress to declare war:

> A more public vetting of the decision to go to war, culminating in a solemn declaration of war by Congress, would most likely ensure stronger public support for the war, by involving the people in the decision and assuring voters that the war had not been launched hastily or under false pretenses. Setbacks and sacrifices might be less surprising and more easily accepted. Because the declaration process would address problems beforehand, it would help us win wars once they started.[45]

The Afghanistan War and the Second Iraq War provide support for Gelb and Slaughter's claim. In both cases, Congress authorized war by statute. The statutes' titles, such as "Authorization for Use of Military Force," were euphemisms for wars that proved far more bloody, prolonged, and expensive than most people had expected. The authors may well be correct in saying that calling war by its name might have prodded elected officials into a more candid public discussion beforehand. The Honest Deal Act would use no such euphemism. Congress and the president would have to authorize "war."

I disagree, however, with Gelb and Slaughter's conclusion that war should always be authorized by declaration rather than by statute. As author and decorated marine veteran Karl Marlentes wrote, "We will find ourselves increasingly embroiled in wars where the primary goal is to restore, or even establish for the first time, civil order and a workable system of justice, not to defeat a clearly defined enemy who is trying to harm us."[46] What is required is candor rather than a declaration of war. If the president fails to disclose the risks, if legislators fail to get the president to disclose the risks, or if legislators fail to disclose their own concerns about the risks, we will blame them for their failures, as President George W. Bush and some legislators discovered to their misery.

To sum up, we can't look to the Constitution to stop the tricks. Most of the tricks do not violate the Constitution, and the Supreme Court has shown little inclination to use it to stop the rest, as I found by trying.[47] The tricks do, however, cleverly frustrate a core purpose of the Constitution: to make members of Congress accountable at the polls for the key decisions of government. This purpose is fundamental to making sure that they serve us and that we are honest with ourselves.

We don't need to amend the Constitution to stop the tricks. The nation avoided the tricks through its first century and a half because we had practices in place that blocked them, not because politicians back then were too upright or too stupid to be tricky. Those practices came in the form of an unwritten constitution that supplemented the written one, much as the United Kingdom today is said to have an "unwritten" constitution. Actually, much of the British constitution is written, but it is done in statutes and other documents rather than in a document called a "constitution." The United States can improve its lowercase-c constitution by enacting the Honest Deal Act.[48]

The Honest Deal Act is not the complete solution to the problems that come from a Congress that uses tricks to promise something for nothing and an electorate that demands it, but it is an essential first step. Yet, no second step is possible until our representatives face up to the chasm between the benefits they promise and the burdens they acknowledge and We the People, in turn, face up to the chasm between the benefits we want and the burdens we are willing to bear.

CHAPTER 9

✮ ✮ ✮

An Action Plan for Us

It's coming to America first,
the cradle of the best and of the worst.
It's here they got the range
and the machinery for change
and it's here they got the spiritual thirst.
It's here the family's broken
and it's here the lonely say
that the heart has got to open
in a fundamental way:
Democracy is coming to the U.S.A.

—Canadian poet-singer-songwriter
Leonard Cohen ("Democracy," 1992)[1]

It *is* "here the family's broken," as Leonard Cohen sang. The Money Trick lets the older generations rob their children and grandchildren. The tricks collectively set off a mad rush to grab from one another, with our "honorable" elected officials advertising their ability to grab on our behalf.

We can get Congress to stop the tricks, but not by urging people to vote against incumbents for tricking us in the *past*. That won't work because we tend to like our own representatives even as we loathe Congress.[2] It also wouldn't be fair because when today's incumbents entered office as freshman legislators, they had to go along with the tricks or be irrelevant. Besides, we have gone along with the trickery.

We should instead vote out those incumbents who refuse to stop the tricks in the *future*. In particular, we should vote out those who refuse to pledge to change the ground rules of Congress to stop the tricks. Without new ground rules, legislators can't stop the tricks, because those who unilaterally forego trickery will find themselves at a disadvantage to those who don't.

And we can get them to pass the Honest Deal Act. For starters, the Five Tricks harm far more voters than they benefit. Consider, for example, who gains and who loses from the debt guarantees that go to the financial giants. Their top executives gain because their compensation goes up with profits, and the Debt Guarantee Trick increases those profits. In contrast, the great bulk of people who work for these firms gain little or no extra compensation because of the debt guarantees. Their pay is based largely on the pay of people doing like work in all kinds of businesses rather than the profitability of the firm at which they work.

Another reason these top executives gain is that, as recipients of big stock options in their own firms, they tend to have disproportionately large investments in these stocks, whose value the Debt Guarantee Trick inflates. In contrast, stockholders other than the top executives tend to have only a small portion of their investments in the shares of the financial giants and so gain little from the subsidies that the Debt Guarantee Trick provides.

Except for the top executives, those who work for or own shares in the financial giants lose far more than they gain from these debt guarantees. They lose because the guarantees imperil the financial system and, in turn, the stock market and economy upon which their livelihoods depend. For the same reason, the guarantees also harm everyone else. Overall, the guarantees for the financial giants harm almost everyone besides the top executives of these firms, who constitute only a tiny portion of the American population.

Yet, perversely, the small number of people benefiting from the guarantees has helped them continue to profit at the public's expense. Precisely because so few people share in this benefit, each one of them gets a big slice and so has a big personal incentive to fight to keep it. They have the means to fight effectively to keep this benefit because they direct the trade associations, lobbyists, and campaign contributions that wield the influence of financial giants in Washington. The rest of us—those on the losing end of the debt guarantee—have so far lacked the organizational means to fight back.

Thus can a tiny organized minority exploit the general public. Each member of the minority has a sufficient stake in the benefit to know the score and cooperate with others in the group to fight to keep it going. And the tiny minority need not come from big business; the agricultural interests that benefit from the federal mandate to put ethanol in gasoline are an example of ones who don't. Political scientists call such small organized groups "concentrated interests" or "special interests."[3] The tricks help special interests get their way at the public's expense, as chapter 5 explained.

Worse still, special interests can often increase their power over time. As Professor Mancur Olson argued in *The Rise and Decline of Nations*, special interests use their superior organization not only to get benefits at the public's expense but also to have changes made to the law that enhance their ability to organize and thus allow them to acquire even-more power in the future. The tendency for special interests to grow their power over time explains why, as Olson showed, nations often decline as their government ages.[4]

Despite this warning of decline, Olson ends his book with a ray of hope: the public can turn the tide of politics against special interests by coming to understand how they get away with hurting the public. As he wrote:

> Ideas certainly do make a difference. May we not then reasonably expect, if special interests are (as I have claimed) harmful to economic growth, full employment, coherent government, equal opportunity, and social mobility, that students of the matter will become increasingly aware of this as time goes on? And that the awareness eventually will spread to larger and larger proportions of the population? And that this wider awareness will greatly limit the losses from the special interests? That is what I expect, at least when I am searching for a happy ending.[5]

Ideas are indeed what allowed the broad public interest to prevail over special interests in the 1970s. The idea that government should protect the public from pollution brought regulation despite large costs being imposed on the well-organized interests in the auto, coal, and other industries.[6] And the idea that the government regulation of airlines, railroads, telephone, and other companies was actually enabling these firms to charge inflated prices brought deregulation that has saved consumers huge sums.

Yet, back in the 1970s, most people had no idea that the Five Tricks had begun. Yes, activists, such as me, called for "power to the people," but by that we meant transferring power and money away from "the establishment" and to the underprivileged. We failed to see that Congress had begun to use the Five Tricks to take power away from We the People.

The time is ripe for the public to see the harm that Five Tricks do to us. We already believe, by more than a two-to-one margin, that the federal government does not have the consent of the governed.[7] Although the public generally does not yet understand the sleights of hand that enable these tricks to work, we have glimpsed the harm that comes from them. To mollify our anger, Congress has passed a succession of statutes:

- Anger about unauthorized or sloppily authorized military campaigns led to the War Powers Act in 1973.
- Anger about deficits led to the budget-balancing statutes of the 1980s and 1990s.
- Anger about mandates to states and localities led to the Unfunded Mandates Reform Act of 1995.
- Anger about regulation led to the Congressional Review Act of 1996.
- Anger about the bailouts of financial giants led to Dodd–Frank.[8]

These statutes have not, however, stopped the tricks. The problem has been that the citizens voicing complaints to Congress haven't insisted on a specific design for new ground rules that would be sufficient to stop the tricks. With the design left to Congress, it has produced reforms that are more apparent than real, at least in the long run.[9]

The mission of this book is to provide an understanding of the sleights of hand that have allowed members of Congress and the presidents to get away with the tricks so that we can insist on making specified changes to the ground rules of legislative politics and finally succeed in stopping them.

We can prevail because we have the *incentive* and the *means* to do so. Our incentive comes from the harm that the tricks do to us. The job of elected officials is to serve us, but under our trick-infested political system, they must do their jobs badly if they want to keep them. Meanwhile, they continue to wield vast power. Officials spend more than a fifth of what the nation earns each year, and through debt guarantees, mandates on states and localities, regulation, and war, they have a huge influence on the rest, too. That people with so much power over our lives do such a poor job is infuriating, and doubly so because we go along with it. Indeed, by continuing to demand something for nothing, we are complicit. As the centuries-old proverb goes, "Fool me once, shame on you, fool me twice, shame on me."

We have the means to succeed. This claim may sound overly hopeful because members of Congress and the presidents are powerful and pay careful attention to what's best for themselves. Yet, we can make their passing the Honest Deal Act what's best for them.

The first step is to tell them that we are on to their sleights of hand, see our own complicity, and ask them to sign a pledge to pass the Honest Deal Act and faithfully implement it. The text of the Honest Deal Pledge is in appendix B. Appendix C provides you with the means to quickly and easily send a message to those elected officials who are dependent upon your support at the polls. It also provides the means to ask your friends to send such messages.

Each one of us who sends this message to politicians will make a substantial difference, because in the end it won't take the concern of that many people to tilt the political balance against the tricks. This is because many sorts of politicians—members of Congress, the president, governors, mayors, other state and local officials, and the candidates for these offices—have reasons to want to stop the tricks.

Members of Congress. Many members of Congress will welcome the Honest Deal Act or at least significant parts of it because the reason they originally got into politics was to do honorable service. To stay in office, they found that they had to twist the truth in order to seem like they had straddled the chasm between the wishes of voters and what is possible. Many of them hate the propensity of Congress to shirk responsibility to the detriment of the nation. Many, as reported in chapter 6, plea to "save us from ourselves." We can say of such members what Dorothy said of the Wizard of Oz, "He was a good man even if he was a bad Wizard."[10]

Nonetheless, it is easy to heap scorn on these members of Congress. I have done so myself. Yet, in writing this book, I have come to believe that we are not entitled to blame them for the trickery until we recognize our own part and propose a way to stop it. Until now, legislators have not been able to save themselves because, as the game of politics is currently played, those who use the Five Tricks are more likely to be reelected and have positions of power in Congress. Those who won't usually get replaced by those who will. For them to tell us of the trickery would be to cast themselves as the bearers of bad tidings. So, trickery has been a rational adaptation to life in Congress as it now works. The Honest Deal Act offers a path to salvation for legislators who want to be able to respect the person they see in the mirror in the morning.

Other legislators may choose to keep up the trickery and the ridiculous posturing it entails because they believe that trickery will ease their reelection. Their hunger to get reelected would, however, similarly force them to support the Honest Deal Act if many voters wanted them to. By pledging support for the Honest Deal Act, they, as well as the challengers who want to take their place, can help themselves win the next election. They won't have to start taking responsibility until later, when the necessity to do so will apply to both parties.

The presidents. The presidents will welcome the Honest Deal Act, except perhaps for the cure for the War Trick, which would deprive them of the power to wage war without securing approval from Congress. While some legislators find the tricks helpful in securing their seats for many terms, presidents are limited to two terms and are often frustrated by the unwillingness of Congress to come to grips with pressing issues before those two terms end.

In addition, by pledging to press for passage of the entire Honest Deal Act, candidates for president can show voters that they support the accountability that is a prerequisite for democracy. We've had successful candidates for president who promised a New Deal and a Fair Deal. Now, let's have one promise an Honest Deal.

Governors, mayors, and other state and local officials. These politicians especially will want to stop the Federal Mandate Trick, which Congress and the presidents use to shift blame to them.

State and local governments, of course, indulge in many of the tricks themselves. For example, many states and local governments use the Money Trick to scandalously underfund public-employee pension plans.

By stopping this trick at the state and local levels, these governments can highlight its use at the federal level. Gina Raimondo, as the Democratic state comptroller of Rhode Island, prompted reform in her state by providing some of the kind of fiscal information that the Honest Deal Act would require at the federal level. The voters subsequently elected her governor in 2014. Some states already have statutes that require the state legislature to vote on important state-agency regulations.[11] Analogs of the Honest Deal Act could thus play a useful role in reforming many states and local governments. State and local officials could use the fact that they support such analogs in running against members of Congress who refuse to pledge to support Honest Deal Act.

As Leonard Cohen sang in his prayer for democracy quoted at the top of this chapter, Americans have the "machinery for change and . . . spiritual thirst" to bring "democracy . . . to the U.S.A." Time and again, voters have insisted that elected officials must act to better realize the ideal expressed in the Declaration of Independence that governments derive their "just powers from the consent of the governed." Although only white, male land owners could vote when the Constitution took effect in 1789, voters were able to get elected officials to, in stages, expand the franchise to eliminate barriers of race, gender, and wealth. That's how we got constitutional amendments granting a right to vote to all races and then to women. That's also how we got the statutes enforcing such rights.[12]

Voters also got elected officials to remove another wart on democracy by eliminating the "spoils system" of government employment, which had long given presidents complete control over who worked in the executive branch. Based on the idea that "to the victor belong the spoils," the spoils system allowed a newly elected president to fire any employee down to the lowest paid clerk or laborer and hire replacements who pledged to pay a portion of their salary to his political party. The spoils system made incumbents less dependent on the consent of the governed. In 1883, after voters came to understand that the spoils system betrayed the public, Congress passed the Pendleton Act, which began the transition to civil service.[13]

History thus suggests that a bottom-up campaign to stop the tricks can work. As Howard Dean put it, "You have the power."[14]

And we have a moral duty to use that power. We call ourselves citizens of a democracy rather than subjects of an oligarchy. We say yes in our hearts when we read the words of the Gettysburg Address, "We here highly resolve ... that government of the people, by the people, for the people, shall not perish from the earth."[15] Yet, the principle behind these words now perishes in the smoke and mirrors of the tricks.

To resolve to do something is not just to prefer it but to feel dutybound to try our best to make it so. Why Lincoln felt so bound, and why he thought we should too, is wonderfully explained in a speech by Professor Leon Kass:

> We are the privileged heirs of a way of life that has offered the blessings of freedom and dignity to millions of people of all races, ethnicities, and religions, and that extols the possibility of individual achievement as far as individual talent and effort can take it. We are also a self-critical nation, whose history is replete with efforts to bring our practices more fully in line with our ideals. And our national history boasts hundreds of thousands of heroic men and women who gave their lives that that nation might live and flourish. To belong to such a nation is not only a special blessing but a special calling: to preserve freedom, dignity, and self-government at home and to encourage their spread abroad. As Abraham Lincoln put it, in a call to perpetuate our political institutions: "*This task of gratitude to our fathers, justice to ourselves, duty to posterity, and love for our species in general, all imperatively require us faithfully to perform.*"[16]

The self-educated Lincoln so stated in a speech that he delivered at the age of twenty-eight shortly after he moved from a rural village to Springfield, Illinois.[17] We, standing on that young man's high shoulders, should see our duty no less clearly. It is a duty to act rather than simply to prefer.

Not only duty but enlightened self-interest should prompt almost all of us to act, including even the top executives of the financial giants. Yes, they would lose their cheap debt guarantees, and we see might even see them muster with a straight face the argument that making their firms pay full freight for those guarantees is contrary to the public interest. Yet, even though these top executives would lose from a bill aimed specially at the financial giants, the Honest Deal Act's proposal to stop all five tricks and thus discourage a wide range of rip-offs and stupidities that afflict the executives as well as their fellow citizens might ultimately result in their gaining on balance. Besides, they too want to be able to respect the person they see in the mirror in the morning. That might even be true of some of the Washington lobbyists and lawyers—the so-called K Street crowd—who gain their income and power from their facility with the tricks.

Most of us, however, have only a small part of our savings invested in shares of one of the financial giants, if any of it at all. The Honest Deal Act would likely reduce the value of these shares initially, but bring gains in many larger ways. Like the shareholders, most of us can imagine some way that the Honest Deal Act might result in our sustaining some loss. For example, it could well lead Congress to phase out the tax break for employer-provided health insurance. That tax break, taken in isolation, cuts the taxes paid by millions of people, myself included. Yet, the tax break cannot be taken in isolation. As chapter 5 showed, the public would gain from ending the tax break, in both saving money and getting better health care. We would also gain from the stopping of the wide range of stupidities and rip-offs that the Five Tricks perpetuate.

So, despite whatever losses we might fear from the Honest Deal Act, we should not lose sight of the many larger ways that we would gain. That, however, is easier said than done.[18] Moreover, we cannot know with any reasonable degree of certainty what changes in policy the Honest Deal Act would bring.

In response to such uncertainty, I can offer this reassurance: My proposals do not tilt for or against spending or taxing, benefits or burdens, war or peace, or any of the rest; rather, they tilt toward making elected officials accountable to us for the consequences they impose. So, ask yourself this question: Do I want my government to be run by officials who are accountable to us on the basis of (a) sound bites or (b) the consequences of their actions? Accountability based upon sound bites is what we have now. Accountability based upon consequences is the direction in which the Honest Deal Act would move us. We should support it out of enlightened self-interest as well as duty.

The Honest Deal Act. Support It Now!

To have a government of the people, by the people, and for the people, we must insist on an honest deal. I wrote this book because I feel a duty to insist. I hope that you do, too. Appendix C provides you with tools to fulfill that duty. The book's Web site, DC-Confidential.org, puts the same tools on the Internet. It also provides a computer "game" that makes it fun to learn about the tricks and how to stop them. Tell your friends about it.

To fulfill your duty and protect yourself and your family, there's no time like the present.

APPENDICES
A Toolkit

Summary of the Honest Deal Act

The Honest Deal Act will contain five titles, each addressed to one of the Five Tricks.

**This summary can be downloaded from
www.dc-confidential.org/honestdeal.**

Title I: Responsibility for Spending and Taxing

To make members of Congress and the president responsible for the gap between spending and revenues that current policies will produce in the long term:

1. The Congressional Budget Office (CBO) shall provide voters with readily understandable information on the size of the financial burdens that current practices will impose upon the people in the long run. The CBO shall have complete autonomy in estimating the size of these burdens.
2. At the conclusion of each Congress and also before each general election, the CBO shall send to citizens a readily understandable letter that states the following kinds of information:
   a. If Congress and the president act now to close the gap between spending and taxation by increasing income taxes on individuals and corporations, revenues from such taxes will have to be increased permanently by _____ %. If they instead act to

close the gap by cutting government expenditures (including Social Security, Medicaid, Medicare, military, and all the other programs), total expenditures will have to be cut permanently by _____%.

b. Congresses and presidents now and in the future will have to choose the extent to which they increase taxes or cut spending, and how to do so, but in the end the impacts will be felt largely by individuals. Assuming that the cost is spread equally among the population, the average tax increase or spending cut for a family of four in the current year will be $_____, with similar amounts each subsequent year.

c. During the most recent Congress, which began in _____ and ended in _____ [(or in the case of a letter sent before a general election) the current Congress, which began in _____ and will end in _____], legislators have taken actions that increased [or decreased, as the case may be] this amount by $_____ per family.

d. The size of the tax increases or spending cuts required to make ends meet will grow larger the longer Congress and the president delay action. If they delay ten years, the size of the required tax increase or spending cut will grow _____% larger.

e. Current spending and taxing policies will not only leave the federal government with insufficient funds to make ends meet but will take funds from future generations to benefit current voters. For more information on the actual impact that the current actions will have on an average person born in a particular year (such as a person born the same year as you, your children, or your grandchildren), see the Congressional Budget Office's Web site at _____.

3. The CBO shall, to the greatest extent possible, have a copy of this letter delivered to each individual of voting age. The Internal Revenue Service, the Social Security Administration, and other government agencies that provide information on benefits shall also include the letter with their own mass communications to the public.

4. To fill in the blanks in its letter, each year the CBO shall adopt a long-term budget model that projects revenues and spending

under current practices. The CBO will make its budget model available to the public in a form conducive to its use in assessing the fiscal impact of various legislative proposals.

Title II: Responsibility for Debt Guarantees

To make members of Congress and the president responsible for the risks that the debt guarantees inflict upon the public:

1. A Debt Guarantee Honesty Commission shall be established. At the end of year one of its operations, the commission shall adopt a list of all existing debt guarantees, explicit and implicit.
2. The commission shall then divide the debt guarantees into three groups to be the subject of proposals made at the end of years two, three, and four. At these times, the commission shall propose:
   a. whether the guarantee could and should be eliminated;
   b. if the guarantee is to be continued, how to set a market-based fee for it, with the fees assigned individually for systemically important (too-big-to-fail) institutions and, to the extent possible, for other debtors as well; and
   c. whether to phase in the discontinuance of the guarantee or a market-based fee and, if so, how.
3. The House and the Senate shall vote on each year's proposals en masse on a fast-track, no-amendment, no-filibuster basis.
4. From the end of year four onward, the Federal Reserve Board shall annually recommend to Congress whether to explicitly guarantee the debts of any institution whose failure would present a systemic risk or whose debts have otherwise become explicitly or implicitly guaranteed. The question for the board would be whether the debts of the institution are explicitly or implicitly guaranteed rather than whether the institution itself is presently at risk. If the board so determines, it shall also recommend how to set a fee for the debt guarantee. The House and the Senate would be required to vote on all such recommendations for the year en masse on a fast-track, no-amendment, no-filibuster basis.

Title III: Responsibility for Federal Mandates

To make members of Congress and the president responsible for the burdens that mandates inflict upon the public:

1. The standing rules of the House and Senate shall be amended to allow each legislator one challenge in each Congress concerning a provision in a floor bill that would harm states or localities failing to do the federal bidding. The challenge would take the form of a point of order and state how the bill should be amended to avoid the harm.

2. The challenge would be resolved by a roll call vote with no debate. Each successful challenge would result in the bill being amended and yield the legislator issuing it another challenge without limit.

Title IV: Responsibility for Regulation

To make members of Congress and the president responsible for major regulations:

1. A major regulation (defined as including regulations that either increase or decrease the regulatory protection available to the public) shall not take effect until approved through the Constitution's legislative process.

2. The House and Senate shall each hold roll call votes on whether to approve major regulations on a fast-track, no-amendment, no-filibuster basis. To further ensure that Congress does not kill major regulations by failing to hold roll call votes by the Honest Deal Act's deadline, such failure should automatically cut off appropriations (including those for salaries, travel expenses, staff, and office expenses) for members of either house that do not meet the deadline until such time as that house cures the failure.

3. A petition signed by a majority in either house would add an extra thirty days to the deadline for a final roll call vote in order to allow time for a hearing on the promulgated rule. (This would not usually be necessary, however, because the Honest Deal Act would come with the expectation that both houses hold hearings when an agency *proposes* a major rule so that the legislators are ready to vote promptly after the agency promulgates the final rule. At

these hearings, the time should be devoted to committee counsel carefully questioning witnesses.)

4. Despite the first point, a major regulation may take effect pending a decision by Congress if the president finds need, but shall cease to take effect if the vote to approve the regulation fails in either the House or the Senate.

5. Courts shall not read approvals of regulations as changing the agency's underlying statutory authority. Approved regulations shall be subject to judicial review.

Title V: Responsibility for War

To make members of Congress responsible for decisions to go to war:

1. In the absence of a declaration of war, a president shall submit a report to Congress within forty-eight hours of deploying the military in an area of ongoing or impending hostilities. The report shall detail the reasons for the mission and its estimated scope.

2. Any member of the armed forces ordered into such an area may bring a lawsuit to enforce this reporting requirement. If the president should have reported but did not, a lower court shall issue a declaratory judgment to that effect. The court's decision would be directly appealable to the Supreme Court.

3. Within twenty days from the time the president submits a report or the courts issue a final order declaring the president should have submitted one, whichever is earlier, no funds otherwise appropriated may be used for the mission (except for the purpose of withdrawing the military) unless Congress had declared war or otherwise explicitly authorized the war.

The Honest Deal Pledge

This pledge can be downloaded from
www.dc-confidential.org/honestdeal.

I pledge that I, [Your Name], will:

1. work to secure passage of the Honest Deal Act (a summary of which is available at www.dcconfidential.org/honestdeal) and

2. faithfully implement the Honest Deal Act; and, in particular,

    a. vote against any maneuver to prevent challenges to federal mandates on state or local governments; oppose any unanimous consent to prevent such challenges; appeal any rulings of the chair to prevent such challenges; and vote to reverse such rulings of the chair; and

    b. work to ensure that the president shall faithfully submit to Congress the report required by the Honest Deal Act within forty-eight hours of introducing the military into an area of ongoing or impending hostilities.

Signature: _____

Name: _____

Address:_____

E-mail:_____

Telephone: _____

Office I hold or for which I am a candidate: _____

Date: _____

Please e-mail signed pledges to pledges@dc-confidential.org.

How You Can Help Trigger Reform

This appendix can be downloaded from
www.dc-confidential.org/action.

Urge Your Representatives in Congress to Pass the Honest Deal Act

You can spur reform by informing the federal officials who want your vote that they should promise to work to pass the Honest Deal Act by taking the Honest Deal Pledge, available at www.dc-confidential.org/action. You can do so in the following ways:

1. In just a few minutes, you can send an e-mail to your representative in the House and your senators. To do so, click the link for this purpose at www.dc-confidential.org/action. The default e-mail message reads as follows, but I urge you, if you can spare the time, to amend it, even if just a little. It should say what you believe and show the recipients that the point of view is your own.

   Dear Politician:

   A half-century ago, elected officials of both parties in Congress and the White House adopted a new system for enacting laws and spending programs—one that lets them take the credit for promising good news while avoiding the blame for the government producing bad results. Because the people we elect avoid accounting to us for what the government actually does to us, we have a federal government that ill serves us.

All this is documented in *DC Confidential: Inside the Five Tricks of Washington*, by David Schoenbrod. The book also shows how Congress can stop the trickery by passing the Honest Deal Act. A summary of the act and a chapter explaining its design is available at www.dc-confidential.org/honestdeal. The Web site also contains computer "games" that are a fun way to learn how the tricks hurt us and how the Honest Deal Act would stop them.

I request that you consider publicly committing yourself to working to enact and faithfully implement the Honest Deal Act by taking the Honest Deal Pledge, which is available at the same link. Please let me know when you make the decision to become involved and also e-mail your signed pledge to pledges@ dc-confidential.org.

Sincerely,

[Your Name]

2. Alternatively, send your own letter or e-mail directly to these officials. If you wish to use the Web site's letter as a starting point, you can copy it from the Web site. There is also a link to get contact information for these officials.
3. Phone these officials' offices in Washington or locally and say that you want them to consider publicly taking the Honest Deal Pledge.
4. Visit any events these officials may be attending in your area, where you can introduce yourself, hand them a copy of the Honest Deal Pledge, and ask them to consider signing it.
5. Finally, sign up to receive updates at the link provided for this purpose at www.dc-confidential.org/action.

Urge Your Friends to Get Involved

After contacting the officials, multiply your efforts by urging your friends to join you in pushing for an honest deal. You can do so easily:

1. Copy the following message from www.dc-confidential.org/action, edit it if you wish, add something personal at the beginning so your friends know it's really from you, and e-mail it to them:

I recently took some steps to help repair the breakdown in our federal government and ask you to join me.

A root cause of the breakdown is this: A half-century ago, elected officials of both parties in Congress and the White House adopted a new system for enacting laws and spending programs, one that lets them take credit for promising good news, while avoiding blame for the government producing bad results. Basically, the people we elect avoid accounting to us for what the government actually does to us. No wonder it's broken!

All of this is documented in a new book, *DC Confidential: Inside the Five Tricks of Washington*, by David Schoenbrod. The book also shows how Congress can stop the trickery by passing the Honest Deal Act. A summary of the act and chapter explaining its design is available at www.dc-confidential.org/honestdeal.

The next step is for some of us to write our representatives in Congress to ask them to pass the Honest Deal Act. I, of course, have done so myself. To find out how you can, too, just go to www.dc-confidential.org/action.

I would be interested to hear how it goes!

Urge Action in Your State and Local Governments

Asking your elected officials to consider supporting the Honest Deal Act and enlisting your friends to do the same are the essentials in the short run. As elections come around, it would be good to also ask candidates running for office to take the Honest Deal Pledge.

For those who want to devote more time to the cause, you can work for passage of analogs of the Honest Deal Act at the state and local levels. Success at these levels, as chapter 9 shows, could help precipitate action at the federal level. People who would like to develop such analogs will find a tool kit at www.dc-confidential.org/action.

Those who would like to work to stop the tricks at any level of government might also find support from the many private nonprofit organizations that advocate for an open, accountable government. Some organizations are listed in appendix D.

Organizations That Call for Accountable and Open Government

The following are among the many organizations that call for open and accountable government in the United States:

- **Center for Effective Government** (http://www.foreffectivegov.org/what-we-do): The center's mission statement is "We particularly focus on effective implementation of critical public protections, improvements in public spending transparency, and reforms that enhance government performance and public oversight of government practices."

- **Common Cause** (http://www.commoncause.org): As the organization describes its work: "Common Cause [battles] for open, honest and accountable government in Washington D.C. and in all 50 states."

- **Federalist Society: Article I Project** (http://www.fed-soc.org/blog/detail/nlc-the-article-i-project): As the society describes the project, "The Article I Project examines the proper role of Congress under Article I of the Constitution."

- **League of Women Voters** (http://lwv.org/content/privatization-position): As the league states, "The LWV believes that transparency, accountability, and preservation of the common good must be ensured."

- **OpenGov Foundation** (http://www.OpenGovFoundation.org): The foundation describes itself as being "dedicated to developing and deploying technologies that support every citizen's ability to participate in their government, and hold it accountable."

- **OpentheGovernment.org** (http://www.openthegovernment.org/we_ believe): The organization's mission statement is, "We believe that transparency is essential to ensuring integrity and accountability in the operation of our governing institutions."
- **Project on Government Oversight** (http://www.pogo.org/): The project describes itself as "a nonpartisan independent watchdog that champions good government reforms. POGO's investigations into corruption, misconduct, and conflicts of interest achieve a more effective, accountable, open, and ethical federal government."
- **ProPublica** (http://www.propublica.org/about/): As ProPublica sees its objective, "Our work focuses exclusively on truly important stories, stories with 'moral force.' We do this by producing journalism that shines a light on exploitation of the weak by the strong and on the failures of those with power to vindicate the trust placed in them."
- **Sunlight Foundation** (http://sunlightfoundation.com/about/): According to the Web site, "The Sunlight Foundation is a nonpartisan nonprofit that advocates for open government globally and uses technology to make government more accountable to all."
- **William and Flora Hewlett Foundation: Madison Initiative** (http://hewlett. org/programs/special-projects/madison-initiative): Hewlett asks, "What will it take for members of the United States Congress to deliberate, negotiate, and compromise in ways that more Americans support? The Hewlett Foundation's Madison Initiative is joining with leaders in and outside of government, nonprofit advocates, academic researchers, and other funders to answer this question."

The following sections list the many organizations that focus on the lack of accountable, open government in specific policy areas.

Taxing and Spending

- **Century Foundation** (http://www.tcf.org/bookstore/detail/dead-men-ruling): The foundation is the publisher of C. Eugene Steuerle's *Dead Men Ruling: How to Restore Fiscal Freedom and Rescue Our Future* (2014).

- **Committee for a Responsible Federal Budget** (http://crfb.org/): The committee considers itself "a bipartisan, non-profit organization committed to educating the public about issues that have significant fiscal policy impact. The Committee is made up of some of the nation's leading budget experts including many of the past Chairmen and Directors of the Budget Committees, the Congressional Budget Office, the Office of Management and Budget, the Government Accountability Office, and the Federal Reserve Board."
- **Peter G. Peterson Foundation** (http://pgpf.org/): Says the foundation, "Our mission is to increase public awareness of the nature and urgency of key fiscal challenges threatening America's future and to accelerate action on them. To address these challenges successfully, we work to bring Americans together to find and implement sensible, long-term solutions that transcend age, party lines and ideological divides in order to achieve real results."

Debt Guarantees

- **American Enterprise Institute** (http://www.aei.org/publication/limiting-systemic-risk-and-too-big-to-fail/): As the country's continuing economic problem is posed by the institute: "There is a growing concern that too-big-to-fail remains an important problem, and the evidence for this belief most often cited is that many of the large financial institutions that were the beneficiaries of government rescues and interventions have actually become larger in the aftermath of the financial crisis."
- **Center for American Progress** (https://www.americanprogress.org/issues/general/news/2014/07/16/93912/the-too-big-to-fail-problem/): As the center sees the present financial situation, "More than five years after the financial crash, the biggest banks are 37 percent larger than they were before, and the debate over what to do about the size of financial institutions continues."
- **Progressive Policy Institute** (http://www.progressivepolicy.org/issues/taking-it-to-the-banks/): The institute states, "Encouraging banks to right-size themselves would make our economy safer from the systemic risk imposed by [some] banks."

Federal Mandates on States and Localities

- **National League of Cities** (http://www.nlc.org/influence-federal-policy/advocacy/regulatory-advocacy): As the league describes its mission, "Because federal rules and regulations often affect local government operations, budgets and development, NLC works to ensure that federal agencies consider the local government perspective when developing regulatory policy."

War

- **Cato Institute** (http://www.cato.org/publications/policy-analysis/congress-surrenders-war-powers-libya-united-nations-constitution): As the institute describes the political climate, "Congress has at times been highly critical of . . . wars but also highly deferential to the president in cases where the wars were brief and popular."
- **Center for American Progress** (https://www.americanprogress.org/issues/ military/ news/2007/03/07/2757/congressional-war-powers-too-many-options-to-forget/): According to the center, "The institutional responsibilities of the Congress with respect to war powers have been hard-fought over the years, and an ample record developed on the many routes by which Congress can have multiple roles and many options for using its war powers."
- **Miller Center, University of Virginia** (http://millercenter.org/policy/commissions/warpowers): As described by the center, "The War Powers Consultation Act . . . calls on Congress to vote up or down on significant armed forces conflicts within 30 days."

Notes

INTRODUCTION

1. Jude Wanniski, "Taxes and a Two-Santa Theory," *National Observer*, March 6, 1976. One such theory was posited by Jude Wanniski, who argued that Republicans should respond to Democrats' promises of benefit increases by promising tax cuts and that they could do so responsibly because the tax cuts would stimulate faster economic growth and thus increase government revenues. Similarly, Democrats sometimes claimed that some of the spending increases that they advocated were investments that would grow the economy and thus increase government revenues.

2. "Beyond Distrust: How Americans View Their Government: Broad Criticism, but Positive Performance Ratings in Many Areas," Pew Research Center "Politics & Policy," November 23, 2015, http://www.people-press.org/2015/11/23/1-trust-in-government-1958-2015/; Peggy Noonan, "America Is So in Play: Donald Trump's Staying Power in the Polls Reflects a Change in the Electorate Only Now Coming into Focus," *Wall Street Journal*, August 27, 2015, http://www.wsj.com/articles/america-is-so-in-play-1440715262.

3. Peter Schuck, *Why Government Fails So Often: And How It Can Do Better* (Princeton, NJ: Princeton University Press, 2014), 2.

4. "Americans Don't Think Incumbents Deserve Reelection," Rasmussen Reports, October 2, 2014, http://www.rasmussenreports.com/public_content/archive/mood_of_america_archive/congressional_performance/americans_don_t_think_incumbents_deserve_reelection; Timothy Penny, *Common Cents: A Retiring Six-Term Congressman Reveals How Congress Really Works—And What We Must Do to Fix It* (Boston: Little, Brown and Company, 1995), 72; Thomas Friedman, "Advice from Grandma," *New York Times*, November 21, 2009, http://www.nytimes.com/2009/11/22/opinion/22friedman.html?_r=0.

CHAPTER 1

1. Bill Dedman, "I-35 Bridge Was Rated among the Nation's Worst: In 2005 Inspection, Minneapolis Span Was Only One Step above 'Intolerable,'"

NBCNews.com, August 3, 2007, http://www.nbcnews.com/id/20102713/ns/us_news-life/t/i--bridge-was-rated-among-nations-worst/#.VFEQpha797Q.

2   Chong Lee, quoted in Keith Ervin, "South Park Bridge on Its Last Legs," *Seattle Times,* July 6, 2006, http://community.seattletimes.nwsource.com/archive/?date=20060706&slug=bridge06m.

3   Joel Connelly, "A New South Park Bridge: The Neighborhood Made It Happen," *Seattle Pi* blog, June 29, 2014, http://blog.seattlepi.com/seattlepolitics/2014/06/29/a-new-south-park-bridge-the-neighborhood-made-it-happen/.

4   "South Park Bridge Funding Rejected," *West Seattle Herald,* February 17, 2010, http://www.westseattleherald.com/2010/02/17/news/south-park-bridge-funding-rejected.

5   "Overview: Executive Summary," 2013 Report Card for America's Infrastructure: American Society of Civil Engineers, accessed October 24, 2016, http://www.infrastructurereportcard.org/a/#p/overview/executive-summary.

6   For three-cents-a-gallon tax, see Federal-Aid Highway Act of 1956, Pub. L. No. 84-627, 70 Stat. 374, 16 U.S.C. § 503 (2006); for 18.4-cents-a-gallon tax, see Omnibus Budget Reconciliation Act of 1993, 103 Pub. L. No. 66, 107 Stat. 312-685 (1993).

7   See, for example, "Final Vote Results for Roll Call 182," Office of the Clerk: U.S. House of Representatives, May 21, 1996, http://clerk.house.gov/evs/1996/roll182.xml; Ashley Halsey III, "15-Cent Increase in Federal Gas Tax Proposed," *Washington Post,* December 4, 2013, http://www.washingtonpost.com/local/trafficandcommuting/15-cent-increase-in-federal-gas-tax-proposed/2013/12/04/548d6d80-5ce9-11e3-95c2-13623eb2b0e1_story.html.

8   Kevin DeGood, *Understanding the Highway Trust Fund and the Perils of Inaction* (Washington, DC: Center for American Progress, 2014), 3, http://cdn.americanprogress.org/wp-content/uploads/2014/02/HTF_factsheet2.pdf.

9   "Final Vote Result for Roll Call 473," Office of the Clerk: U.S. House of Representatives, July 31, 2014, http://clerk.house.gov/evs/2014/roll473.xml; Frank Wooten, "Still Reeling Down the Road to Ruin," *Post and Courier,* November 24, 2014, http://www.postandcourier.com/article/20141125/PC16/141129661/1177/still-reeling-down-the-road-to-ruin.

10 See Highway and Transportation Funding Act of 2014, H.R. Rep. No. 113-5021 (2014) (Congressional Budget Office Rep.), http://www.cbo.gov/sites/default/files/45522-hr5021a.pdf; Highway and Transportation Funding Act of 2014, H.R. Rep. No. 113-520, § IV, at 22 (2013–14) (Ways and Means Committee Rep.), https://www.congress.gov/congressional-report/113th-congress/house-report/520/1.

11 Carol Roberts, quoted in Vipal Monga, "Welcome to the World of 'Pension Smoothing': New Bill Extends Provision That Allows Firms to Delay Making Pension Contributions," *Wall Street Journal,* August 11, 2014, http://online.wsj.com/articles/welcome-to-the-world-of-pension-smoothing-1407800119.

12 Josh Barro, "'Pension Smoothing': The Gimmick Both Parties in Congress Love," *New York Times,* July 31, 2014, http://www.nytimes.com/2014/07/31/upshot/pension-smoothing-the-gimmick-both-parties-in-congress-love.html?_r=0; Linda Killian, "A Pension 'Fix' That Isn't," *Wall Street Journal,*

July 18, 2014, http://blogs.wsj.com/washwire/2014/07/18/a-pension-fix-that-isnt/; "Congress Irresponsibly Takes 'Pension Smoothing' from Exception to Habit," *Washington Post*, August 19, 2014, http://www.washingtonpost.com/opinions/congress-takes-pension-smoothing-from-exception-to-habit/2014/08/19/387caa2a-23e5-11e4-86ca-6f03cbd15c1a_story.html.

13 Congress's 1974 law: Employee Retirement Income Security Act of 1974 (ERISA), Pub. L. No. 93-406, 88 Stat. 829 (1974); quoted in Kenneth Quinnell, "The Rich Get Richer, Everyone Else Loses in Possible Hostess Liquidation," AFL-CIO, November 19, 2012, http://www.aflcio.org/Blog/Corporate-Greed/The-Rich-Get-Richer-Everyone-Else-Loses-in-Possible-Hostess-Liquidation.

14 John Ehrhardt and Zorast Wadia, "Milliman 100 Pension Funding Index," Milliman, October 2014, http://us.milliman.com/uploadedFiles/insight/2014/pfi-october-2014.pdf. Pension Benefit Guaranty Corporation, *Helping Secure Retirements: PBGC Annual Report 2013* (Washington, DC: Pension Benefit Guaranty Corporation), 4, accessed September 19, 2016, http://www.pbgc.gov/documents/2013-annual-report.pdf: The PBGC insures both single and multi-employer pension plans. The gimmick applies to single-employer pension plans. Hostess's employees were covered by both single- and multiple-employer pension plans.

15 For fiscal consequences and pension risk, see 160 Cong. Rec. 120, S5024, S5032 (July 29, 2014) (remarks of sens. Robert Corker and Barbara Boxer); on the failure to respond, see 160 Cong. Rec. 110, H6245-61 (July 15, 2014); 160 Cong. Rec. 120, S5021-39 (July 29, 2014); 160 Cong. Rec. 122, H7169-76 (July 31, 2014); *id.* at S5209; H.R.113-520 (2014). There was no Senate committee report.

16 "PBGC Pension Insurance: We've Got You Covered," Pension Benefit Guaranty Corporation, accessed September 19, 2016, http://www.pbgc.gov/wr/find-an-insured-pension-plan/pbgc-protects-pensions.html.

17 Joshua Gotbaum, quoted in "PBGC Responds to Study on PBGC Premium Increases," Pension Benefit Guaranty Corporation, May 14, 2014, http://www.pbgc.gov/news/press/releases/pr14-06.html; Pension Benefit Guaranty Corporation, *Annual Report: Fiscal Year 2014* (Washington, DC: Pension Benefit Guaranty Corporation), 109, http://www.pbgc.gov/Documents/2014-annual-report.pdf#page=5.

18 Quote from annual report: Pension Benefit Guaranty Corporation, *Annual Report 2014*, 51; for doubts about corporation in annual report, see Alex J. Pollock, "A Federal Guarantee Is Sure to Go Broke," *Wall Street Journal*, November 30, 2014, http://www.wsj.com/articles/alex-j-pollock-a-federal-guarantee-is-sure-to-go-broke-1417387173.

19 Howell E. Jackson, "Counting the Ways: The Structure of Federal Spending" (Discussion Paper 583, Harvard Law School, Cambridge, MA, March 2007), 21, http://www.law.harvard.edu/programs/olin_center/papers/pdf/Jackson_583.pdf.

20 For diverse data suggesting that transportation spending is not targeted to the most critical projects, see Greg Ip, "Quality, Not Just Quantity, of Infrastructure Needs Attention," *Wall Street Journal*, May 20, 2015, http://www.wsj.com/articles/quality-not-just-quantity-of-infrastructure-needs-attention-1432138724.

21 The transportation-spending statute that Congress enacted in 2015 is also full of gimmicks. See Joan Lowy, "Obama Signs 5-Year Infrastructure Spending

Bill," *Monterey Herald* "Transportation," December 4, 2015, http://www.montereyherald.com/article/NF/20151204/NEWS/151209898.

22   For a perspective on the fiscal gap from the right, see Jagadeesh Gokhale, "Fiscal and Generational Imbalances and Generational Accounts: A 2012 Update" (Working Paper 12, Cato Institute, Washington, DC, November 13, 2012), 6–7, http://www.cato.org/publications/working-paper/fiscal-generational-imbalances-generational-accounts-2012-update; for a perspective from the left, see C. Eugene Steuerle, *Dead Men Ruling: How to Restore Fiscal Freedom and Rescue Our Future* (New York: Century Foundation Press, 2014), 80.

23   As the legal philosopher and professor Jeremy Waldron wrote, "The agent-accountability that is involved in democracy puts the onus of generating… transparency and the conveying of the information that accountability requires *on the persons being held accountable.* … The agents owe the principal an account." Jeremy Waldron, "Accountability: Fundamental to Democracy" (Public Law Paper 14-13, New York University School of Law, April 2014), 31, http://papers.ssrn.com/sol3/papers.cfm?abstract_id=2410812 (emphasis in original).

24   Oscar Wilde, *Lady Windermere's Fan* (Seattle: CreateSpace, 2015), 56.

25   "New Low: Only 25% Think Their Member of Congress Deserves Reelection," Rasmussen Reports, June 25, 2014, http://www.rasmussenreports.com/public_content/archive/mood_of_america_archive/congressional_performance/new_low_only_25_think_their_member_of_congress_deserves_reelection.

26   Barack Obama, quoted in Michael D. Shear, "Obama Lesson: 'Shovel Ready' Not So Ready," *The Caucus* blog, *New York Times*, October 15, 2010, http://thecaucus.blogs.nytimes.com/2010/10/15/obama-lesson-shovel-ready-not-so-ready/?_php=true&_type=blogs&_r=0; White House citation: Executive Office of the President, Council of Economic Advisors, *The Economic Impact of the American Recovery and Reinvestment Act: Five Years Later; Final Report to Congress* (February 2014), 8, 34, White House: President Barack Obama, http://www.whitehouse.gov/sites/default/files/docs/cea_arra_report.pdf; Philip K. Howard, *The Rule of Nobody: Saving America from Dead Laws and Broken Government* (New York: Norton, 2014), 156.

27   Bruce Ackerman, *The Decline and Fall of the American Republic* (Cambridge, MA: Belknap, 2010), 63; for a similar perspective from the right, see F. H. Buckley, *The Once and Future King: The Rise of Crown Government in America* (New York: Encounter Books, 2014).

28   Ackerman, *American Republic*, 39.

29   David R. Mayhew, *The Imprint of Congress* (New Haven, CT: Yale University Press, 2017); for studies on consequences of a strong executive and weak legislature, see Buckley, *Once and Future King*, chs. 7–8, app. C.

30   Anthony King, "Running Scared," *Atlantic*, January 1997, http://www.theatlantic.com/magazine/archive/1997/01/running-scared/376754/.

31   On the agreement on policy, see, for example, Ralph Nader, *Unstoppable: The Emerging Left-Right Alliance to Dismantle the Corporate State* (New York: Nation Books, 2014); Morris P. Fiorina and Samuel J. Abrams, *Disconnect: The Breakdown of Representation in American Politics* (Norman: University

of Oklahoma Press, 2009), ch. 1. Whether the electorate itself has become somewhat more polarized is a separate question.

* Figure 2: "Social Justice Alert: RIP South Park Bridge," Grow and Resist, accessed December 8, 2016, http://growandresist.com/social-justice-alert-rip-south-park-bridge/.

CHAPTER 2

1 Alexander Hamilton, James Madison, and John Jay, *The Federalist Papers*, ed. Ian Shapiro (New Haven, CT: Yale University Press, 2009), 42–47.

2 "For so work the honey-bees / Creatures that by a rule in nature teach / The act of order to a peopled kingdom." William Shakespeare, *Henry V* (New York: Penguin Group, 1999), act 1, sc. 2, 15. Thomas D. Seeley, *Honeybee Democracy* (Princeton, NJ: Princeton University Press, 2010), chs. 1–7: Seeley later used Shakespeare's passage in *Honeybee Democracy* as an epigram about how wild honeybees decide where to locate their hives and applied it to how scientists go about deducing how they make decisions.

3 Even though swarms generally choose well, less than one in four of the newly located colonies survive the next winter, and picking a mediocre location makes the odds much worse. In contrast, more than three in four of the established colonies survive the winter.

4 James Madison, "Debates in the Federal Convention of 1787" (transcript, June 6, 1787), TeachingAmericanHistory.org, http://teachingamericanhistory.org/convention/debates/0606-2/.

5 U.S. Const. art. I, § 5, cl. 3, § 8; the Constitution's requirement for Congress: Hamilton et al., *Federalist Papers*, 47–53; A. F. Pollard, *The Evolution of Parliament* (London: Longmans, 1968), 180.

6 See Hamilton et al., *Federalist Papers*, 47–53.

7 Domestic manufacturers quote: "Memorial of Sundry Manufacturers, Mechanics, and Friends to National Industry, of the State of Connecticut," in 42 Annals of Cong. 3124–28 (1824); Webster quote: Daniel Webster, "Letter to Mr. Isaac P. Davis," in *The Private Correspondence of Daniel Webster* (Boston: Little, Brown and Company, 1857), 383; on the compromise legislation, see Mark Thornton and Robert Ekelund, *Tariffs, Blockades, and Inflation: The Economics of the Civil War* (Lanham, MD: Rowman & Littlefield, 2004), 20.

8 Robert H. Wiebe, *Self-Rule: A Cultural History of American Democracy* (Chicago: University of Chicago Press, 1995), 21, quote on 68; for a discussion of voting on hard choices, see, for example, Daniel Walker Howe, *What Hath God Wrought* (New York: Oxford University Press, 2007), 272–73 (on tariffs); 365 (on spending and taxing); and ch. 4 (on war). Ibid., 576. In general, voters back then knew where their representatives stood on the hard choices, and legislators were candid about those decisions. Wiebe described it this way: "By the late 1820's, as Alexis de Tocqueville noted, it was already American practice in politics to 'strip off…whatever conceals it from sight, in order to view it more closely and in the broad light of day.'" Wiebe, *Self-Rule*, 21.

9 For a discussion of literacy, see Wiebe, *Self-Rule*, 67; on newspapers and foreign visitors, see Howe, *What Hath God Wrought*, 227; Howe quote in ibid., 231.

10 On the desire to be fair, see, for example, Jonathan Haidt, *The Righteous Mind:*

Why Good People Are Divided by Politics and Religion (New York: Pantheon Books, 2012); James Q. Wilson, *The Moral Sense* (New York: Free Press Paperbacks, 1997); on the experiments of modern behavioral scientists, see ibid., 35–49.

11 On Coco Chanel offering perfume to GIs, see Tilar J. Mazzeo, *The Secret of Chanel No. 5: The Intimate History of the World's Most Famous Perfume* (New York: HarperCollins, 2010), 161–63; on Truman, ibid., 157.

12 I need not get into the debate on the role of nature versus nurture in promoting fairness. For a discussion of the role of nature versus nurture in this area, see, for example, Nicholas Wade, *A Troublesome Inheritance* (New York: Penguin Books, 2013), ch. 3; Haidt, *Righteous Mind*, ch. 1.

13 As the scientists wrote, "Our findings suggest that relatively minor acts of dishonesty by in-group members can have a large influence on the extent of dishonesty." Francesco Gino, Shahar Ayal, and Dan Ariely, "Contagion and Differentiation in Unethical Behavior: The Effect of One Bad Apple on the Barrel," *Psychological Science* 20 (March 2009), 398, http://people. duke.edu/~dandan/webfiles/PapersDisHonesty/Contagion%20and%20 Differentiation.pdf.

14 David Schoenbrod, *Power without Responsibility: How Congress Abuses the People through Delegation* (New Haven, CT: Yale University Press, 1993), 26–31.

15 My recollections are corroborated by those of a much-more-central figure in these events—Senator Hubert Humphrey's legislative assistant, John G. Stewart. John G. Stewart, "When Democracy Worked: Reflections on the Passage of the Civil Rights Act of 1964," *New York Law School Law Review* 59 (2014–15).

16 For a further discussion of the "I have a dream" passage, see Clarence B. Jones and Stuart Connelly, *Behind the Dream: The Making of the Speech that Transformed a Nation* (New York: St. Martin's Griffin, 2011), 112; quote from Clarence Jones, speaking in "Remembering the Dream, Renewing the Dream," YouTube video, 2:25, from a panel hosted at the New York Law School Law Review Symposium, September 13, 2013, posted by New York Law School, https://www.youtube.com/watch?v=fR_44BevHQ4&feature=youtu. be&t=1h31m15s.

17 Clarence B. Jones, in Jones and Connelly, *Behind the Dream*, 138.

18 Clarence B. Jones, in ibid., 130.

19 Robert A. Caro, *The Passage of Power: The Years of Lyndon Johnson IV* (New York: Vintage Books, 2012), 349, 486, 489, 600–601.

20 Ibid., 568. Twenty-seven Republicans voted to stop the filibuster, while only six voted against.

21 Ibid., 564.

22 Benjamin Page and Robert Shapiro, *The Rational Public: Fifty Years of Trends in American Policy Preferences* (Chicago: University of Chicago Press, 1992), 319.

23 "The Voice of Public Choice: James Buchanan, Who Died on January 9th, Illuminated Political Decision-Making," *Economist*, January 19, 2013, http:// www.economist.com/news/finance-and-economics/21569692-james- buchanan-who-died-january-9th-illuminated-political-decision-making.

24 Esa Saarinen, "Philosophy for Managers: Reflections of a Practitioner," in *Systems Intelligence: A New Lens on Human Engagement and Action*, ed. Raimo P. Hamalainen and Esa Saarinen (Helsinki: Systems Analysis Laboratory Helsinki University of Technology, 2008), 11–12, http://sal.aalto.fi/publications/pdf-files/rsaa08.pdf. I am indebted to Professor Esa Saarinan for the conductor analogy, which he applied in a nongovernmental context.

25 James Q. Wilson, "Interest and Deliberation in the American Republic, or, Why James Madison Would Never Have Received the James Madison Award," *Political Science and Politics* 23 (1990).

26 Alexis de Tocqueville, *Democracy in America*, Vol. 1, trans. Harvey C. Mansfield and Delba Winthrop (New York: Vintage Books, 2000), 55.

27 Abraham Lincoln, "The Gettysburg Address" (speech, November 19, 1863), Abraham Lincoln Online "Speeches & Writings," http://www.abrahamlincolnonline.org/lincoln/speeches/gettysburg.htm.

28 On Lincoln's resolution that the government "shall not *perish*": ibid. (emphasis added). On the end of property qualification, see Wiebe, *Self-Rule.* 30; Alexander Keyssar, *The Right to Vote: The Contested History of Democracy in the United States* (New York: Basic Books, 2009), 29. On the pairing of liberty and equality, consider the first two sentences of the Gettysburg Address: "Four score and seven years ago our fathers brought forth on this continent, a new nation, *conceived in liberty*, and *dedicated to the proposition that all men are created equal.* Now we are engaged in a great civil war, testing whether that nation, or any nation *so conceived* and *so dedicated,* can long endure." Lincoln, "Gettysburg Address" (emphasis added). See also Garry Wills, *Lincoln at Gettysburg* (New York: Simon & Schuster, 1992).

29 On immigrants' capacity for leadership, see Jane Addams, *Twenty Years at Hull House* (New York: New American Library, 1961), 89. Hull House described its purpose as providing a "center for the higher civic and social life." "Chicago's Hull House—circa 1910," Virginia Commonwealth University: Social Welfare History Project, accessed November 14, 2016, http://socialwelfare.library.vcu.edu/settlement-houses/hull-house-circ-1910/. For quote: Addams, *Twenty Years at Hull House*, 45.

30 Page and Shapiro, *Rational Public*, 389, 394, 397, quote on 384; see also Martin Gilens, *Affluence & Influence: Economic Inequality and Political Power in America* (Princeton, NJ: Princeton University Press, 2012), 40.

31 Jeremy Waldron, *The Dignity of Legislation* (Cambridge, UK: Cambridge University Press, 1999), 2.

* Figure 5: "Jane Addams Biography: Philanthropist, Women's Rights Activist, Anti-War Activist" (1860–1935)," bio., accessed November 6, 2016, http://www.biography.com/people/jane-addams-9176298.

CHAPTER 3

1 Michael Bloomberg, quoted in Associated Press, "Mayor Bloomberg Outlines Plan to Balance United States Budget," *Huffington Post*, November 8, 2011.

2 For support for the assertions about Senator Muskie's problem, how it gave rise to the Clean Air Act, and problems in the act's implementation, see my much-lengthier treatment of these subjects in David Schoenbrod, *Saving Our*

Environment from Washington (New Haven, CT: Yale University Press, 2005), chs. 3–5.

3   John C. Esposito and Ralph Nader, *Vanishing Air: The Ralph Nader Study Group Report on Air Pollution* (New York: Grossman, 1970), vii–ix, 293.

4   For an argument that delegation undermines accountability, see Adam Hill, "Does Delegation Undermine Accountability? Experimental Evidence on the Relationship between Blame Shifting and Control," *Journal of Empirical Legal Studies* 12 (2015).

5   E. Donald Elliott, Bruce A. Ackerman, and John C. Millian, "Towards a Theory of Statutory Evolution: The Federalization of Environmental Law," *Journal of Law, Economics & Organization* 1 (1985), 327–38.

6   116 Cong. Rec. 42, 381 (1970) (statements of Edmund Muskie) (emphasis added).

7   On automakers' reputation, see, for example, Ralph Nader, *Unsafe at Any Speed: The Designed-In Dangers of the American Automobile* (New York: Grossman, 1965).

8   For Congress's ability to shift the blame for the unpopular consequences of the Clean Air Act, see Schoenbrod, *Saving Our Environment*, chs. 3–5. For Congress's ability to shift the blame for the unpopular consequences of statutes that delegate, see, in general: (1) David Mayhew, *Congress: The Electoral Connection* (New Haven, CT: Yale University Press, 1974), 132. As Mayhew described the situation, "In a large class of legislative undertakings the electoral payment is for positions taken rather than for effects." (2) Morris Fiorina, "Legislative Choice of Regulatory Forms: Legal Process or Administrative Process?," *Public Choice* 39 (1982). (3) Hill, "Does Delegation Undermine Accountability?," 4. As Hill described: "Even in these cases, where the agent is effectively powerless to change the outcome, participants blame principals significantly less than in cases where the principal brings about the outcome directly." On the findings of political scientists, see sources cited in David Schoenbrod, "Statutory Junk," Emory Law Journal Online (forthcoming, 2017).

9   William Nelson, *The Roots of American Bureaucracy: 1830–1900* (Cambridge, MA: Harvard University Press, 1982), 6, 82–112, 140–44. Some scholars believe that Congress delegated law-making authority from the beginning of the republic. See, for example, Jerry L. Mashaw, *Creating the Administrative Constitution: The Lost One Hundred Years of American Administrative Law* (New Haven, CT: Yale University Press, 2012). Others argue that the practice began much more recently. See Philip Hamburger, *Is Administrative Law Unlawful?* (Chicago: University of Chicago Press, 2014), ch. 6.

10   Herbert Croly, *The Promise of American Life* (Norwood, MA: Norwood, 1965), 276. Such sentiments continued. As Robert Wiebe wrote, "Thurman Arnold's *Folklore of American Capitalism* (1937), often cited as the New Deal's most significant commentary on government, derisively dismissed the very thought of popular rule." Wiebe, *Self-Rule*, 207. On captains of industry and socialists, see ibid.

11   For more on this topic, see, for example, Theodore J. Lowi, *The End of Liberalism* (New York: Norton, 1969).

[12] See, for example, 44 Fed. Reg. 33, 116 (June 8, 1979); 44 Fed. Reg. 46, 275 (Aug. 7, 1979); 44 Fed. Reg. 53, 144 (Sept. 12, 1979); 45 Fed. Reg. 55, 134 (Aug. 18, 1980).

[13] Schoenbrod, *Saving Our Environment*, 36–38.

[14] For support about the assertions of the benefits from further cuts in pollution and a discussion of the false assumptions that Congress built into the statute, see William F. Pedersen and David Schoenbrod, "The Overwhelming Case for Clean Air Act Reform," *Environmental Law Reporter* 43 (November 2013); for an argument that the EPA overestimates the harm resulting from the particulates in the air, see, for example, Art Fraas and Randall Lutter, "Uncertain Benefits Estimates for Reductions in Fine Particulate Concentrations," *Risk Analysis* 33 (2013).

[15] Rule to Reduce Interstate Transport of Fine Particulate Matter and Ozone (Interstate Air Quality Rule), 69 Fed. Reg. 4566 (Jan. 30, 2004).

[16] *Clean Air Act Amendments of 1977: Hearings Before the Subcommittee on Environmental Pollution of the Committee on Environment and Public Works*, 95th Cong., 1st Session, 8 (Feb. 11, 1977) (statement of Edmund Muskie, Senator of Maine).

[17] Fraas and Lutter, "Uncertain Benefits Estimates," 442. Fraas and Lutter posited that there may be a safety threshold for fine particulates at a level well below the EPA health-based air-quality goal.

[18] See, for example, Michael A. Livermore and Richard L. Revesz, "Rethinking Health-Based Environmental Standards," *New York University Law Review* 89 (2014), http://www.nyulawreview.org/issues/volume-89-number-4/rethinking-health-based-environmental-standards.

[19] For the interstate origins of pollution, see, for example, Owen R. Cooper, Andrew O. Langford, David D. Parrish, and David W. Fahey, "Challenges of a Lowered U.S. Ozone Standard," *Science* 348 (June 5, 2015), http://science.sciencemag.org/content/348/6239/1096.

[20] On the supposed opportunity for states, see 116 Cong. Rec. 42, 381 (1970).

[21] Committee on Air Quality Management in the United States, National Research Council, *Air Quality Management in the United States* (Washington, DC: National Academies Press, 2004), 128.

[22] For an opinion on how Congress could shoulder responsibility, see David Schoenbrod, Richard B. Stewart and Katrina Wyman, *Breaking the Logjam: Environmental Protection That Will Work* (New Haven, CT: Yale University Press, 2012), ch. 5; for a discussion of acid rain legislation, see ibid., 6–8, 36–39.

[23] R. Shep Melnick, *Regulation and the Courts: The Case of the Clean Air Act* (Washington, DC: Brookings Institute Press, 1983), 149–51.

[24] Transcript: Barack Obama, speaking in "Barack Obama on FOX News Sunday," *Fox News*, April 28, 2008, http://www.foxnews.com/story/2008/04/28/transcript-barack-obama-on-fox-news-sunday/.

[25] Schoenbrod et al., *Breaking the Logjam*, 82–83.

[26] For information on the discussion in *Breaking the Logjam*'s report and book, and how to purchase the publications, see "Breaking the Logjam: Environmental Reform for the New Congress and Administration," New York Law School, http://www.breakingthelogjam.org.

[27] Howard, *Rule of Nobody*, 104–10.

[28] For a discussion of the literature, see, for example, Fiorina and Abrams, *Breakdown of Representation*, chs. 1–6.

[29] For Medicaid and Medicare statutes, see "Total Medicaid Spending, FY 2015," Henry J. Kaiser Family Foundation, http://kff.org/medicaid/state-indicator/total-medicaid-spending/; for the Clean Air Act, see Schoenbrod, *Saving Our Environment*, chs. 14, 16.

[30] Stephen Breyer, *Breaking the Vicious Circle: Toward Effective Risk Regulation* (Cambridge, MA: Harvard University Press, 1995).

[31] Ibid., chs. 1–2; see also, for example, Cass Sunstein, *Risk and Reason: Safety, Law, and the Environment* (Cambridge, UK: Cambridge University Press, 2002), viii; Daniel A. Farber, *Eco-Pragmatism: Making Sensible Environmental Decisions in an Uncertain World* (Chicago: University of Chicago Press, 1999), 73.

[32] Ralph Nader described this sense of fairness as "the common core of people's humanity, which finds expression in factual realities, and the many senses of fairness and fair play that appear right where people are interacting every day—their workplaces, neighborhoods, marketplaces, public spaces, and the all-encompassing physical environment." Nader, *Unstoppable*, 16.

CHAPTER 4

[1] U.S. Const., art. I, § 8, cl. 7. In referring to taxes, I am including tariffs and other measures to raise revenue.

[2] On quote concerning Constitution requiring Congress to provide a statement, see id., art. I, § 8, cl. 2, cl. 7. Howe, *What Hath God Wrought*, 499: The debt was retired in 1835 for the only time in history. Ibid., 365: So strong was the sense that the budget should be balanced except in emergency situations that those who wanted less government spending fought to reduce government receipts, because it was assumed that a cut in revenue would force a cut in spending. Ibid., 409: Although land sales also financed spending, they were not thought of as a drain on the future but rather as a way of building the future.

[3] Franklin Delano Roosevelt, "Campaign Address on the Federal Budget at Pittsburgh, Pennsylvania" (speech, October 19, 1932), American Presidency Project "Franklin D. Roosevelt," http://www.presidency.ucsb.edu/ws/index.php?pid=88399; on post–World War II surpluses, see Office of Management and Budget, *Historical Tables: Budget of the U.S. Government: Fiscal Year 2011* (Washington, DC: U.S. Government Printing Office, 2010), 21–22, White House: President Barack Obama, accessed October 26, 2016, https://www.whitehouse.gov/sites/default/files/omb/budget/fy2011/assets/hist.pdf.

[4] John F. Kennedy, "Special Message to the Congress on Taxation" (speech, April 20, 1961), American Presidency Project "John F. Kennedy," http://www.presidency.ucsb.edu/ws/?pid=8074. The tax cut came when President Johnson signed it into law. Revenue Act of 1964, Pub. L. No. 88-272.

[5] John Maynard Keynes, *The General Theory of Employment Interest and Money* (New York: Harcourt, 1936), 128–30.

[6] Lyndon B. Johnson, "First State of the Union Address" (speech, January 8, 1964), American Rhetoric: Online Speech Bank, http://www.americanrhetoric.com/speeches/lbj1964stateoftheunion.htm.

7   For a brief account of the unraveling of the deficit-control scheme, see Thomas Mann and Norman Ornstein, *It's Even Worse Than It Looks: How the American Constitutional System Collided with the New Politics of Extremism* (New York: Basic Books, 2012), 121–22.

8   Jacob S. Hacker and Paul Pierson, *Winner-Take-All Politics: How Washington Made the Rich Richer—and Turned Its Back on the Middle Class* (New York: Simon & Schuster, 2010), 215. The bipartisan Committee for a Responsible Federal Budget explained some of the gimmicks in its report *Avoiding Budget Gimmicks* (Washington, DC: Committee for a Responsible Federal Budget, June 2015), http://crfb.org/sites/default/files/2015gimmickchartbook.pdf.

9   Alan Blinder, "Four Deficit Myths and a Frightening Fact: We Don't Have a Generalized Overspending Problem. We Have a Humongous Health-Care Problem," *Wall Street Journal*, January 19, 2012, http://online.wsj.com/news/articles/SB10001424052970204468004577164820504397092.

10   15 U.S.C. §§ 1601–67f (2012).

11   M. L. Cross, "Constitutional or Statutory Provisions Prohibiting Municipalities or Other Subdivisions of the State from Subscribing to, or Acquiring Stock of, Private Corporation," *American Law Reports* 152 (1944).

12   Federal Deposit Insurance Corporation, *A Brief History of Deposit Insurance in the United States* (Washington, DC: Federal Deposit Insurance Corporation, September 1998), 1, http://www.fdic.gov/bank/historical/brief/brhist.pdf.

13   For Yogi Berra quote, see Todd Richissin, "8 Top 'Yogi-isms' from 'The Great No. 8,' Baseball's Yogi Berra," *Montclair Patch*, September 23, 2015. On increased limits, see Federal Deposit Insurance Corporation, *Brief History of Deposit Insurance*, 68. See, generally, Kenneth L. Peoples, Emanuel Melichar, Eric P. Thor, Paul T. Prentice, and Gregory D. Hanson, *Anatomy of an American Agricultural Credit Crisis: Farm Debt in the 1980s* (New York: Rowman & Littlefield, 1992); "History of the 80s, Volume 1: An Examination of the Banking Crises of the 1980s and Early 1990s," Federal Deposit Insurance Corporation, last modified June 5, 2000, https://www.fdic.gov/bank/historical/history/vol1.html; R. Dan Brumbaugh Jr., *Thrifts under Siege: Restoring Order to American Banking* (New York: Ballinger, 1999); James R. Barth, *The Great Savings and Loan Debacle* (Washington, DC: American Enterprise Institute, 1991).

14   For all quotes (emphasis added to each), see Urs W. Birchler, "'Never Again!'—the Dynamics of Bank Bailouts" (working paper, University of Zurich, July 10, 2014), 2, http://www.scribd.com/doc/241350083/Urs-Birchler-Never-Again-20140710#scribd.

15   "United Fidelity Bank, fsb, Evansville, Indiana, Assumes All of the Deposits of Highland Community Bank, Chicago, Illinois," Federal Deposit Insurance Corporation, January 23, 2015, https://www.fdic.gov/news/news/press/2015/pr15007.html.

16   According to Liz Marshall, Sabrina Pellerin, and John Walter: "61 percent of the liabilities of the financial system are subject to explicit or implicit protection from loss by the federal government. This protection may encourage risk-taking, making financial crises and bailouts more likely." Liz Marshall, Sabrina Pellerin, and John Walter, "Bailout Barometer: How Large Is the Financial Safety Net?," Federal Reserve Bank of Richmond, last updated February 3, 2016,

https://www.richmondfed.org/publications/research/special_reports/safety_net/index.cfm.

[17] Ed Koch, quoted in Irvin Molotsky, "Koch Tells Fellow Mayors Reasons to Beware of Mandated Programs," *New York Times*, January 25, 1980, §§ 2, 3.

[18] For a catalog of the side effects of federal grants and mandates, see, for example, James L. Buckley, *Saving Congress from Itself: Emancipating the States and Empowering Their People* (New York: Encounter Books, 2014), ch. 3.

[19] See Charles Austin Beard, *The Office of Justice of the Peace in England: In Its Origin and Development* (New York: Burt Franklin, 1904), 116–18, 120–22; U.S. Const., art. I, § 4, cl. 1; art. IV, § 4; on state militias, see: art. I, § 8, cl. 15–16; art. II, § 2, cl. 1.

[20] On Congress lacking the power to mandate states, see, for example, New York v. United States, 505 U.S. 144, 145, 161 (1992). On states lacking the power to interfere with federal activities, such as by entering into treaties or violating constitutionally guaranteed rights or constitutionally ordained policies, see U.S. Const., art. I, § 10, cl. 1–3; art. IV, §§ 1–3; art. V. For constitutional rights enforceable against the states, see, for example, U.S. Const., amends. XIII–XV. Congress has the power to enforce these amendments but not to seek to do more. City of Boerne v. Flores, 521 U.S. 507, 535 (1997).

[21] For separate federal and state governments, see Tocqueville, *Democracy in America*, 56; for source of quote and Congress not coercing states, see ibid., 250.

[22] Ross Sandler and David Schoenbrod, *Democracy by Decree* (New Haven, CT: Yale University Press, 2003), 13–34. In this book, Ross Sandler and I noted that the Watergate scandal brought changes in Congress that eroded the discipline that political parties had imposed on individual legislators.

[23] *New York*, 505 U.S. 144, at 168–69; see also Printz v. United States, 521 U.S. 898, 922–23 (1997).

[24] Schoenbrod, *Saving Our Environment*, 23–28, 39–51.

[25] Ibid., 39–51.

[26] For the current version of the statute, see Clean Air Act § 173(a) (4), 42 U.S.C. § 7503 (2012).

[27] *Id.* at §§ 179, 7509 (2012). Virginia v. Browner, 80 F.3d 869, 882 (4th Cir. 1996). Virginia v. Browner upheld the highway funds cut-off. On states generally knuckling under, see, for example, James E. McCarthy, *Highway Fund Sanctions for Clean Air Act Violations* (report for Congress, Washington, DC: Congressional Research Service/Library of Congress, October 22, 1997), http://research.policyarchive.org/490.pdf.

[28] Jonathon Sizemore to author, memorandum, December 1, 2015.

[29] On the growth in federal grants, see Buckley, *Saving Congress from Itself*, ch. 2. For a discussion of methods that Congress uses to coerce, see Paul L. Posner, *The Politics of Unfunded Mandates: Whither Federalism?* (Washington, DC: Georgetown University Press, 1998). The Supreme Court case that struck down a mandate is National Federation of Independent Business v. Sebelius, 132 S.Ct. 2566, 2634 (2012), in which Justice Ginsberg (dissenting) wrote: "Prior to today's decision . . . the Court has never ruled that the terms of any grant

crossed the indistinct line between temptation and coercion." For a discussion
of the case's uncertain impact, see, for example, Lynn A. Baker, "The Spending
Power after NFIB v. Sebelius," *Harvard Journal of Law and Public Policy* 37
(2014); Michael S. Greve, "Coercion, Conditions, and Commandeering: A Brief
Note on the Medicaid Holding of NFIB v. Sibeilus," *Harvard Journal of Law and
Public Policy* 37 (2014).

30   William J. Clinton, "Remarks on Signing the Unfunded Mandates Reform
     Act of 1995" (speech, March 22, 1995), American Presidency Project "William
     J. Clinton," http://www.presidency.ucsb.edu/ws/?pid=51131; on other ways to
     define mandates, see Advisory Commission on Intergovernmental Relations,
     *The Role of Federal Mandates in Intergovernmental Relations: A Preliminary
     ACIR Report for Public Review and Comment,* (January 1996), 11–12, A-27,
     University Libraries, http://www.library.unt.edu/gpo/acir/Mandates.html.

31   For Clinton quote, see Clinton "Unfunded Mandates Reform Act"; on the
     demise of the commission, see John Kincaid, "The U.S. Advisory Commission
     on Intergovernmental Relations: Unique Artifact of a Bygone Era," *Public
     Administration Review* 71 (March–April 2011); the point-of-order provision
     is in 2 U.S.C. § 1501 (2012); on exemptions, see 2 U.S.C. § 1503 (2012); on the
     paucity of points of order over the years, see Robert Jay Dilger and Richard
     Beth, *Unfunded Mandates Reform Act: History, Impact, and Issues* (Washington,
     DC: Congressional Research Service, July 9, 2015), 15–16, http://www.fas.org/
     sgp/crs/misc/R40957.pdf.

32   Breyer, *Breaking the Vicious Circle*, chs. 1–2; see also, for example, Sunstein, *Risk
     and Reason*, viii; Farber, *Eco-Pragmatism*, 73–74.

33   U.S. Const., art. I, § 8, cl. 1, 3. Schoenbrod, *Power without Responsibility*, 155–57:
     Laws are rules of private conduct—rules that regulate society. The Constitution
     does not prevent, and the Supreme Court has never held, that Congress may
     not delegate the making of the rules that regulate how government administers
     itself, its property, and its money.

34   Gibbons v. Ogden, 22 U.S. 1, 196 (1824).

35   On the application of legislated rules, see Cargo of the Brig Aurora v. United
     States, 11 U.S. 382 (1813); on statutes regulating steamboat safety, see Mashaw,
     Creating the Administrative Constitution, 187–208; on legislators dealing with
     the important issues versus the details, see Wayman v. Southard, 23 U.S. 1, 43
     (1825).

36   On the progressive era thinking, see, for example, Robert Rabin, "Federal
     Regulation in Historical Perspective," *Stanford Law Review* 38 (1986), 1206–8,
     1212–15, 1225–29, 1231–36; for the "intelligible principle," see J. W. Hampton Jr.,
     & Co. v. United States, 276 U.S. 394, 409 (1928); for a case upholding a statute
     telling agencies to regulate in the public interest, see Whitman v. American
     Trucking Associations, 531 U.S. 457, 491–96 (2001).

37   On the Court deferring to Congress, see *id*. at 474–75, which explains that
     the Supreme Court has "almost never felt qualified to second-guess Congress
     regarding the permissible degree of policy judgment that can be left to those
     executing or applying the law."

38   Administrative Procedure Act, Pub. L. 79-404, 60 Stat. 237 (1946) (current
     version at 5 U.S.C. § 500 et seq. (2012)).

[39] Eric Posner and Adrian Vermeule, *The Executive Unbound: After the Madisonian Republic* (Oxford, UK: Oxford University Press, 2010). Posner and Vermeule argued that the accountability of the president as executive makes up for the loss of accountability in the legislative process. In this section, I take issue with them.

[40] See, for example, Lisa Heinzerling, "Ozone Madness," *Grist*, September 4, 2011, http://grist.org/article/2011-09-03-ozone-madness/. Professor Heinzerling was a key member of President Obama's team at the EPA.

[41] Posner and Vermeule's *Executive Unbound* is a spirited defense of the president being unbound by legislative power. The authors argue that the Madisonian ideal in which the legislature makes the law and the executive branch implements it is impossible because there are too-many choices that legislated law must address in advance. See *Executive Unbound*, 4–5. I agree, but disagree with their making the leap from that position to their conclusion that "there is no pragmatically feasible alternative to executive government under current conditions." Ibid., 5. Although chapter 3 of the book reaches this conclusion, the argument boils down to the observation that legislation to constrain executive power has failed to achieve much so far. They do not, however, deal with suggestions such as John Ely's that teeth should be put into the War Powers Act or James Landis's that Congress should be made responsible for major regulations (both discussed in chapter 8). The problem is not that legislators cannot constrain the executive branch to some degree but that they do not want to constrain it because it would require them to be accountable. Posner and Vermeule go on to argue that the executive, although unbound by legislative power, is nonetheless bound in other ways. They mention running for reelection, but of course have to acknowledge that that presidents in their second term cannot run for reelection. See ibid., 12.

As a fallback, Posner and Vermeule mention the desire of presidents to be well regarded in history and the extraordinary scrutiny to which presidential candidates are subject. See ibid., ch. 4. On this basis, they claim that presidents will tend to pursue public-regarding objectives rather than maximizing their own power. Even if this is true, there is nothing in Posner and Vermeule's account that keeps presidents from using the tricks to hide the unpopular consequences of the steps they take to achieve popularity. To use an example that they mention, President George W. Bush used irresponsible means to gain popularity by supporting prescription drugs for Medicare recipients. See ibid., 145.

Posner and Vermeule also argue that presidents and presidential candidates will try to boost their popularity by making government more transparent and therefore more accountable. See ibid., 145. That is true, but only to an extent. As chapter 6 shows, President Obama's first official act was to issue a policy of "transparency and open government," but his administration hid the Office of Management and Budget model that would have revealed an embarrassing fiscal future. Until voters demand transparency across the board, presidents will support transparency selectively.

[42] Frank Newport, "Congress Retains Low Honesty Rating," Gallup, December 3, 2012, http://www.gallup.com/poll/159035/congress-retains-low-honesty-rating.aspx.

43 Penny, *Common Cents*, 72.

44 Penn Jillette, "Who's the Real Illusionist? Penn Jillette on How Modern Politics Resembles a Vegas Magic Act," *Wall Street Journal*, September 10, 2011, http://online.wsj.com/news/articles/SB10001424053111903285704576560482965329702.

45 Ibid.; L. Frank Baum, *The Annotated Wizard of Oz: The Centennial Edition* (New York: Norton, 2000), 282.

CHAPTER 5

1 Roald Dahl, *The Enormous Crocodile* (New York: Random House, 2012).

2 The $6,000 estimate is discussed later in this chapter.

3 26 U.S.C. § 3501(b) (2006).

4 Paul Starr, *The Social Transformation of American Medicine* (New York: Basic Books, 1984), 294–310.

5 For wage regulations, see United States Department of Labor, *The Termination Report of the National War Labor Board, Industrial Disputes and Wage Stabilization in Wartime*, Vol. 1 (Washington, DC: U.S. Government Publishing Office, 1949), 380–81. Robert B. Helms, "Tax Policy and the History of the Health Insurance Industry" (paper presented at a conference sponsored by Tax Policy Center and the American Tax Policy Institute, Brookings Institution, Washington, DC February 29, 2008), 7, https://www.aei.org/wp-content/uploads/2011/10/healthconference-helms.pdf: The War Labor Board said it had ruled to exclude health insurance to simplify its job and did not consider the long-term consequences for health care. For the IRS's exclusion of health insurance from taxable income, see ibid., 7–9; Special Ruling, 433 Standard Fed. Tax Serv. (CCH), ¶ 6587 (November 24, 1943).

6 On the continuation of the tax exclusion, see Helms, "Tax Policy," 7; on tax rates, see United States Census Bureau, *Biennial Edition: Historical Statistics of the United States, Colonial Times to 1970*, part I (Washington, DC: Department of Commerce, September 1975), 1095, http://www.census.gov/library/publications/1975/compendia/hist_stats_colonial-1970.html; on employer-provided coverage as unique to health care and the tax break as the leading cause, see Helms, "Tax Policy," 11, 17.

7 See Samuel Shem, *The Spirit of the Place* (New York: Berkley Publishing Group, 2008). This novel, by Harvard Medical School Professor Stephen Berger writing under a pen name, provides a moving portrait of such a medical practice.

8 For a summary of the writing about fee increases in health care, see Helms, "Tax Policy," 21–22; Sandeep Jauhar, *Doctored: The Disillusionment of an American Physician* (New York, Farrar, Straus and Giroux, 2014), 10; on the increasing income of physicians, see United States Census Bureau, *Historical Statistics*, 176.

9 Health Maintenance Organization Act of 1973, Pub. L. No. 93-222, 87 Stat. 914 (1973) (codified at 42 U.S.C. § 300e). Reacting to the spiraling health care costs that it helped cause, Congress added to the trend toward bureaucratic control of the medical practice by requiring large employers to offer employees an HMO option. Quote from Jauhar, *Doctored*, 11.

10 Rita A. Mariotti, "Doctors and Patients Both Are Losing under 'Managed Care,'" *Star-News*, January 19, 1997, http://news.google.com/newspapers?n

id=1454&dat=19970119&id=nLFOAAAAIBAJ&sjid=RRUEAAAAIBAJ&
pg=2453,1325848.

[11] Ibid.

[12] David Zimmerman, interviews by the author, n.d.

[13] Ibid.

[14] Congressional Budget Office, *Private Health Insurance Premiums and Federal Policy* (Washington, DC: Congressional Budget Office, February 11, 2016), https://www.cbo.gov/sites/default/files/114th-congress-2015-2016/reports/51130-Health_Insurance_Premiums.pdf.

[15] For doctors' hours, income, and expenses in dealing with insurance companies see Jauhar, *Doctored*, 12–13; on administrators' salaries, see Elizabeth Rosenthal, "Medicine's Top Earners Are Not the M.D.s," *New York Times*, May 17, 2014, http://www.nytimes.com/2014/05/18/sunday-review/doctors-salaries-are-not-the-big-cost.html; on administrative costs, see Uwe E. Reinhardt, "Why Does US Health Care Cost So Much? (Part II: Indefensible Administrative Costs)," *Economix* blog, *New York Times*, November 21, 2008, http://economix.blogs.nytimes.com/2008/11/21/why-does-us-health-care-cost-so-much-part-ii-indefensible-administrative-costs/?scp=2&sq=Uwe%20Reinhardt&st=cse; for President Obama's request to control health care costs: "Remarks by the President at the Annual Conference of the American Medical Association," White House: President Barack Obama "Speeches & Remarks," June 15, 2009, http://www.whitehouse.gov/the_press_office/Remarks-by-the-President-to-the-Annual-Conference-of-the-American-Medical-Association/.

[16] Jauhar, *Doctored*, 6, 13–15.

[17] Joint Economic Committee, *How the Tax Exclusion Shaped Today's Private Health Insurance Market* (Washington, DC: Joint Economic Committee, December 17, 2003), 3, http://www.jec.senate.gov/public/_cache/files/bffc53a6-d2f4-4312-b195-a4938e6bed2b/healthtaxexclusion.pdf.

[18] Joint Committee on Taxation, *Background Materials for Senate Committee on Finance Roundtable on Health Care Financing* (Washington, DC: Joint Committee on Taxation, May 8, 2009), 9, https://www.jct.gov/publications.html?func=startdown&id=3557.

[19] Seth Hanlon, "Tax Expenditure of the Week: Tax-Free Health Insurance," Center for American Progress, January 12, 2011, http://www.americanprogress.org/issues/open-government/news/2011/01/12/8899/tax-expenditure-of-the-week-tax-free-health-insurance/.

[20] On diverse policy makers pushing for phasing out the tax break, see, for example, Pete Domenici and Alice Rivlin, *Domenici-Rivlin Debt Reduction Task Force Plan 2.0* (Washington, DC: Bipartisan Policy Center, December 3, 2012), 5, http://bipartisanpolicy.org/wp-content/uploads/sites/default/files/D-R%20 Plan%202.0%20FINAL.pdf; for Wyden's bill, see Healthy Americans Act, S. 391, 111th Cong. (2007).

[21] For problems leading President Obama to enact the Affordable Care Act, see "Remarks by the President at the Annual Conference of The American Medical Association," White House: President Barack Obama "Briefing Room," June 15, 2009, https://www.whitehouse.gov/the-press-office/remarks-president-annual-conference-american-medical-association. For more about

the Cadillac tax, see the Patient Protect and Affordable Care Act, Pub. L. No. 111-148, 124 §§ 119, 4980I (2010). Tevi D. Troy and Mark Wilson, *The Impact of the Health Care Excise Tax on U.S. Employees and Employers* (Washington, DC: American Health Policy Institute, 2014), 1, 3, http://www.americanhealthpolicy. org/Content/documents/resources/Excise_Tax_11102014.pdf: Even by 2020, the Cadillac tax would produce only $13 billion, less than a twentieth of the revenue lost because of the tax break. For Republicans' failure to do away with the tax break, see Ramesh Ponnuru and Yuval Levin, "A Conservative Alternative to ObamaCare: To Avoid a Lurch to the Left If the Current Law Fails, the Time Is Right to Present Sensible, Market-Oriented Reforms," *Wall Street Journal*, November 13, 2013, http://www.wsj.com/articles/SB100014240 52702304448204579182203093952642; Laura Meckler, "Republicans Shy Away from Their Own Health Plan," *Wall Street Journal*, December 9, 2013, http:// www.wsj.com/articles/SB10001424052702303330204579248321886920780.

[22] John Micklethwait and Adrian Woolridge, *The Fourth Revolution: The Global Race to Reinvent the State* (New York: Penguin Books, 2014), ch. 5. The value of this exclusion grew to $434 billion in 2012, fully 3 percent of GDP.

[23] Hacker and Pierson, *Winner-Take-All Politics*, 291; Kevin Bogardus, "Labor Unions Lobby against 'Cadillac' Tax," *Hill*, December 8, 2009, http://thehill. com/business-a-lobbying/71293-labor-unions-lobby-against-cadillac-tax. Such powerful interests "saw their main concerns addressed" at the outset of the drafting of the Affordable Care Act.

[24] Schuck, *Why Government Fails So Often*, 128–54. Schuck showed how legislators motivated to serve constituents could do a much-better job of designing legislation to fulfill this function.

[25] Lee Hamilton, "Will the House Come to Order?," *American Interest* 2 (September 2006), http://www.the-american-interest.com/2006/09/01/ will-the-house-come-to-order/.

[26] Ryan Grim and Sabrina Siddiqui, "Call Time for Congress Shows How Fundraising Dominates Bleak Work Life," *Huffington Post*, January 8, 2013, http://www.huffingtonpost.com/2013/01/08/call-time-congressional-fundraising_n_2427291.html.

[27] Interview with senior Capitol Hill staffer, 2009. Interview was conducted in confidentiality, and per mutual agreement name of interviewee is withheld.

[28] For an example of this story, see John R. Silber, *Seeking the North Star: Selected Speeches* (Boston: Godine, 2014), 36–37.

[29] See, for example, Hacker and Pierson, *Winner-Take-All Politics*; Steven M. Teles, "Kludgeocracy in America," *National Affairs* 17 (Fall 2013), http://www. nationalaffairs.com/publications/detail/kludgeocracy-in-america; Steven M. Teles, "The Scourge of Upward Redistribution," *National Affairs* 25 (Fall 2015), http://www.nationalaffairs.com/publications/detail/the-scourge-of-upward-redistribution; Schuck, *Why Government Fails So Often*, 22–23 (collecting studies). Systematic studies Schuck compiled by both liberal and conservative policy analysts show that policies that are publicized as benefiting the general public actually benefit well-organized interests.

[30] See Hacker and Pierson, *Winner-Take-All Politics*, 17–18.

[31] Ibid., 97.

32 For unions and membership-based clubs, see ibid., chs. 5–6; for ideological organizations, see ibid., 143–46.

33 Quote in ibid., 44; James Bessen, "Accounting for Rising Corporate Profits: Intangibles or Regulatory Rents" (Working Paper 16-18, Boston University School of Law & Economics, May 11, 2016), https://www.bu.edu/law/working-papers/accounting-for-rising-corporate-profits-intangibles-or-regulatory-rents/: Political activity and regulatory rents account for a large share of the increase in corporate profits especially since 2000.

34 First quote: Jacob Hacker and Paul Pierson, "Winner-Take-All Politics: Public Policy, Political Organization, and the Precipitous Rise of Top Incomes in the United States," *Politics & Society* 38 (2010), 173; second quote: Hacker and Pierson, *Winner-Take-All Politics*, 113.

35 Jonathan Rauch, *Governments End: Why Washington Stopped Working* (New York: PublicAffairs, 1999), 12–15. See, generally, Neomi Rao, "Administrative Collusion: How Delegation Diminishes the Collective Congress," *New York University Law Review* 90 (November 2015).

36 Ibid., 118.

37 For reaction to the 1989 prescription drug provisions, see Andrea Stone, "Rosty's 'Catastrophic' Moment over Health Care Was a First," Illinois Single-Payer Coalition, August 11, 2010, http://ilsinglepayer.org/article/rostys-catastrophic-moment-over-health-care-was-first; for consequences of the 2003 prescription drug provisions, see Congressional Budget Office, *A Detailed Description of CBO's Cost Estimate for the Medicare Prescription Drug Benefit* (Washington, DC: Congressional Budget Office, July 2004), http://www.cbo.gov/sites/default/files/cbofiles/ftpdocs/56xx/doc5668/07-21-medicare.pdf.

38 There is disagreement as to whether the polarization stems from voters or leaders as well as disagreement about its causes. For a general discussion of the polarization, see James Q. Wilson, *American Politics, Then & Now: And Other Essays* (Washington, DC: American Enterprise Institute, 2010), 84; Fiorina and Abrams, *Breakdown of Representation*. I don't need to take a position on this disagreement because the tricks affect both voters and legislators. Blame for polarization is also pinned on gerrymandering. For an argument that gerrymandering is not a major cause and a compendium of other causes, see Mann and Ornstein, *It's Even Worse Than It Looks*.

39 Hacker and Pierson, *Winner-Take-All Politics*, 159.

40 For the salutary effects of legislatures spending more time in Washington, see Norman Ornstein and Thomas E. Mann, *The Broken Branch: How Congress Is Failing America and How to Get It Back on Track* (Oxford, UK: Oxford University Press, 2008), 169–70; Mann and Ornstein, *It's Even Worse Than It Looks*, 232.

41 Mann and Ornstein, *It's Even Worse Than It Looks*; for the opinion of experts in psychology, see Jonathan Haidt, *Righteous Mind* (2012), 275; Evan Bayh, "Why I'm Leaving the Senate," *New York Times*, February 20, 2010, http://www.nytimes.com/2010/02/21/opinion/21bayh.html?pagewanted=all; Hamilton, "Will the House Come to Order?"

42 Fifty-nine percent of "political insiders" believe that the public doesn't "know

enough about the issues facing Washington to form wise opinions about what should be done." James A. Barnes, "Six of Ten Political Insiders Believe Public is Ill-Informed," *National Journal*, March 24, 2011, http://www. nationaljournal.com/politics/six-of-ten-political-insiders-believe-public- is-ill-informed-20110324.

43 On voters wielding great power, see King, "Running Scared"; Waldron, "Accountability," 28.

44 Letter from Thomas Jefferson to Pierre Samuel du Pont de Nemours (April 24, 1816), in *The Essential Jefferson* (Indianapolis: Hackett, 2006), 230. The recipient of the letter, Pierre Samuel du Pont de Nemours, was a French aristocrat and the progenitor of one of America's first industrial powerhouses.

45 In recounting his reluctant acceptance of the rising power of elites at the dawn of the twentieth century, Henry Adams wrote, "Nothing could surpass the nonsensity of trying to run so complex and so concentrated a machine [that is, the United States government and economy] by Southern and Western farmers in grotesque alliance with city day-laborers." Henry Adams, *The Education of Henry Adams* (New York: Penguin Books, 1995), 328.

46 Michael Patrick Hearn, quoted in L. Frank Baum, *The Annotated Wizard of Oz: The Centennial Edition* (New York: Norton, 2000), 44n20. Hearn viewed Baum's purpose as giving pleasure to children rather than expressing political viewpoints. To me, however, it is not surprising that hints of Baum's political attitudes crept into his books. On Dorothy and her allies, see ibid., 351. As to the film version, Hearn, quoted in ibid., 306. Quote from ibid., 321.

47 As professors Jacob Gersen and Matthew Stephenson claimed: "Effective accountability mechanisms can decrease, rather than increase, an agent's likelihood of acting in her principal's interests. The problem, which we call 'over-accountability,' . . . is essentially an information problem: sometimes even a fully rational but imperfectly informed principal (e.g., the citizens) will reward 'bad' actions rather than 'good' actions by an agent (e.g. the President)." Jacob Gersen and Matthew Stephenson, "Over-Accountability," *Journal of Legal Analysis* 6 (2014), 1. The authors reached this conclusion based on the assumption that the principal's lack of information could result in an accountable agent acting contrary to the principal's interest. They did not, however, demonstrate equal interest in the possibility that a lack of accountability would produce perverse results for the principal. Here is one example that should sound familiar: an agent wins popularity in the short term by handing out benefits to citizens without disclosing that they will have to pay later. Although the authors did acknowledge in passing that accountability in the hands of imperfectly informed principals does not always produce "perverse results" (ibid., 222), they failed to show that such accountability usually leads to perverse rather than beneficial results. In discussing each of the Five Tricks, I show how the hiding of responsibility for costs, risks, and other unpopular consequences by our agents in Congress and the White House does routinely lead to perverse results.

Professors Gersen and Stephenson also stated that "accountability . . . is not an end in itself" but rather only a means to increase the welfare of the principal. Ibid., 232. Others have disagreed, including the people who signed their names to the Declaration of Independence's proposition that governments derive "their just Powers from the Consent of the Governed" as well as Abraham Lincoln, Jane Addams, and the many modern Americans who have resolved to preserve not only government "for the people," but also government "of the people" and "by the people."

CHAPTER 6

1   "Pink Floyd Lyrics: 'Mother,'" AZLyrics.com, accessed November 15, 2016, http://www.azlyrics.com/lyrics/pinkfloyd/mother.html.

2   Barnes, "Public Is Ill-Informed."

3   *The State of The U.S. Economy: Hearing Before the Committee on the Budget House of Representatives*, 112th Cong., 1st Session (Feb. 9, 2011) (testimony of Ben Bernanke, Chairman, Board of Governors of the Federal Reserve System), http://www.gpo.gov/fdsys/pkg/CHRG-112hhrg64726/html/CHRG-112hhrg64726.htm. Yellen stated, "We can see in for example CBO's very-long-term projections that . . . there is more work to do to put fiscal policy on a sustainable course. . . . Over the long term deficits will rise to unsustainable levels relative to the economy and putting in place a package of reforms—I know these are very controversial matters—but that would probably help confidence." *The Economic Outlook: Hearing Before the Joint Economic Committee Congress of the United States*, 113th Cong., 2nd Session, 20–21 (May 7, 2014) (testimony, Janet Yellen, Chairperson, Federal Reserve System), http://www.gpo.gov/fdsys/pkg/CHRG-113shrg88497/pdf/CHRG-113shrg88497.pdf. For top politicians, see Christopher Demuth, "Our Democratic Debt," *National Review*, June 21, 2014, https://www.nationalreview.com/nrd/articles/381873/our-democratic-debt.

4   Jackson, "Structure of Federal Spending," 19–20.

5   See Emily Teipe, *America's First Veterans and the Revolutionary War Pensions* (Lewiston, NY: Edwin Mellen, 2002). Early Congresses did provide some pensions to Revolutionary War veterans, but in far-smaller amounts relative to gross domestic product than the benefits promised today. According to C. Eugene Steuerle, "For most of American history—from the founding of the republic to at least the end of World War II . . . the president and Congress created and funded programs mostly on a year-to-year basis, extending them only after considering other ways to use available revenue." Steuerle, *Dead Men Ruling*, 5–9.

6   For the statute and the Yucca Mountain facility, see Richard Stewart and Jane Stewart, *Fuel Cycle to Nowhere: U.S. Law and Policy on Nuclear Waste* (Nashville: Vanderbilt University Press, 2012), 56–83; for the court decision and its consequences, see Ralph Vartabedian, "Tiny Nuclear Waste Fee Added Up to Billions," *Los Angeles Times*, March 15, 2014, http://www.latimes.com/nation/la-na-nuclear-waste-20140515-story.html.

7   For the financial structure of the 1935 legislation, see Jagadeesh Gokhale, *Social Security: A Fresh Look at Policy Alternatives* (Chicago: University of Chicago Press, 2010), part 1; Frankin Delano Roosevelt, quoted in Arthur M. Schlesinger Jr., *The Coming of the New Deal* (New York: Houghton Mifflin, 1958), 308. Initially, the contributions were put into a Social Security account,

but after that a 1939 statute created the "Federal Old-Age and Survivors Insurance Trust Fund." 42 U.S.C. § 401 (2014).

8 Richard M. Nixon, "Nixon's Statements on Social Security: Statement on Signing the Social Security Amendments of 1972—October 30, 1972," Social Security "President Nixon," http://www.ssa.gov/history/nixstmts.html#1972; Jackson, "Counting the Ways," 27.

9 Congressional Budget Office, *2015 Long-Term Budget Outlook* (Washington, DC: Congressional Budget Office, June 16, 2015), 2, https://www.cbo.gov/publication/50250.

10 Peter R. Fisher, "Remarks of Under Secretary of the Treasury Peter R. Fisher to the Columbus Council on World Affairs . . . ," U.S. Department of the Treasury "Press Center," November 14, 2002, https://www.treasury.gov/press-center/press-releases/Pages/po3622.aspx.

11 For the statute requiring financial report, see 31 U.S.C., § 331(e) (1) (2014).

12 For the 2015 Financial Report, see Department of the Treasury, *Financial Report of the United States Government: Fiscal Year 2015* (Washington, DC: Department of the Treasury, February 25, 2016), 22, https://www.fiscal.treasury.gov/fsreports/rpt/finrep/fr/15frusg/02242016_FR(Final).pdf.

13 Quote from "Statement of the Comptroller General of the United States," in ibid., 43. Paul Krugman, "The Fiscal Fizzle: An Imaginary Budget and Debt Crisis," *New York Times*, July 20, 2014, http://www.nytimes.com/2014/07/21/opinion/Paul-Krugman-An-Imaginary-Budget-and-Debt-Crisis.html. Krugman drew solace from the fact that the debt-to-GDP ratio was somewhat higher during World War II. Yet, the reason the nation had a high ratio then is because it was responding to a major challenge. The comptroller general thought that the high ratio that we have now could render us unable to meet a some new challenge.

14 For release of the 2005 report under the Bush administration, see Department of the Treasury, *Financial Report of the United States* (Washington, DC: Department of the Treasury, 2006), https://www.fiscal.treasury.gov/fsreports/rpt/finrep/fr/06frusg/06frusg.pdf. An e-mail from William Mills, associate librarian for information services, to the author, dated August 26, 2013, shows that the Obama administration did its best to hide the 2012 report, and the result is that there was no significant press coverage in the weeks after its release.

15 Long-term fiscal sustainability quote: Department of the Treasury, *Financial Report 2015*, n.p.; foundation for economic growth and prosperity quote: Jacob J. Lew, "A Message from the Secretary" (February 25, 2016), in ibid., n.p.

16 As Dr. Gokhale put it, this "intergenerational 'chain-letter' funding framework implies a constant renewal of federal obligations to successive generations as their current payroll taxes extinguish benefit obligations to current retiree generations that were created earlier." Gokhale, "2012 Update." Chris Cox and Bill Archer, "Why $16 Trillion Only Hints at the True U.S. Debt: Hiding the Government's Liabilities from the Public Makes It Seem That We Can Tax Our Way Out of Mounting Deficits. We Can't," *Wall Street Journal*, November 26, 2012, http://online.wsj.com/news/articles/SB100014241278873233532045781273740390876 36: Cox and Archer, two retired members of Congress, here made the

case that government does not reveal anything as far as the true extent of our
fiscal shortfall.

17   For the difference in fiscal gaps between reports, see Department of the
    Treasury, *Financial Report 2015*, 6; for quotes, see ibid., 37, 43.

18   "A Message from the Secretary of the Treasury: A Citizen's Guide," in
    Department of the Treasury, *Financial Report 2015*, 6.

19   Jagadeesh Gokhale and Kent Smetters, *Fiscal and Generational Imbalances:
    New Budget Measures for New Budget Priorities* (Washington, DC: American
    Enterprise Institute, 2003). The presses of the Brookings Institution, the
    Massachusetts Institute of Technology, Oxford University, and the University
    of Chicago have published some of their other books and top-tier economics
    journals have published their articles.

20   Barack Obama, "Transparency and Open Government: Memorandum for
    the Heads of Executive Departments and Agencies," White House: President
    Barack Obama, January 21, 2009, http://www.whitehouse.gov/the_press_office/
    TransparencyandOpenGovernment/.

21   National asset quote from Obama, "Transparency and Open Government,
    Memorandum for the Heads of Executive Departments and Agencies,"
    White House: President Barack Obama "Briefing Room," accessed
    November 15, 2016, https://www.whitehouse.gov/the_press_office/
    TransparencyandOpenGovernment"; e-mail stating that information is not
    available to the general public from Sylvia Mathews Burwell, director of the
    Office of Management and Budget, to author, August 26, 2013.

22   Gokhale, "2012 Update," 2, 8, 16, 19. The 9 percent figure is based upon CBO's
    "alternative"—that is, realistic—projections.

23   Ibid., 22.

24   See chapter 5 of this book, as well as, for example, David Cay Johnston,
    Perfectly Legal (New York: Penguin Group, 2005); Micklethwait and
    Wooldridge, *Fourth Revolution*, ch. 9.

25   John Bresnahan and Jake Sherman, "Budget Agreement Reached," *Politico*,
    December 10, 2013, http://www.politico.com/story/2013/12/budget-deal-
    update-patty-murray-paul-ryan-100960. Congress claimed that the $23 billion
    in savings were to be achieved, in part, by denying a cost-of-living increase
    in military pensions. However, Congress later reinstated the cost-of-living
    increase. Jennifer Liberto, "Senate Votes to Restore Military Pensions," CNN
    "Money," February 12, 2014, http://money.cnn.com/2014/02/12/news/economy/
    military-pensions-senate.

26   As Steuerle explained: "The largest and most important growing programs
    are designed so that when the economy grows faster, they grow faster as well."
    Steuerle, *Dead Men Ruling*, 80. Alice Rivlin, "Rising Debt—Not a Crisis, But a
    Serious Problem to Be Managed," Brookings, September 8, 2016, https://www.
    brookings.edu/testimonies/rising-debt-not-a-crisis-but-a-serious-problem-
    to-be-managed/. Other thoughtful analysts have also concluded that current
    spending and taxing policies will lead to fiscal disaster. See, for example,
    Laurence J. Kotlikoff and Scott Burns, *The Clash of Generations: Saving
    Ourselves, Our Kids, and Our Economy* (Cambridge, MA: MIT Press, 2012).

27 See, for example, Micklethwait and Wooldridge, *Fourth Revolution*, chs. 7–8; Nader, *Unstoppable*, chs. 1–3; Schuck, *Why Government Fails So Often*, ch. 1.

28 Erskine Bowles and Alan Simpson, "Bowles & Simpson: Debt Solution Must Be Bipartisan," *USA Today*, last modified September 21, 2012, http://usatoday30.usatoday.com/news/opinion/forum/story/2012-09-20/simpson-bowles-deficit-commission/57819842/1.

29 Department of the Treasury, *Financial Report 2015*, 6.

30 The states spent $415 billion to provide Medicaid health care in fiscal year 2012. The Kaiser Family Foundation Web site reports Medicaid health care costs borne by states exclusive of administrative costs at Laura Snyder and Robin Rudowitz, "State Fiscal Conditions and Medicaid: 2014 Update," Henry J. Kaiser Family Foundation, April 4, 2014, http://kff.org/report-section/state-fiscal-conditions-and-medicaid-2014-update-issue-brief-8572/. Richard Ravitch, *So Much to Do: A Full Life of Business, Politics, and Confronting Fiscal Crises* (New York: PublicAffairs, 2014), 230.

31 For a discussion of the coming crisis, see Richard Ravitch and Paul A. Volcker, *Final Report* (New York: State Budget Crisis Task Force, January 14, 2014), http://www.statebudgetcrisis.org/wpcms/. For infrastructure, see ibid., 18. The General Accountability Office forecasted that "state and local governments would need to make substantial policy changes" to close the gap between spending and revenues. U.S. Government Accountability Office, *State and Local Governments' Fiscal Outlook: 2015 Update* (Washington, DC: U.S. Government Accountability Office, December 16, 2015), 1, http://www.gao.gov/assets/680/674205.pdf.

32 Ravitch, *So Much to Do*, 237.

33 Viral V. Acharya, Matthew Richardson, Stijn van Nieuwerburgh, and Lawrence J. White, *Guaranteed to Fail: Fannie Mae, Freddie Mac, and the Debacle of Mortgage Finance* (Princeton, NJ: Princeton University Press, 2011), 17. As stated by the statute: "Neither the enterprises nor the Banks, nor any securities or obligations issued by the enterprises or the Banks, are backed by the full faith and credit of the United States." 12 U.S.C. § 4501(4) (2014).

34 For assurances to lenders, see Gretchen Morgenson and Joshua Rosner, *Reckless Endangerment: How Outsized Ambition, Greed, and Corruption Led to Economic Armageddon* (New York: Times Books, 2011), 66; for federal bank regulations, see James R. Hagerty, *The Fateful History of Fannie Mae: New Deal Birth to Mortgage Crisis Fall* (Charleston, SC: History Press, 2012), 40–41.

35 For safe lending practices, see Hagerty, *Fateful History*, 48; for the limited supply of safe mortgages, see Morgenson and Rosner, *Reckless Endangerment*, 42.

36 12 U.S.C. § 1452 (2014).

37 For buying riskier mortgages, see Morgenson and Rosner, *Reckless Endangerment*, 35, 52–53; Acharya et al., *Guaranteed to Fail*, 33; Hagerty, *Fateful History*, 63; for legislation, see Federal Home Loan Mortgage Corporation Act of 1970, Pub. L. No. 91-351, 12 U.S.C. § 1451 (2014); for increasingly vigorous enforcement, see Peter J. Wallison, *Hidden in Plain Sight: What Really Caused the World's Worst Financial Crisis and Why It Could Happen Again* (New York: Encounter Books, 2015), ch. 7.

[38] For disreputable lenders, see Morgenson and Rosner, *Reckless Endangerment*, 53–56; for rising home prices, see Acharya et al., *Guaranteed to Fail*, 33.

[39] For interest expense saved and dividends, see Wayne Passmore, *The GSE Implicit Subsidy and the Value of Government Ambiguity* (Washington, DC: Federal Reserve Board, 2005), 3; for the fancy trappings of Fanny, see Hagerty, *Fateful History*, 52, 83.

[40] Morgenson and Rosner, *Reckless Endangerment*, 26; see also pp. 35, 59–60 and Acharya et al., *Guaranteed to Fail*, 35.

[41] Acharya et al., *Guaranteed to Fail*, 35.

[42] Morgenson and Rosner, *Reckless Endangerment*, 5.

[43] For capital requirements, see Acharya et al., *Guaranteed to Fail*, 24. Regulations have required Fannie and Freddie to have even-less cushion on the mortgages they guarantee. Leading up to the housing crash that began in 2006–07, the companies had only $1 in shareholder capital for every $72 of debts or guarantees. Ibid., 26.

[44] For managers keeping their bonanzas, see Hagerty, *Fateful History*, 199. However, to the extent the bonuses were paid in company stock that the executives still held, they lost along with other shareholders when the value of the stock tanked. Ibid., 197.

[45] For the government's need to pay, see ibid., 16; Henry M. Paulson Jr., *On the Brink: Inside the Race to Stop the Collapse of the Global Financial System* (New York: Business Plus, 2010), 159.

[46] For the $130 billion estimate, see *The Budgetary Cost of Fannie Mae and Freddie Mac and Options for the Future Federal Role in the Secondary Mortgage Market: Hearing Before the House Committee on the Budget*, 112th Cong., 1st Session, 7–8 (June 2, 2011) (testimony of Deborah Lucas, Assistant Director for Financial Analysis). Nick Timiraos, "Cost of Bailing Out Fannie and Freddie Expected to Fall Sharply," *Wall Street Journal*, October 26, 2012, http://online.wsj.com/article/SB10001424052970204598504578080770443540656.html. As the housing market recovered, the estimated cost to the government diminished.

[47] Hagerty, *Fateful History*, 18, 90, 203–4.

[48] Johnson aide, quoted in ibid., 40; Acharya et al., *Guaranteed to Fail*, 5.

[49] Fannie and Freddie claimed for decades that their role in promoting home ownership was the envy of the rest of the world, yet few other countries have emulated it. Per capita home ownership is higher in many other countries than it is in the United States. Ibid., 123; Hagerty, *Fateful History*, 101. Mortgage interest rates compared to the applicable risk-free rate are higher in the United States than they are in most other developed countries. Dwight M. Jaffee, "A Privatized U.S. Mortgage Market," Conference on the GSEs, Housing, and the Economy, January 24, 2011, http://www.rhsmith.umd.edu/files/Documents/Centers/CFP/2011/jaffee.pdf: This paper compares mortgage rates to the applicable risk-free rate. For the .07 percent reduction, see Morgenson and Rosner, *Reckless Endangerment*, 251; for the benefits of the savings going mainly to the well-to-do, see Acharya et al., *Guaranteed to Fail*, 8–9.

[50] Edward DeMarco, quoted in Mary Kissel, "The Man Who Took on Fannie Mae: How a Career Bureaucrat Became the Target of the

Housing Lobby and the White House for Trying to Avoid a Repeat of 2008," *Wall Street Journal*, July 12, 2014, http://www.wsj.com/articles/mary-kissel-the-man-who-took-on-fannie-mae-1405119923.

[51] For debt guarantees contributing to the bubble, see Acharya et al., *Guaranteed to Fail*, 28, 44–45; Christopher DeMuth, "Debt and Democracy." Remarks at Hudson Institute Trustees Dinner, New York, March 19, 2012, 8 (on file with the author).

[52] For Wall Street emulating Fannie, Freddie, and Ginnie Mae, see Morgenson and Rosner, *Reckless Endangerment*, ch. 3. So lucrative were mortgage lending and the securitization of mortgages that some of the mortgage lenders like Countrywide started packaging and selling their own mortgage-backed securities and some Wall Street firms started their own mortgage-lending operations. See Acharya et al., *Guaranteed to Fail*, 49.

[53] For a discussion of nineteenth-century banking requirements, see Niall Ferguson, "The Descent of Finance," *Harvard Business Review*, July 1, 2009; Houman B. Shadab, "Credit Risk Transfer Governance: The Good, the Bad, and the Savvy," *Seton Hall Law Review* 42 (2012): Assets-to-capital ratios include forms of capital other than equity, so that assets-to-equity ratios would be even higher.

[54] As a team of Stanford business school professors concluded, "The availability of explicit or implicit government guarantees of bank debt creates a bias towards choosing risky strategies to exploit the guarantees, providing shareholders with nice returns if they succeed and saddling the government with the losses if they fail." Anat R. Admati, Peter M. DeMarzo, Martin F. Hellwig, and Paul C. Pfleiderer, "Fallacies, Irrelevant Facts, and Myths in the Discussion of Capital Regulation: Why Bank Equity is Not Socially Expensive" (Research Paper 13-7, Stanford University Graduate School of Business, October 22, 2013), 22, https://www.gsb.stanford.edu/sites/default/files/research/documents/Fallacies%20Nov%201.pdf. Charles Calomiris, "How to Regulate Bank Capital," *National Affairs* 10 (Winter 2012), 50, http://www.nationalaffairs.com/publications/detail/how-to-regulate-bank-capital.

[55] For disagreement about the cause of the meltdown, see, for example, Financial Crisis Inquiry Commission, *Final Report of the National Commission on the Causes of the Financial and Economic Crisis in the United States* (Washington, DC: U.S. Government Printing Office, January 2011), https://www.gpo.gov/fdsys/pkg/GPO-FCIC/pdf/GPO-FCIC.pdf (compare the majority and dissenting reports). Three books put substantial, even primary, blame on government housing policy starting with Fannie and Freddie: (1) Morgenson and Rosner, *Reckless Endangerment*, 4–5; (2) Hagerty, *Fateful History*, 204; and (3) Acharya et al., *Guaranteed to Fail*, 2, 98. Other books dismiss or ignore Fannie and Freddie, including Paul Krugman, *The Return of Depression Economics and the Crisis of 2008* (New York: Norton, 2009), 162. For a critique of Krugman's argument, see Christopher DeMuth, "Government Regulation and the Financial Crisis of 2008" (paper presented at the Transformation of American Government conference, Hertog Foundation, Washington, DC, March 13, 2013), 23–36. Others blame the Commodities Futures Modernization Act of 2000 for allowing the speculative trading of credit default swaps (CDSs). See Lynn A. Stout, "Derivatives and the Legal Origin of the 2008 Credit Crisis,"

Harvard Business Law Review 1 (2011), 1. For a contrary view, see Shadab, "Credit Risk Transfer Governance," 1016–17.

For quote, see Acharya et al., *Guaranteed to Fail*, 49. Morgenson and Rosner similarly concluded that because Fannie was "the leader in housing finance, its actions set the tone for private-sector lenders across the nation." Morgenson and Rosner, *Reckless Endangerment*, 38–39. Wallison, *Hidden in Plain Sight*, 7: Besides, as Peter Wallison pointed out, Fannie and Freddie bought Wall Street's mortgage-backed securities with money borrowed under the cover of the debt guarantees in order to hold enough mortgages for low- and moderate-income families to comply with the government's affordable-housing requirements. Acharya et al., *Guaranteed to Fail*, 24. Moreover, federal banks encouraged the banks to hold Fannie and Freddie's mortgage-backed securities.

[56] For Morgenson and Rosner quotes, see *Reckless Endangerment*, 10; for campaign contributions, see ibid., 12; for additional points, see: ibid., 72 (discusses charities), 64, 68–71 (discusses giving jobs to the relatives, companions, and former staffers of legislators); ibid., 61–65, 68 (reviews setting up offices in key congressional districts to facilitate a "patronage scheme" and to exert pressure on Congress); ibid., 187–88 (looks at the referral of legislators to Fanny's close ally Countrywide, so that it could be given sweetheart mortgages); ibid., 71–74, 83 (examines the hiring of "academics to write favorable studies about [Fannie's] role in the mortgage market," effectively putting these academics on long-term retainer to keep them from doing studies attempting to prove the contrary); ibid., 22 (looks into donations to antipoverty groups such as ACORN, which then switched from lobbying against Fannie and Freddie to lobbying on their behalf).

[57] Barney Frank, quoted in Peter J. Wallison, "Five Years Later: Don't Mention the Feds; Washington and the Media Are Peddling a Narrative That Discounts the Government's Role in the Financial Crisis," *Wall Street Journal*, September 18, 2013, http://online.wsj.com/article/SB10001424127887324576304579073111289821626.html.

[58] Wall Street Reform and Consumer Protection Act, 111 Pub. L. No. 203, §§ 331–36 (2010); 12 U.S.C. § 5301 (2014).

[59] Peter Conti-Brown, "Elective Shareholder Liability," *Stanford Law Review* 64 (2012), 417–18; for a discussion of the literature on Dodd–Frank, see ibid., 418–27.

[60] Ibid., 419–25. The statute calls the covered firms "systemically important."

[61] For a discussion of these warnings, see Conti-Brown, "Elective Shareholder Liability," 421–25.

[62] Neel Kashkari, *Lessons from the Crisis: Ending Too Big to Fail* (transcript of speech, Brookings Institution, February 16, 2016), 4–5, http://www.brookings.edu/~/media/events/2016/02/16-kashkari/kashkaribrookings2162016.pdf. The transcript discusses, inter alia, breaking up big banks.

[63] Conti-Brown, "Elective Shareholder Liability," 411n3 (note discusses past debt guarantees). As for the future of the debt guarantees, see, for example, Luigi Zingales, "How Political Clout Made Banks Too Big to Fail," Bloomberg View, May 29, 2012, http://www.bloombergview.com/articles/2012-05-29/how-political-clout-made-banks-too-big-to-fail. Kenichi Ueda and Beatrice Weder

di Mauro, "Quantifying Structural Subsidy Values for Systemically Important Financial Institutions" (Working Paper 12/28, International Monetary Fund, May 2012), http://www.imf.org/external/pubs/ft/wp/2012/wp1228.pdf. A 2012 IMF working paper finds that the perception that the government would come to the rescue of the creditors of large financial institutions cuts their borrowing costs by eighty basis points.

[64] See Zingales, "Too Big to Fail." The statute does, however, give officials tools to deal with the insolvency of financial firms that could be far superior to the previously available options.

[65] See Gretchen Morgenson, "One Safety Net That Needs to Shrink," *New York Times*, November 3, 2012, http://www.nytimes.com/2012/11/04/business/one-safety-net-that-needs-to-shrink.html?_r=0; Gretchen Morgenson, "Don't Blink, Or You'll Miss Another Bailout," *New York Times*, February 16, 2013, http://www.nytimes.com/2013/02/17/business/dont-blink-or-youll-miss-another-bank-bailout.html?pagewanted=all.

[66] For Dodd–Frank, see Acharya et al., *Guaranteed to Fail*, 2–3; for share of mortgage market financed by Fannie and Freddie, see Congressional Budget Office, *Transitioning to Alternative Structures for Housing Finance* (Washington, DC: Congressional Budget Office, December 2014), 1, https://www.cbo.gov/publication/49765. The government is now taking Fannie and Freddie's profits, but that is not a fee geared to the size and riskiness of its debt.

[67] For regulation getting weaker, see Calomiris, "How to Regulate Bank Capital," 56–57; Joe Light, "Mortgage Giants Set to Loosen Lending: Fannie, Freddie near Deal to Lift Limits; Concerns Persist," *Wall Street Journal*, October 17, 2014, http://www.wsj.com/articles/fannie-freddie-close-to-agreement-that-could-reduce-lender-penalties-1413561203.

[68] John H. Cochrane, "Running on Empty: Banks Should Raise More Capital, Carry Less Debt—and Never Need a Bailout Again," *Wall Street Journal*, March 1, 2013, http://online.wsj.com/article/SB10001424127887324048904578318064208389202.html?KEYWORDS=bank+capital; Calomiris, "How to Regulate Bank Capital," 56. The crises preceding the debt guarantee were not only much less frequent but also much smaller relative to countries' economies.

[69] Howard, *Rule of Nobody*.

[70] In describing the lengths of the statute and of regulations, I assumed, for the sake of comparison, that *DC Confidential* would have about 420 words per page.

[71] Howard, *Rule of Nobody*, 124.

[72] For the compliance of big firms, see J. B. Ruhl, James Salzman, Kai-Sheng Song, and Han Yu, "Environmental Compliance: Another Corporate Integrity Crisis or Too Many Rules?," *Natural Resources & Environment* 17 (2002); for the compliance of small firms, see Charles Murray, *By the People: Rebuilding Liberty without Permission* (New York: Penguin Random House, 2015), chs. 2, 9.

[73] For a scholar on the right who makes such a proposal, see Murray, *By the People*, chs. 2, 9; for a scholar on the left making such a proposal, see Cass R. Sunstein, *Simpler: The Future of Government* (New York: Simon & Schuster, 2013), 35.

74   See, for example, Robert G. Kaiser, *Act of Congress: How America's Essential Institution Works, and How It Doesn't* (New York: Knopf, 2013), ch. 1.

75   Haidt, *Righteous Mind*, 86 (emphasis in original).

76   *Federal Debt: Testimony Before the Joint Economic Committee* (written testimony, Mitchell E. Daniels Jr.).

*   Figure 8: United States Department of the Treasury, *Financial Report 2015*, 5.

*   Figure 9: Ibid., 6.

CHAPTER 7

1   Congress has made it more difficult to act by requiring that its members conduct open-door negotiations, but a task force of the American Political Science Association found that we should have transparency as to the decisions that Congress makes rather than transparency on the negotiations to reach those decisions. Jane Mansbridge and Cathie Jo Martin, eds., *Negotiating Agreement in Politics* (Washington, DC: American Political Science Association, December 2013), ch. 5, http://www.apsanet.org/Portals/54/ APSA20Files/publications/MansbridgeTF_FinalDraft.pdf. The Honest Deal Act would do nothing to bar closed-door negotiations.

2   For examples of the disagreement, compare, for example, Lawrence Lessig, *Republic, Lost: How Money Corrupts Congress—and a Plan to Stop It* (New York: Grand Central Publishing, 2011), ch. 15; Robert G. Kaiser, *So Damn Much Money: The Triumph of Lobbying and the Corrosion of American Government* (New York: Random House, 2010), ch. 24. For a brief explanation of some of the reasons that campaign finance reform is so complicated and an argument that Lessig's proposals are insufficient, see Mann and Ornstein, *It's Even Worse Than It Looks*, 120.

3   As Lessig pointed out, "In a whole host of ways, legislative power can be exercised without a trace. And where it is exercised without a trace, the [relationship between campaign contributions and roll call votes] cannot map cause and effect." Lessig, *Republic, Lost*, 150.

  There are also other flaws of Congress that I have not mentioned. In *It's Even Worse Than It Looks*, Mann and Ornstein make dozens of proposals to remedy these flaws. My own proposals would not get in the way of any of theirs, with the possible exception of what they suggest in the section "Shifting Authority Between and Within the Branches." Here, the only possible conflict between my work and theirs would be with my proposal on the Regulation Trick, but even with this, I make use of the following recommendation based on *their book*: I use the base closing model of agency recommendation combined with fast-track up or down votes in Congress. See Mann and Orstein, *It's Even Worse Than It Looks*, 131–63.

  Professor Noveck showed that the government could produce better consequences for citizens by making greater use of the expertise. See Beth Simone Noveck, *Smart Citizens, Smarter Government: The Technologies of Expertise and the Future of Government* (Cambridge, MA; Harvard University Press, 2015). Professor Schuck presented many other proposals to help Congress produce better consequences for citizens. Stopping the tricks would give Congress more of an incentive to produce better consequences for the people. See Schuck, *Why Government Fails So Often*.

⁴ U.S. Const., art. I, § 8, cl. 11.

⁵ These wars include the War of 1812, the Mexican-American War (1846), the Spanish-American War (1898), World War I (1917), and World War II (1941).

⁶ For Quasi War, see Gordon S. Wood, *Empire of Liberty: A History of the Early Republic, 1789–1815* (New York: Oxford University Press, 2009), 245–46; Alexander Hamilton, "Publius," *Federalist* 25, December 21, 1787; see also Philip Bobbitt, "War Powers: An Essay on John Hart Ely's War and Responsibility: Constitutional Lessons of Vietnam and Its Aftermath," *Michigan Law Review* 92 (1994).

⁷ For the general practice of presidents not waging war, see, for example, John Hart Ely, *War and Responsibility: Constitutional Lessons of Vietnam and Its Aftermath* (Princeton, NJ: Princeton University Press, 1993), 9–10, 104; Louis Fisher, *Presidential War Power*, 3rd ed. (Lawrence: University Press of Congress, 2013), xiii–xv; Raoul Berger, *Executive Privilege: A Constitutional Myth* (Cambridge, MA: Harvard University Press, 1974), 85–87; Alexander M. Bickel, "Congress, the President and the Power to Wage War," *Chicago-Kent Law Review* 48 (1971), 133–35.

For arguments about whether the practice of the president seeking authorization from Congress was consistently followed, see, for example, John Yoo, *Crisis and Command: The History of Executive Power from George Washington to George W. Bush* (New York: Kaplan, 2009); Robert H. Bork, "Address: Erosion of the President's Power in Foreign Affairs," *Washington University Law Review* 68 (1990). Those who argue that the country should be able to wage war without affirmative Congressional approval claim that there are many examples of it having done so before 1950. Yet, the vast majority of these occurrences "involved landings to protect American property or lives abroad. Generally undertaken during periods of disorder or civil unrest when local authorities could no longer provide protection against ordinary outlawry, these landings were, at least superficially, intended to maintain strict neutrality between contesting political factions." "Congress, the President, and the Power to Commit Forces to Combat," *Harvard Law Review* 81 (1968), 1788.

Moreover, in many of these instances, military commanders took action without presidential approval so that if these instances can be considered precedent for military commanders embarking on campaigns without congressional authorization, they can also be considered precedent for them embarking on campaigns with neither presidential nor congressional authorization. See John Hart Ely, "Suppose Congress Wanted a War Powers Act That Worked," *Columbia Law Review* 88 (1988), 1389n34.

Perhaps the most cited counterexample to combat requiring congressional authorization is the first Barbary War (1801–05). The claim is that in the period between President Thomas Jefferson taking office in 1801 and his getting authorization from Congress in 1802, he launched offensive military action. Yet, whatever one can say of President Jefferson's subordinates, he consistently took the position that without congressional authority, he could act only defensively. See, for example, Frank Lambert, *The Barbary Wars: American Independence in the Atlantic World* (New York: Hill and Wang, 2005), ch. 5. Lambert wrote of Jefferson, "He instructed the navy to engage any enemy vessel that attacked American shipping, but not to pursue corsairs in offensive engagements nor to take them as prizes." Ibid., 126.

8   For presidents' lip service to not waging war, see, for example, Ely, *War and Responsibility*, 9–10; Fisher, *Presidential War Power*, 38–47, 57; Berger, *Executive Privilege*, 75–85; Francis D. Wormuth and Edwin B. Firmage, *To Chain the Dog of War: The War Power of Congress in History and Law* (Chicago: University of Illinois Press, 1986), vii; Arthur M. Schlesinger Jr., *The Imperial Presidency* (Boston: Houghton Mifflin, 2004), 421; Janet Cooper Alexander, "John Yoo's War Powers: The Law Review and the World," *California Law Review* 100 (2012), 346; Abraham Sofaer, "The Presidency, War and Foreign Affairs: Practice under the Framers," *Law and Contemporary Problems* 40 (1976), 36–37; Joseph R. Biden Jr. and John B. Ritch III, "The War Power at a Constitutional Impasse: A 'Joint Decision' Solution," *Georgetown Law Journal* 77 (1988), 380; for Mexican-American War, see Howe, *What Hath God Wrought*, 762–64, 797–99, 813, 828–29.

9   Harry S. Truman, "The President's News Conference" (June 29, 1950), American Presidency Project "Harry S. Truman," http://www.presidency.ucsb.edu/ws/?pid=13544; Mark W. Clark, *From the Danube to the Yalu* (Blue Ridge Summit, PA: TAB Books, 1989), 369.

10 For the need to ask Congress for funds, see Bobbitt, "War Powers," 1390; for funding a navy to fight Naval War, see Wood, *Empire of Liberty*, 245–46.

11 Schlesinger, *Imperial Presidency*, xxvii; Ely, *War and Responsibility*, ix; Robert Gates, *Duty: A Memoir of a Secretary at War* (New York: Vintage Books, 2014), 51.

12 Winston S. Churchill, *My Early Life* (New York: Touchstone, 1930), 232.

13 Ely, *War and Responsibility*, 15–21.

14 Lyndon Johnson, quoted in ibid., 53; for how Congress responded to the challenges in Southeast Asia, see ibid., chs. 2–5.

15 On voters' opinions about going to war in Southeast Asia, see Irving Wallace and David Wallechinsky, *The People's Almanac* (Garden City, NY: Doubleday, 1975), 828; for assertions about the statute requiring presidents to get congressional approval,, see Ely, *War and Responsibility*, 46–49, 53, 62.

16 On the requirement to report, see War Powers Resolution, 50 U.S.C. §§ 1541–48 (2014). (The War Powers Resolution is also known as the War Powers Act.) "This resolution will prevent any Tonkin Gulf resolution; it will prevent any de facto declaration of a war by the funding of a war": 119 Cong. Rec. H9648 (daily ed., Nov. 7, 1973) (statement of Rep. Robert Drinan) (Drinan also discusses the importance of producing reports). 50 U.S.C. § 1547(a) requires the authorization to be explicit. An appropriation of funds without explicit approval won't suffice. Congress could of course repeal the requirement in an appropriations bill, but that repeal would itself have to be explicit. See Tennessee Valley Authority v. Hill, 437 U.S. 153, 189 (1978), which states: "There is nothing in the appropriations measures, as passed, which states that the Tellico Project was to be completed irrespective of the requirements of the Endangered Species Act. These appropriations, in fact, represented relatively minor components of the lump-sum amounts for the *entire* TVA budget. To find a repeal of the Endangered Species Act under these circumstances would surely do violence to the 'cardinal rule ... that repeals by implication are not favored'" (emphasis in original). On the action-forcing purpose of the deadline, see Ely, *War and Responsibility*, 48.

17 Richard F. Grimmett, *War Powers Resolution: After Thirty-Six Years* (Washington, DC: Congressional Research Service, 2010), 49–69. Instead of submitting a report that starts the sixty-day clock, presidents submit other paperwork.

18 For candidate Obama's insistence on getting authorization, see Charlie Savage, "Barack Obama's Q&A," boston.com, December 20, 2007, http://www.boston.com/news/politics/2008/specials/CandidateQA/ObamaQA/; for President Obama not seeking authorization, see "Letter from the President regarding the Commencement of Operations in Libya," White House: President Barack Obama "Briefing Room," March 21, 2011, http://www.whitehouse.gov/the-press-office/2011/03/21/letter-president-regarding-commencement-operations-libya; for congressional leaders urging the president to intervene without giving them responsibility, see Charlie Savage, *Power Wars: Inside Obama's Post-9/11 Presidency* (New York: Little, Brown, and Company, 2015), 637; for Gates on "act of war," see *Operation Odyssey Dawn and U.S. Military Operations in Libya: Hearings Before the Committee on Armed Services*, 112th Cong., 1st Session, 15 (March 31, 2011), https://www.gpo.gov/fdsys/pkg/CHRG-112hhrg65802/pdf/CHRG-112hhrg65802.pdf; for Gates on the gall of members of Congress, see Gates, *Duty*, 513.

19 50 U.S.C. 1546(c): An even-more-impractical alternative for stopping the war is for Congress to refuse to appropriate funds for the Department of Defense. The statute does contain a provision stating that the president must cease hostilities if the House and the Senate each pass a resolution to that effect. U.S. Const., art I, § 7, cl. 2–3; I.N.S. v. Chadha, 462 U.S. 919 (1983): But the courts would likely find that provision to be in violation of the constitutional provision that requires Congress to present the bills it passes to the president for signature. This constitutional flaw has given presidents an excuse to defy the reporting provision.

20 Ely, *War and Responsibility*, 54; 141 Cong. Rec. S3971 (1995) (statement of Senator Joseph Biden).

21 For popular agreement that legislators need to take part of the responsibility for going into Libya in 2011, see "Just 26% Favor Continued Military Action in Libya," Rasmussen Reports, June 13, 2011, http://www.rasmussenreports.com/public_content/politics/general_politics/june_2011/just_26_favor_continued_military_action_in_libya. This article states that at the time of the intervention, 59 percent of likely US voters agreed that President Obama should get the approval of Congress if he wanted to continue US military action in Libya. Twenty-one percent didn't think congressional approval was needed. Another 20 percent were not sure. For agreement on legislators' responsibility about going into Syria in 2013, see Hart Research Associates, "Study #13336: NBC News Survey," question 12, Public Opinion Strategies, August 28–29, 2013, http://pos.org/documents/nbc_syria.pdf.

22 Leslie H. Gelb and Anne-Marie Slaughter, "Declare War: It's Time to Stop Slipping into Armed Conflict," *Atlantic Monthly*, November 1, 2005, http://www.theatlantic.com/magazine/archive/2005/11/declare-war/304301/.

23 Caspar W. Weinberger, "The Uses of Military Power" (remarks delivered to the National Press Club, Washington, DC, November 28, 1984), PBS *Frontline*, http://www.pbs.org/wgbh/pages/frontline/shows/military/force/weinberger.html; Barack Obama, quoted in Savage, "Barack Obama's Q&A."

[24] For Obama's 2012 announcement, see James Ball, "Obama Issues Syria a 'Red Line' Warning on Chemical Weapons," *Washington Post*, August 20, 2012, http://www.washingtonpost.com/world/national-security/obama-issues-syria-red-line-warning-on-chemical-weapons/2012/08/20/ba5d26ec-eaf7-11e1-b811-09036bcb182b_story.html; for Obama's 2013 reaction to Assad, see Barack Obama, "Statement by the President on Syria," White House: President Barack Obama "Briefing Room," August 31, 2013, http://www.whitehouse.gov/the-press-office/2013/08/31/statement-president-syria; for Obama's 2014 quote, see Barack Obama, "Statement by the President on ISIL," White House: President Barack Obama "Briefing Room," September 10, 2014, http://www.whitehouse.gov/the-press-office/2014/09/10/statement-president-isil-1.

[25] *Secretary of Defense Ash Carter Opening Statement on Counter-ISIL, House Armed Services Committee*, 114th Cong., 1st Session (Dec. 1, 2015), http://docs.house.gov/meetings/AS/AS00/20151201/104236/HHRG-114-AS00-Wstate-CarterA-20151201.pdf; Phil Klay, "What I'll Tell My Son about Fighting in the Iraq War," *PBS NewsHour*, December 1, 2015, http://www.pbs.org/newshour/bb/what-ill-tell-my-son-about-fighting-in-the-iraq-war/.

CHAPTER 8

[1] Katharine Lee Bates, "America the Beautiful" (song, 1913), USA Flag Site, accessed November 17, 2016, http://www.usa-flag-site.org/song-lyrics/america/.

[2] Gokhale, "2012 Update"; see also Steuerle, *Dead Men Ruling*, 80.

[3] The reason that coming up with a precise number is impossible is that there is uncertainty about factors such as the rate of interest that the government must pay when it seeks to borrow, growth in productivity, the rates at which people are born and die, the portion of the population that seeks work, economic booms and busts, natural catastrophes, and wars. Congressional Budget Office, *2015 Long-Term Budget Outlook*. The CBO argued that because such uncertainty may make the future tougher than the past, rational government officials should make projections in order to discern whether the government can sustain itself despite the unexpectedly tough times that will result from the uncertainty. Ibid., 108.

[4] Philip Joyce, *The Congressional Budget Office: Honest Numbers, Power, and Policymaking* (Washington, DC: Georgetown University Press, 2011), 213–19. See also Philip Joyce, *The Congressional Budget Office at Middle Age* (Washington, DC: Brookings Institution, February 17, 2015), https://www.brookings.edu/research/the-congressional-budget-office-at-middle-age/. In *The Congressional Budget Office*, Professor Joyce argues that the CBO should pay more attention to the long-term fiscal outlook.

[5] The cost would increase because of both (1) actions by Congress and (2) other changes, such as natural catastrophes or changes in the state of the national or international economy. Both types of changes would be reflected in the total cost, but for the purposes of holding elected officials accountable for actions that happen in a current Congress, the CBO should report the increase and decrease resulting from the first type only.

[6] For activities, including purely informational ones, that Congress may delegate to agents, see Bowsher v. Synar, 478 U.S. 714, 754 (1986).

7   For intergenerational consequences, see Gokhale, *Social Security*; Laurence J.
     Kotlikoff and Scott Burns, *The Coming Generational Storm: What You Need to
     Know about America's Economic Future* (Cambridge, MA: MIT Press, 2005);
     Gokhale, "2012 Update," 25.

8   Christopher DeMuth Sr., "The Real Cliff: The Staggering Debt from Decades of
     Continuous Government Borrowing Is About to Come Due," *Weekly Standard*,
     December 24, 2012, http://www.weeklystandard.com/articles/real-cliff_666593.
     html; Micklethwait and Wooldridge, *Fourth Revolution*, 11, 122–24.

9   Charles Lindblom, "The Science of Muddling Through," *Public Administration
     Review* 19 (Spring 1959).

10   For difficulty enforcing balanced budget requirements in the states, see Donald
     Tobin, "The Balanced Budget Amendment: Will Judges Become Accountants?
     A Look at State Experiences," *Journal of Law & Politics* 12 (Spring 1996).

11   For the inevitability of guarantees, see Conti-Brown, "Elective Shareholder
     Liability," 423–25 This article provides a summary of the literature.

12   For quote by the director of the agency regulating Fannie and Freddie, see
     Alex J. Pollock, "GSE Debt Growth Leaves U.S. Taxpayers Exposed," American
     Enterprise Institute, June 20, 2011, http://www.aei.org/publication/gse-
     debt-growth-leaves-u-s-taxpayers-exposed/; Christopher Dodd, quoted in
     Tami Luhby, "U.S. Plan to Save Fannie and Freddie: Paulson and Bernanke
     Proposal Would Give Mortgage Finance Giants Bigger Line of Credit with
     Treasury and Open NY Federal Reserve Lending Window," CNN "Money,"
     last modified July 14, 2008, http://money.cnn.com/2008/07/13/news/economy/
     fannie_freddie_sunday/.

13   Acharya et al., *Guaranteed to Fail*, 7–8. Acharya, Richardson, Van
     Nieuwerburgh, and White, the four NYU business school professors previously
     mentioned, showed how to implement the principle that the beneficiaries
     of guarantees should pay a market-based fee. They sensibly emphasized that
     the private firms providing a share of the guarantee must be vetted to ensure
     creditworthiness. Ibid., 8.

14   For the riskiness of debt, see, for example, Admati et al., "Why Bank Equity Is
     Not Expensive"; Charles W. Calomiris, "Bank Capital Requirement Reform:
     Long-Term Size and Structure, the Transition, and Cycles" (position paper
     presented at the Shadow Open Market Committee Symposium on Escaping
     from Stagnation: Macroeconomic Policies for Sustainable Growth, New
     York, October 21, 2011), http://shadowfed.org/wp-content/uploads/2011/10/
     Calomiris-SOMCOct2011.pdf. For an argument in favor of a prolonged
     transition to tougher capital requirements, see Admati et al., "Why Bank
     Equity Is Not Expensive," 59: The Stanford business school professors argued
     that even if these firms are made to pay the full price for their guarantees,
     and thus deprived of their hidden subsidies, regulations should nonetheless
     be imposed that require them to have more of a cushion. Ibid., 3: Over the
     past century, the ratio of bank capital to assets grew from 4:1 or below to 10:1
     for commercial banks and 30:1 for investment banks. Ferguson, "Descent of
     Finance," 3–4. There are debates as to whether and how to increase bank capital
     that I don't get into here because my recommendations focus on getting rid of
     the tricks.

15   As already explained, debt guarantees could not be eliminated for too-big-to-fail firms unless the firms were made far smaller.

16   The Defense Base Closure and Realignment Commission proposes which bases to close, and its proposal will take effect unless Congress votes to the contrary. (For information on the commission, see the Defense Base Closure and Realignment Commission's Web site: http://www.brac.gov/.) My suggestion is that the Debt Guarantee Honesty Commission's proposal would take effect only if enacted.

17   See, for example, Kashkari, "Lessons from the Crisis," which discusses, inter alia, breaking up big banks. Other proposals for dealing with the systemic risk posed by financial giants include having them raise a far-larger portion of their funds through equity rather than borrowing and making the banks' own shareholders personally liable for their debts. An example of this suggestion is in Conti-Brown, "Elective Shareholder Liability."

18   "Section 2—Instant Replay: Article 1. Coaches' Challenge," in "Rule 15. Officials and Instant Replay," NFL "Operations," accessed November 3, 2016, http://operations.nfl.com/the-rules/2015-nfl-rulebook/#rule-15.-officials-and-instant-replay. In NFL games, each team gets to challenge two rulings made during the game. The challenge results in officials reviewing their call by instant video replay. If the first two challenges are successful, the team gets a third.

The concept of adding "provisions in a bill that threaten to do harm to states or localities if they fail to do the federal bidding" would require careful definition in the statute. The provision should include harsher treatment of residents triggered by a state or locality not complying with federal standards. Congress could vote to inflict punishment on states or localities that fail to do the federal bidding and might well do so where there is a strong federal purpose, but individual legislators would have to take responsibility for this decision. Excluded from the concept should be sanctions to punish violations of constitutional prohibitions, such as Congress denying education grants to states that violate the equal protection clause's prohibition of school segregation as defined by the courts. This exclusion would require the prohibition to be as defined by the courts to keep Congress from creating expansive definitions of constitutional rights in order to gain the ability to coerce the states without taking responsibility. See Marci A. Hamilton and David Schoenbrod, "The Reaffirmation of Proportionality Analysis under Section 5 of the Fourteenth Amendment," *Cardozo Law Review* 21 (1999). Cf. City of Boerne v. Flores, 521 U.S. 507 (1997).

A bill could be insulated against points of order by Congress doing as Professor Greve suggested: "The proclivity of state governments to accept federal funds and the attached strings is exacerbated by an oft-observed financial asymmetry: states can opt out of federal grants-in-aid but not the taxes that pay for those grants. . . . If a state declines participation in a federal funding program, (Congress could and should provide) that state's citizens will receive a tax rebate—proportionate to their home state's federal tax share and their individual payments—on the following year's tax return." Michael S. Greve, "Washington and the States: Segregation Now," American Enterprise Institute 17 (May 2003), 7–8, http://www.aei.org/wp-content/uploads/2011/10/17-FedO-May-2003.pdf.

An ironclad rule in favor of such opt-outs would be subject to the objection that there are some tasks that must get done (such as maintenance of interstate highways) but which the states arguably can do more efficiently. Perhaps, however, Greve's suggestion could be a default rule that Congress could subsequently override.

In the Honest Deal Act, each legislator would get one initial challenge in each Congress, but unlike in the NFL, there would be no limit on the number of additional challenges that a legislator could pose. In the House, this could be accomplished through a rule that might be worded as follows:

"Section 1: It shall be out of order for the House to consider legislation with a provision that harms states or localities that fail to do the federal bidding without a separate roll call vote on the provision. When the preceding point of order is properly raised, the chair will ask, 'Should the legislation be amended as described in the point of order?' If the point of order is upheld, the legislation shall be amended and the legislation shall proceed to a vote.

Section 2: It shall also be out of order for the House to consider a rule from the rules committee limiting points of order under section 1 of this rule.

Section 3: It shall be out of order for a member in a congress who was not upheld on a point of order under sections 1 or 2 of this rule to raise another point of order under sections 1 or 2 in the same Congress."

Voters would and should regard how legislators vote on a challenge to a ruling on a point of order under section 1 as reflecting their position on whether to amend the bill as described in the point of order.

[19] Buckley, *Saving Congress from Itself*, chs. 2–4.

[20] James Landis, *The Administrative Process* (New Haven, CT: Yale University Press, 1938), 76.

[21] *I.N.S.*, 462 U.S. 919.

[22] Stephen Breyer, "The Legislative Veto after Chadha," *Georgetown Law Journal* 72 (1984), 793–95. Breyer was showing that Congress could take on the job of voting on regulations, rather than arguing that it should do so. For a neat explanation of why the constitutional concerns raised about Breyer's approach are insubstantial, see Jonathan H. Adler, "Placing 'REINS' on Regulations: Assessing the Proposed REINS Act," *NYU Journal of Legislation and Public Policy* 16 (2013), 24–29.

[23] Congressional Responsibility Act of 1995, H.R. 2727, 104th Cong. (1995). This bill, unlike my present proposal and Landis's original proposal, was not limited to major regulations.

[24] Congressional Review Act, 5 U.S.C. §§ 801–8 (2006). The Congressional Review Act has had little impact because members of Congress prefer to avoid responsibility and presidents are almost certain to veto bills that repeal regulations that their administrations have promulgated. For further discussion on this, see, for example, "The Mysteries of the Congressional Review Act," *Harvard Law Review* 122 (2009), http://cdn.harvardlawreview.org/wp-content/uploads/pdfs/vol_122_the_mysteries.pdf.

[25] The current House bill is Regulations from the Executive in Need of Scrutiny Act, H.R. 427, 114th Cong. (July 28, 2015). For the Affordable Care Act provision, see *id.*, § 804(2) (B).

[26] Howard Dean, with the assistance of Judith Warner, *You Have the Power: How to Take Back Our Country and Restore Democracy in America* (New York: Simon & Schuster, 2006).

[27] Ackerman, *American Republic.*

[28] The new version of REINS, to its credit, would also apply only to major regulations. That would be an improvement over the Congressional Responsibility Act. Agencies may be tempted to fragment major regulations into nonmajor ones to evade votes in Congress, but existing statutes would in some instances keep agencies from doing so by defining the scope of regulations that agencies must issue. Moreover, such evasions would run the risk that courts would invalidate their supposedly nonmajor regulations by disguising them as major ones. Experience gained from the Honest Deal Act would give a better sense of whether it would be feasible to lower the threshold for regulations to be voted on, and may suggest some selective process by which members of Congress could own or disown some of the more important new nonmajor regulations.

[29] The list of bills on 112 symbolic public laws passed by Congress is taken from an e-mail from Nicole Jolicoeur and Laura Rion to David Schoenbrod, September 27, 2016.

[30] Ackerman, *American Republic*, 39. Here, Ackerman was stating a broad principle rather than addressing the Congressional Responsibility Act.

[31] Waldron, *Dignity of Legislation*, 159.

[32] For our proposal, see Schoenbrod et al., *Breaking the Logjam*, ch. 4; for economic analysis, see Jared Carbone, Richard D. Morgenstern, Roberton C. Williams III, and Dallas Burtraw, "Getting to an Efficient Carbon Tax: How the Revenue Is Used Matters," Resources for the Future, January 13, 2014, http://www.rff.org/research/publications/getting-efficient-carbon-tax-how-revenue-used-matters; for conservatives' approach to establishing market-based incentives, see, for example, N. Gregory Mankiw, "The Key Role of Conservatives in Taxing Carbon," *New York Times*, September 4, 2015, http://www.nytimes.com/2015/09/06/upshot/the-key-role-of-conservatives-in-taxing-carbon.html; Sarah Kent and Justin Scheck, "Carbon-Tax Debate Brings Together Unusual Allies: Oil Giants Line Up with Environmentalists, As Natural Gas Offers Emissions Edge over Coal," *Wall Street Journal*, November 30, 2015, http://www.wsj.com/articles/carbon-tax-debate-brings-together-unusual-allies-1448936246; for the progressivity of taxation, see Roberton C. Williams III, Dallas Burtraw, and Richard Morgenstern, "The Impact of a US Carbon Tax across Income Groups and States," Resources for the Future, September 24, 2015, http://www.rff.org/research/publications/impacts-us-carbon-tax-across-income-groups-and-states.

[33] For obsolete statutes, see, for example, Gregg Easterbrook, "Let's Modernize Our Environmental Laws," *New York Times*, October 7, 2015, http://www.nytimes.com/2015/10/08/opinion/why-can-the-epa-regulate-smog-but-not-greenhouse-gases.html; Howard, *Rule of Nobody.*

[34] For a proposal to deal with the existing regulations from the Progressive Policy Institute, see Michael Mandel and Diana G. Carew, "A Politically and Technically Feasible Approach for Handling Regulatory Accumulation,"

Progressive Policy Institute, May 21, 2014, http://www.progressivepolicy.org/
issues/economy/a-politically-and-technically-feasible-approach-for-handling-
regulatory-accumulation/.

35 U.S. Const., art. II, § 2, cl. 1; for Eisenhower's take on the need to get
    congressional approval, see Ely, *War and Responsibility*, 47; for Ely quote,
    see ibid., 3; for others putting forth the argument that the president does not
    need congressional authorization, see, for example, John C. Yoo, "War and the
    Constitutional Text," *University of Chicago Law Review* 69 (2002); for an able
    summary of the two schools of thought, see Bobbitt, "War Powers," 1370–76.

36 Bobbitt, "War Powers," 1370–76; for a discussion of the power of Congress
    to cut off war funding, see John Yoo, *The Powers of War and Peace: The
    Constitution and Foreign Affairs after 9/11* (Chicago: University of Chicago
    Press, 2005), 159; U.S. Const., art. I, § 9, cl. 7; see also U.S. Const., art. I, § 8, cl.
    12–13.

37 Ely, *War and Responsibility*, 132–38, 47–67, 115–31.

38 Bruce Ackerman, "Can the Supreme Court Force Congress to Own the War
    on ISIS? Judicial Intervention May Be the Only Way Left to Break the Political
    Impasse on Authorizing Obama's Use of Force," *Atlantic*, August 25, 2015,
    http://www.theatlantic.com/politics/archive/2015/08/supreme-court-and-
    isis/402155/. Bruce Ackerman argued that the courts would decide a case
    brought by individual soldiers in harm's way.

39 Ely described an emergency as a situation in which "a clear threat to
    national security has developed so rapidly as to preclude Congress's advance
    consideration of such authorization, or keeping the pendency of the United
    States' response to such a threat a secret prior to its initiation is clearly essential
    to its military effectiveness."

    Ely also proposed that the action could be brought by any member of
    Congress. The DC Circuit in a split decision ruled that members of Congress
    lack standing to sue under the War Powers Resolution. Campbell v. Clinton,
    203 F.3d 19 (D.C. Cir. 2000), *cert. denied*, 531 U.S. 815 (2000). The Honest Deal
    Act should authorize members of Congress to sue because a new case may
    produce a different outcome.

    For the willingness of courts to decide, see Ely, *War and Responsibility*,
    47–67.

    Bobbitt, "War Powers," 1391. As Bobbitt noted, Congress should include a
    provision in the Combat Authorization Act stating that appropriations bills
    should not be read to countermand this provision of the Combat Authorization
    Act unless it explicitly states as much. Such legislated canons of interpretation
    should be honored by the courts. See Nicholas Quinn Rosenkranz, "Federal
    Rules of Statutory Interpretation," *Harvard Law Review* 115 (2002). Ely's version
    does not have such a canon of interpretation, but it should be added.

40 There is, of course, the risk that candidates would so pledge but then
    rationalize their way out of honoring that pledge. Bruce Ackerman has
    proposed an antidote to such rationalization without involving the courts:
    He suggested a "Supreme Executive Tribunal" constituted so as to be free of
    presidential control. Ackerman, *American Republic*, 141–80.

41   Yoo quote: Yoo, *Crisis and Command*, 350. John Yoo, "War, Responsibility, and the Age of Terrorism," *Stanford Law Review* 57 (2004): In this journal article, Professor Yoo argued that requiring congressional authorization as a matter of constitutional law would render the decision-making process too inflexible for a changing world. My own proposal is to require congressional approval through a statute that can be more readily changed than constitutional doctrine.

42   Yoo, *Crisis and Command*, 363. As Yoo pointed out, "It is impossible to answer counterfactual questions." Ibid., 363. Eliot A. Cohen, "The Stakes on the Syria Vote: America's Credibility as a Guarantor of International Order Is on the Line," *Wall Street Journal*, September 2, 2013, http://www.wsj.com/articles/SB10001424127887324432404579049261525066516.

43   Jide Nzelibe and John Yoo, "Rational War and Constitutional Design," *Yale Law Journal* 115 (2006); for a discussion of groupthink, see Peter M. Shane, *Madison's Nightmare: How Executive Power Threatens American Democracy* (Chicago: University of Chicago Press, 2009), 56–81.

44   Ackerman, *American Republic*, 39.

45   Gelb and Slaughter, "Declare War." Analyses by several serving and retired military officers reach the same conclusion. As Joseph Gallagher put it: "If this nation declared war when it engaged in war, as the Constitution requires, the United States would wage fewer of them—and be far better positioned to win them." Joseph V. Gallagher III, "Unconstitutional War: Strategic Risk in the Age of Congressional Abdication," *Army War College Review* 41 (Summer 2011), 33. http://www.carlisle.army.mil/USAWC/parameters/Articles/2011summer/Gallagher.pdf.

46   The Constitution specifically mentions ways that Congress can authorize the use of hostilities other than by declaring war: "To declare War, grant Letters of Marque and Reprisal, and make Rules concerning Captures on Land and Water." U.S. Const., art. I, § 8, cl. 11. Karl Marlentes, *What It Is Like to Go to War* (New York: Atlantic Monthly Press, 2011), 252.

47   I did what I could to get the courts to stop the Regulation Trick but fell short. See David Schoenbrod, "Politics and the Principle that Elected Legislators Should Make the Laws," *Harvard Journal of Law and Public Policy* 26 (2002), http://digitalcommons.nyls.edu/cgi/viewcontent.cgi?article=1244&context=fac_articles_chapter. The Constitution provides even-less hope of curing most of the other tricks.

48   Philip Howard proposed a constitutional amendment that would help deal with some of the ill effects of the Regulation Trick, but, as he acknowledged, amending the Constitution is extremely difficult. Howard, *Rule of Nobody*, part II. For a thoughtful discussion of small-*c* constitutionalism and the many statutes that are part of it, see William N. Eskridge Jr. and John A. Ferejohn, *A Republic of Statutes: the New American Constitution* (New Haven, CT: Yale University Press, 2010).

CHAPTER 9

1   Leonard Cohen, "Democracy" (song, 1992), French Leonard Cohen site, accessed November 1, 2016, http://www.leonardcohensite.com/songs/

democracy.htm. Cohen called democracy "the greatest religion the West has produced." Leonard Cohen, *Leonard Cohen on Leonard Cohen: Interviews and Encounters*, ed. Jeff Burger (Chicago: Chicago Review Press, 2014), 294.

2   See, for example, Jeffrey M. Jones, "Record-Low 21% Say Most in Congress Deserve Re-Election: Slim Majority Still Say Their Own Member Deserves Re-Election," Gallup, August 9, 2011, http://www.gallup.com/poll/148904/record-low-say-congress-deserve-election.aspx.

3   A seminal work on concentrated interests is Mancur Olson, *The Logic of Collective Action* (Cambridge, MA: Harvard University Press, 1965), which was published around the time Congress began to use the tricks in earnest. See also Hacker and Pierson, "Public Policy, Political Organization, and Rise of Top Incomes."

4   Mancur Olson, *The Rise and Decline of Nations: Economic Growth, Stagflation, and Social Rigidities* (New Haven, CT: Yale University Press, 2008).

5   Ibid., 237.

6   See, generally, Schoenbrod, *Saving Our Environment*.

7   "19% Think Federal Government Has Consent of the Governed," Rasmussen Reports, April 11, 2014, http://www.rasmussenreports.com/public_content/politics/general_politics/april_2014/19_think_federal_government_has_consent_of_the_governed.

8   For the origins of the War Powers Act, see, for example: *War Powers Legislation: Hearings Before the Committee on Foreign Relations*, 92nd Cong., 1st Session, March 8, 1971 (statements of J. W. Fulbright, Senator of Arkansas, at 58; Claiborne Pell, Senator of Rhode Island, at 125; Robert Taft Jr., Senator of Ohio and US Representative, at 261; and statement of Charles Mathias, Senator of Maryland, at 336). Thornburgh discussed polls that show that 75 percent of Americans would go as far as to support a constitutional amendment to balance the federal budget. For the origins of budget-balancing statutes, see, for example, Dick Thornborn, "Gramm-Rudman-Hollings and the Balanced Budget Amendment: A Page of History," *Harvard Journal on Legislation* 25 (1988), 615; for the origins of the Unfunded Mandates Reform Act, see 141 Cong. Rec. 7, S833–34 (1995) (comments of Senator Robert Dole); for the origins of the Congressional Review Act, see, for example, James T. O'Reilly, "EPA Rulemaking after the 104th Congress: Death from Four Near-Fatal Wounds?," *Environmental Lawyer* 3 (1996), 5–10; for the origins of Dodd-Frank, see, for example, chapter 6 of this book.

9   Members of Congress played the critical role in designing these illusory ground-rule statutes. See, for example, Ely, *War and Responsibility*, 48–49; Robert Keith and Bill Heniff Jr., *The Budget Reconciliation Process: House and Senate Procedures* (New York: Nova Science, 2006), 1–6; Posner, *Politics of Unfunded Mandates*, 180–207; "The Mysteries of the Congressional Review Act," *Harvard Law Review* 122 (2009), 2176–83.

10   For "save us from ourselves" quote, see Bowles and Simpson, "Debt Solution Must Be Bipartisan"; for Dorothy quote, see Baum, *Annotated Wizard of Oz*, 310.

11   On state finances in general, see chapter 6; on the inadequate funding of pension plans in particular, see Andrew G. Biggs, "Public Sector Pensions: How

Well Funded Are They, Really?," American Enterprise Institute, July 19, 2012, https://www.aei.org/publication/public-sector-pensions-how-well-funded-are-they-really/; on state statutes calling for votes on agency regulations, see, for example, Florida, Fla. Stat. Ann. § 120.541(3) (2010 West).

12 U.S. Const., amends. XV, XIX. See also Wiebe, *Self-Rule*, 100, 164–65, which discusses the Fifteenth and Nineteenth Amendments. Public support for the rights of African Americans preceded, rather than followed, presidential, judicial, and congressional action. Rasmussen wrote of the Civil Rights Act of 1964 that like "other great events in American history, the attitudes of Americans changed first and the actions of politicians lagged behind." Scott Rasmussen, *The People's Money: How Voters Would Balance the Budget and Eliminate the Federal Debt* (New York: Threshold Editions, 2013), 32. See also Caro, *Passage of Power*, 558–70; Wiebe, *Self-Rule*, 243–57.

13 Francis Fukuyama, *Political Order and Political Decay: From the Industrial Revolution to the Globalization of Democracy* (New York: Farrar, Straus and Giroux, 2014), ch. 10.

14 Dean, *You Have the Power*.

15 Lincoln, "Gettysburg Address."

16 Leon Kass, "The Other War on Poverty: Finding Meaning in America" (remarks delivered at the Irving Kristol Lecture at the American Enterprise Institute Annual Dinner, May 2, 2012), http://www.aei.org/publication/the-other-war-on-poverty-finding-meaning-in-america/ (emphasis added).

17 Abraham Lincoln, "Lyceum Address," Abraham Lincoln Online "Speeches & Writings," January 27, 1838, http://www.abrahamlincolnonline.org/lincoln/speeches/lyceum.htm.

18 Dan Ariely, Joel Huber, and Klaus Wertenbroch, "When Do Losses Loom Larger Than Gains?," *Journal of Marketing Research* 42 (2005). As researchers have found, people in psychological experiments value avoiding the loss of a dollar more than they value gaining one.

Acknowledgments

I must thank an unusually large number of people because writing *DC Confidential* took an unusually long time. Eight years ago, I began to write a book on how politicians trick voters. Eight years is three times longer than it took me to write any previous book. Yet *DC Confidential* took even longer than that because it ended up incorporating many elements from a book that I began and put aside more than twenty years ago. That book was on how many voters want to believe politicians' promises of something for nothing.

I needed eight years to complete *DC Confidential* because I sought to explain the trickery in terms that voters who do not work in politics can readily understand. The trickery works through complexity and voters have lives to live and so have only limited patience for fathoming the intricacies. Thus I had to find ways to make clear the inherently unclear. Also, I sought to show how the trickery infects government broadly and that required educating myself about many complex topics.

I won't even try to thank the many people who graciously helped me more than eight years ago, with a sole exception. Twenty years ago, New York Law School Dean Harry Wellington told me that he thought that although few people could explain such complexity in a way that had visceral appeal, I could. That bucked me up as the years went by.

Over the past eight years, three people have provided continuing counsel: Ross Sandler, my litigation partner at the Natural Resources Defense Council and current colleague and friend at New York Law School; Christopher DeMuth, my former colleague at the American Enterprise Institute and current friend; and David Johnson, my former colleague at New York Law School and current friend and collaborator.

Many other people have done me the favor of critiquing chapters or, in some cases, the whole book. They include: Bruce R. Adler, Joseph Antos, Richard Chused, Howard Dean, Richard A. Epstein, Stephen Fineberg, Jagadeesh Gokhale, Deecy Gray, Philip K. Howard, Sandeep Jauhar, Lynn Johnston, James H. King, Jethro Lieberman, David I. Levine, Jamie Maunz, Brian Mannix, Lawrence M. Mead, Eugene Meyer, Norman Ornstein, Marcus Peacock, Edward Pinto, Alex Pollock, Edward Purcell, Sabeel Rahman, Thomas Ranieri, Neomi Rao, Jonathan Rauch, Dean Reuter, Esa Saarinen, Helen Sandalls, Houman Shadab, John G. Stewart, Richard B. Stewart, Peter Wallison, Adam White, Katrina M. Wyman, John Yoo, and David Zimmerman. Deborah Paulus-Jagric, a student and research assistant of mine a quarter century ago, who has helped with all my books since then, not only critiqued the entire book but also prepared the index.

I also benefitted from reactions to presentations that I made at the Henry Salvatori Center at Claremont-McKenna College; the Federalist Society; the Advanced Environmental Law Seminar at New York University School of Law; the Wallace Stegner Center for Land, Resources and the Environment at the S. J. Quinney College of Law, University of Utah; the Environmental Law Center at Vermont Law School; and the Manuscript Society at Yale University. Attending the last of these talks was Annie Shi, then a Yale undergraduate, who would soon be graduating and starting a job in New York. She volunteered to help with the book after work and gave me much wise counsel.

Along the way, I benefitted from the advice and information provided by Gerard Alexander, Andrew Biggs, Suzanne Davidson, Kim Dennis, Susan Dudley, Annette Gordon-Reed, Michael Greve, Jonathan Haidt, Kevin Hassett, Charles John Jackson, Melanie Kirkpatrick, William R. Levi, G. Tracy Mehan III, Jeffrey Miron, Daniel Mitchell, Beth Noveck, Veronique Rodman, Amity Shlaes, and Mark Steinmeyer.

New York Law School deans Anthony Crowell and Richard Matasar were stalwart supporters and advisors throughout. Other law school colleagues who generously helped include Silvia Alvarez, Michael Blanco, Regina Chung, Nancy Guida, William Mills, Michael Roffer, and especially my faculty assistant, Jennifer Morgan.

New York Law School students Paul Accomando, Cynthia Claytor, Hannah Faddis, Andrew Ford, Nicole Jolicoeur, Will Kostas, Alicia Langone, Laura Rion, Jonathan Sizemore, and Melissa Witte provided careful research assistance and advice on the manuscript in the spirit of intellectual partnership.

Will Kostas was an unusually helpful research assistant, because, prior to coming to the law school, he had worked for years in Congress. Because of his knowledge of Capitol Hill and excellent judgment, I have continued to seek his help after graduation and he has responded graciously. He is an ongoing advisor.

My agent, Peter W. Bernstein, provided wise counsel throughout.

I am also grateful to the people at Encounter Books, starting with Roger Kimball and his colleagues, including especially Lauren Miklos, Heather Ohle, and Sam Schneider. Jana Weinstein provided careful copy editing.

Connected to this book is the Web site DC-Confidential.org. On the site are computer "games" that provide an entertaining way to learn about the Five Tricks. David Johnson is the coauthor of these games and Scott Rossi of Tactile Media made them fun to use. Stephen Fineberg, my dear friend starting in third grade, did the illustrations that grace the games, the Web site, and the book. Regina Chung and Roberto Alvarez of New York Law School designed and built the site. David Moore and Beth Noveck gave me valuable technical advice.

The biggest debt of all goes to my loving partner, Jan Selby.

I ask forgiveness from anyone whom I may have overlooked.

I met the three mentors to whom I dedicated this book in this order: First, Neal D. Peterson, who was my boss when I was on the staff of Senator and then–vice president Hubert H. Humphrey. Then, Spottswood W. Robinson, III, the judge for whom I clerked and previously the litigator for the Virginia plaintiffs in *Brown v. Brown of Education*. And last, John Doar, my boss at the Bedford-Stuyvesant Restoration antipoverty program and previously the champion of the Civil Rights Division of the Department of Justice in the fight for civil rights. Each of them modeled dedication to fairness, professionalism, and courage. They are departed, but still with me.

Index

Acid rain, 48–50, 51
Ackerman, Bruce, 18, 152, 153, 159
Affordable Care Act, 86, 87; Regulations from the Executive in Need of Scrutiny Act (REINS) and, 151

Blame shifting by Congress, 6, 12, 15, 45, 67; debt guarantees and, 116–17, 120; EPA and, 43–44, 48–49, 51, 53; Five Tricks as enabling, 3–4, 74, 76–77, 88–89, 92; presidents and, 74–75, 130–31, 133–37, 160; regulation and, 70, 71–72, 75, 92; states and, 47–48, 51, 52–53, 65, 67–70, 111, 166–67; taxing and spending and, 52, 57, 59–62, 145
Budget, federal: deficits and, 15, 139–45
Bush, George H. W.: Debt Guarantee Trick and, 64, 113; pollution control and, 49
Bush, George W.: Debt Guarantee Trick and, 113; Money Trick and, 60, 93, 105, 107; war and, 134, 160

Campaign contributions, 6, 40, 62, 88, 89, 90, 119, 129–30, 162
Cap and trade, 49–51
Carter, Jimmy, 44
Civil Rights Act (1964), 29–33, 40, 52
Clean Air Act (amendments of 1970): accomplishments of, 46, 50–51; burdens imposed by, 40, 43–45, 89;

citizens' suits and, 43; duties imposed by, 41; EPA and, 40–41, 43, 72, 73; failures of, 45, 50; false assumptions in, 46–48; lead in gas and, 43–45; states and, 67
Clean Air Act (amendments of 1977): federal highway grants and, 68–69; states and, 48, 67–68
Clean Air Act (amendments of 1990): acid rain and, 48–50; cap and trade and, 49–51; climate change and, 154–55; regional conflicts enacting, 49
Clinton, William: Debt Guarantee Trick and, 113; federal mandates and, 69–70; Somalia and, 136
Congress: accountability and, 16, 23, 124, 126, 129, 132, 150–56; approval ratings of, 17; budget deficits and, 145; claiming credit and, 15, 45; Clean Air Act (1970) and, 41, 43, 44–46, 47–48; Clean Air Act (1977) and, 48, 67–69; Clean Air Act (1990) and, 48–51; Congressional Budget Office and, 60, 103, 141; debt guarantee subsidies and, 117, 147; Debt Guarantee Trick and, 62, 64, 125, 126, 145; EPA and, 41, 43, 44–45, 46–48, 51; executive infringement of, 18; Federal Mandate Trick and, 65–70, 110–11, 123–25, 148–49; Five Tricks and, 2–6, 20, 52–55, 76–77, 92–94, 126, 130; health